An Expendable Squadron

Roy Conyers Nesbit had a long and distinguished career as a leading aviation historian. He served as an air observer with 217 Squadron in 1941 and 1942 and was chairman of the Beaufort Aircrews Association. His many books include The Royal Air Force: An Illustrated History From 1918, RAF in Camera, The Battle of Britain, The Battle For Europe, Arctic Airmen, Eyes of the RAF, The Battle of the Atlantic, Ultra Versus U-Boats, Reported Missing, The Battle for Burma *and* The Strike Wings. *Roy Nesbit died in 2014, while this book was in production.*

An Expendable Squadron

The Story of 217 Squadron, Coastal Command, 1939–1945

Roy Conyers Nesbit

Pen & Sword
AVIATION

First published in Great Britain in 2014 by
Pen & Sword Aviation
an imprint of
Pen & Sword Books Ltd
47 Church Street
Barnsley
South Yorkshire
S70 2AS

ISBN 978 1 47382 328 0

A CIP catalogue record for this book is available from the British
Library

Typeset in Ehrhardt by
Mac Style Ltd, Bridlington, East Yorkshire
Printed and bound in the UK by CPI Group (UK) Ltd,
Croydon, CRO 4YY

Pen & Sword Books Ltd incorporates the imprints of Pen &
Sword Archaeology, Atlas, Aviation, Battleground, Discovery,
Family History, History, Maritime, Military, Naval, Politics,
Railways, Select, Transport, True Crime, and Fiction, Frontline
Books, Leo Cooper, Praetorian Press, Seaforth Publishing and
Wharncliffe.

For a complete list of Pen & Sword titles please contact
PEN & SWORD BOOKS LIMITED
47 Church Street, Barnsley, South Yorkshire, S70 2AS, England
E-mail: enquiries@pen-and-sword.co.uk
Website: www.pen-and-sword.co.uk

Contents

Acknowledgements   vi

Chapter 1   The Problems of Training   1

Chapter 2   South-Western Approaches   19

Chapter 3   Operational Beginnings   53

Chapter 4   The German Battlecruisers   74

Chapter 5   Bombing, Mining, Patrolling and on Standby   93

Chapter 6   French Ports Under Occupation   121

Chapter 7   New Beauforts and New Stations   148

Chapter 8   The Last Three Years   178

Appendices

A   Junkers Ju 88 at RAF Chivenor   210
B   Kenneth Campbell's Victoria Cross   213
C   Beaufort Aircrews Association   216
D   Air-Laid Mines and U-boats: Coastal Waters of
      Western France   222
E   Air-Laid Mines and Enemy Surface Vessels: Coastal
      Waters of Western France   225
F   St Eval Church   227
G   Memorial at Westminster Abbey   233
H   Roll of Honour No 217 Squadron   235

Bibliography   245
Index   246

Acknowledgements

I am extremely grateful to those who have helped and encouraged me with detailed research into British and French records and books, including the discovery of relevant photographs. They are: Tim Carroll; Mrs Annette Crossley; Roger Hayward; Dr Jacques Ilias; Dr René Jaloustre; Mme Genevieve Moulard; Air Cdre Graham R. Pitchfork.

My thanks are also due to those who provided photographs for the book. They are: *Aeroplane Monthly*; Archives de Bordeaux; Archives Départmentales de la Charente Maritime; Archives Municipale de Brest; Archiv Petrick; Arthur Aldridge; Sidney Bemrose; Bundesarchiv Koblenz; A. Richard Chapman; Stanley Clayton; Mrs Peggy Connell-McDowell; the late Jefferson H. Cresswell; the late Chris Davies; the late G. Alan Etheridge; the late Jack Gibson; Mrs E. Godfrey; Charles Hamlin; the late Günther Heinrich; the late Norman Hearn-Phillips; Zdenek Hurt; the late John E. Porter; Mark Postlethwaite; Jean-Louis Roba; the late Arthur H. Simmonds; St Eval Chruch; Mrs Nina Stimson; the late Francis A.B. Tams; the late Georges Van Acker; the late Eddie G. Whiston; Michael Whiston.

Finally, I should like to thank Mrs Jane Cowderoy for having the patience to check each chapter of my book, together with the captions of photographs, and to correct errors, inducing those caused by my poor typing ability.

Chapter 1

The Problems of Training

At 11.00 hours on Saturday 3 September 1939 many families in the UK were gathered around their wireless sets. They were listening to the gloomy voice of their Prime Minister, Neville Chamberlain, announcing that no reply had been received from Herr Hitler to his ultimatum delivered three days before and that 'in consequence, this country is at war with Germany'.

The air raid sirens wailed immediately after he finished, in what was obviously a demonstration, followed by the 'all clear'. Although not unexpected, this announcement must have been received with dismay by those with direct experience of the carnage of The Great War (as the First World War was known in those days). For some of the younger generation, however, it provided a welcome opportunity.

At this time, I was a few weeks beyond my eighteenth birthday, living with my parents and three brothers in a suburban house in Woodford Green, Essex. This was on the northern fringe of Epping Forest and only a short train ride to the City of London, where our father held a position in the Bank of England. We lived comfortably as a middle-class family. The secure position of our father had insulated us from inter-war unemployment and the Great Depression of the early 1930s. Moreover, all four boys had gained scholarships to schools which brought them up to Matriculation standard.

My employment was that of a junior clerk in Lloyds Bank, Fenchurch Street in London. In many respects this was an enviable occupation of the time, being secure, reasonably well paid and with good prospects. However, the work seemed so dreary and monotonous that I longed for something more adventurous. I had read copiously about the exploits of pilots in the Great War and studied books about the modern RAF. I had looked enviously at the fighter aircraft in the airfield of North Weald, near Epping, and had recently applied to join the RAF Volunteer Reserve (RAFVR), under the impression that this would be a part-time occupation – although no reply had been received.

It had been obvious for months that war was inevitable, despite the occasion in September 1938 when Chamberlain returned from a conference with Hitler in Munich, waving a piece of paper which he said assured us of 'peace in our time'. Since then, German had invaded Czechoslovakia and now had invaded Poland. It was time for me to act.

As soon as the sirens sounded the all-clear I telephoned a former school-friend who lived nearby. We had already discussed our course of action and duly cycled about five miles to Romford, where we knew that a recruitment centre was open on Sundays. At the beginning of the war, the age of conscription was twenty years – although it was soon reduced to eighteen. Conscripted entrants could be drafted into any branch of the armed services but those who volunteered could apply for whatever branch they chose. Thus we signed forms for training as pilots in the RAFVR.

On the next morning, I reported my action to the sub-manager at Lloyds Bank. He seemed displeased, presumably thinking I should have asked his permission beforehand and that he might have to find a replacement at short notice, but this did not worry me for I was looking forward to a great adventure. I did not have to wait long, for to my delight I received an official letter on the next day, telling me to report to RAF Uxbridge in Middlesex for an examination.

On arrival, I was first given an intensive medical examination. This had been anticipated and I had previously purchased from HM Stationery Office a copy of Air Publication 130 entitled *The Medical Examination for Fitness for Flying* and had practised all the relevant exercises. For instance, I could hold my breath for 90 seconds and carry out the necessary number of press-ups on the floor. I was a somewhat skinny youth but quite strong for my size and weight, with plenty of stamina and good eyesight.

The staff could find nothing wrong with me and I was passed on for interview. My scholastic record had been somewhat patchy, with a mixture of distinctions, credits, passes and one failure (in Latin). However, while at Lloyds Bank I had passed some of the subjects in Part I of the Associated Institute of Bankers examinations, by studying in the evenings and at weekends. We could sit for these subjects piecemeal over several years. When all those in Parts 1 and 2 had been passed, our names would include the magic letters AIB, thus providing entry to managerial positions. This minor achievement seemed to interest the RAF interviewer, as well as my father's position in the Bank of England. It is possible that they had an influence on my wartime RAFVR service, for I was frequently picked out for extra administrative duties.

After the interview I was sworn in at the lowest rank in the RAF, Aircraftman Second Class, being designated in the category of Aircrew (Under Training).

Several of the other applicants were rejected for minor disabilities, such as colour blindness, and some were so dejected that they had tears in their eyes. Together with other successful entrants, I was sent to a hut for the night preparatory to 'kitting out'. There was little to do except eat a rather unappetising meal and listen to bawdy RAF songs sung by airmen in nearby huts, memorising the words for future use.

On the following day, I received a series of injections and was then provided with kit which included an ancient uniform which buttoned up to the neck, instead of the modern version with lapels which was worn with a shirt and black tie. To my surprise, I was then told to go home and await further orders.

I expected my mother to be proud when she saw me in uniform but instead she looked shocked. It took me some time to realise that she must have been thinking of her two brothers, one of whom had lost a leg on the Western Front and the other who suffered permanently from what was known as 'shell shock' in those days, as well as my father's elder brother who had been killed in the Second Battle of Ypres. Moreover, my elder brother had enlisted in the Territorial Army (TA) some months before and had already been called up. My two younger brothers, who were twins, were below military age but would become eligible in a couple of years.

Of course, I immediately notified Lloyds Bank of my RAF enlistment. The authorities were gratifyingly patriotic, for they continued to credit my bank account with my salary, less the small payment I received as an Aircraftman Second Class. I was duty-bound to notify them of any increase in my rank and pay, and did so meticulously when these events happened.

For fourteen long weeks I fretted at home, reading anything that concerned flying training but bewildered by the 'Phoney War' that persisted between the Anglo-French and German forces on the Western Front. Finally, I was ordered to report back to RAF Uxbridge on New Year's Day 1940, and went off enthusiastically to war in my ancient uniform, carrying an Airman's Diary for 1940 and a 'Stop-a-Shot' steel mirror in my left breast pocket, both of these articles having been given to me by my father, who was a veteran of the Great War.

At Uxbridge I joined a group of other recruits and found that we were all promoted to the rank of Leading Aircraftman, equivalent to Lance-Corporal in the British army. It was interesting to find that some of these recruits were not resident in the UK but had travelled from different parts of the Commonwealth and then volunteered. There was even one who lived in South

America. We were all provided with modern uniforms, with a propeller on each sleeve to denote our new rank, and each given a white flash to be worn in the front of the forage cap, indicating a status of 'u.t. pilot', with the 'u.t.' meaning 'under training'.

Thus equipped, thirty of us were sent by train to Cambridge, where parts of the some of the university's colleges had been taken over by the RAF to form a scattered and make-shift Initial Training Wing (ITW), although not given that title. Instead, we became 11 Flight, C Squadron, Downing College, and were billeted three to each bedroom in the former students' quarters in one of the blocks surrounding a quadrangle. The weather was freezing cold and no heating was provided, although there were fireplaces without fuel. We rapidly discovered that the best way to keep reasonably warm was to put sheets of newspapers between our bed blankets.

Our days were spent with early morning drill in the quadrangle, followed by intensive work in a lecture hall. The drill was conducted by a steely-eyed corporal who barked orders at us in the time-honoured service fashion, scathing about our efficiency and continually demanding smarter behaviour. We expected this process and did not resent it or even dislike the corporal. All of us had experienced the strict discipline which was common in the schools of those days. This was merely a somewhat different version and in any event we wanted to behave like smart servicemen.

Soon after our arrival we were given another series of injections during the afternoon. On this occasion the medical officer stuck the needles into our chests instead of our arms and the outcome was rather painful. We had to parade with full packs on the following morning and there was thick snow on the ground. The effect of the injections took hold on some recruits who felt dizzy and collapsed on the snow, while the others continued to march and step over their bodies. I was little affected, and the scene reminded me of a painting which hung in my grandmother's drawing room, entitled 'Napoleon's Retreat from Moscow'. Our worthy corporal was forced to dismiss the Flight.

On other occasions we joined Flights from other colleges on route marches in lanes threading through the surrounding countryside. I enjoyed these occasions in the crisp winter air, although our efforts to sing bawdy RAF songs while marching were quickly silenced by the officer leading the parade. On one occasion we were ordered to wear our gas masks and double-march the last stretch back to our colleges, so that we all arrived red-faced and breathless. The purpose of this was not explained to us.

The wireless operator in a Lockheed Hudson signalling with an Aldis lamp to the crew of another aircraft. (Author's collection)

The lectures were also similar to schooldays but covering subjects such as navigation, signals including Morse Code, aero engines, armoury including RAF machine-guns, meteorology, aircraft recognition and RAF organisation. Some trainees found the contents difficult but I was anxious to learn every subject and applied myself diligently, being helped to some extent by my previous studies at home. There were periodic tests, marked in a similar way to children's school, and my results were rated as excellent.

The course was supposed to last for about eight weeks, after which we should have been posted elsewhere to Elementary Flying Training School (EFTS) and learnt how to fly, but nothing happened when the time arrived. Thus the drill and the lectures began all over again, to our frustration. Winter turned into Spring and the 'Phoney War' continued on the Western Front, although there was some activity in the air and major problems in the Atlantic Ocean with German capital ships and U-boats.

When we dared to query our situation, we were told that all EFTSs were full and that no places were available for us. Of course we knew that the RAF was split into Bomber Command, Fighter Command, Coastal Command and Training

A large draft of aircrew volunteers leaving Britain for training in Canada in their various specialisms.
(Author's collection)

Command, plus a Maintenance Group. All had embarked on programmes of expansion, but we did not know that Training Command had planned primarily on a huge programme overseas in the Commonwealth. This had begun on 17 December 1939 when the Empire Air Training Scheme was agreed. It was centred mainly in Canada but other schools were set up in Australia and New Zealand.

These training schools provided instructors from their own citizens but the UK was sending flying instructors as well as aircraft. Eventually there were twenty-five EFTSs, twenty-five Service Flying Training Schools (SFTSs), fourteen Air Observer Schools (AOSs), fourteen Bombing and Gunnery Schools (B&GSs) and two Navigation Schools. Apart from these, Southern Rhodesia had already set up its own Air Training Scheme, with some help from the UK.

This huge Empire Air Training Scheme began after we trainees at Cambridge had joined the RAFVR, and we were still destined for scantier facilities within the UK. Moreover, there was a shortage of qualified flying instructors in our home Training Command. A highly successful method adopted by the private training school of Marshalls in Cambridge was to 'cream off' the best of their pupil pilots and to train them as instructors. This was later adopted by the RAF, often to the dismay of the trainees who had expected to fly operationally, but they had to obey orders. But this method was not employed by the RAF in April 1940.

The German Blitzkrieg began on 10 May and we read with incredulity of the rapid retreat of the Anglo-French forces. We became aware that the war was likely to last for a very long time. Then, on 19 May, we at last received our postings, being broken up into small parties and sent to various airfields. I was part of a group sent to RAF Upwood, near Ramsey in Huntingdonshire, under the impression that we were to begin flying training. But it turned out to be an operational station, part of Bomber Command's No 8 Group, and our duty was that of ground gunners.

I was introduced to my gun pit, surrounded by sandbags and equipped with an ancient Lewis gun which looked like a relic from the Great War. My function was to sit there for hours on end, gazing at the sky and hoping that a German aircraft would appear to end the boredom. However, I was glad to see the machine-gun, for I was left-handed. This was regarded as a serious disability in those days. As a small boy in elementary school I had been forced by an inspector to change my writing to the right hand, a procedure which had sent me temporarily from top of the class to the bottom. While at Downing College, we had had a session on a nearby rifle range, and I was ordered to fire right-handed. This restriction did not apply to machine-guns.

Days went by with no activity, but one early morning I went out to my gun pit and found that there was a crater nearby, the sandbags were scattered and the Lewis gun was missing. Many years later, I researched this matter at the Public Record Office and found that sixteen bombs had been dropped during the night, killing one airman. Evidently I had slept through this episode while in the barrack block some distance away.

I went to the control tower and asked for another machine-gun, but was told that my posting had come through at last and that I was to report to the EFTS at RAF Prestwick, near Ayr in Scotland. This was much to my liking and I immediately set off. Prestwick proved to be a grass airfield, marked out with a single runway, and the trainers were de Havilland Tiger Moths, the delightful biplanes which resembled fighters of the Great War.

The splendid de Havilland Tiger Moth first entered service with the RAF in 1932 as an initial trainer for pilots. It continued in that role for twelve years. Some examples remain in private hands and are regarded with much affection. (Aeroplane Monthly)

My first flight took place on 18 June, with a sergeant instructor. He seemed to loath his work and had the manner of a drill instructor, sitting in the front seat barking orders over the intercom which had to be obeyed instantly. We began with take-offs, circuits and landings, but it was difficult to acquire the feel of the aircraft with the constant stream of snarling instructions: Nevertheless, on subsequent and intermittent days, we flew higher and went into rolls, spins and loops, all with little chance of my getting an independent feel of response from the rudder bar and control column.

By this time the Battle of Britain had begun, and in retrospect it seems possible that most of the better instructors had been posted away to convert on to Hurricanes and Spitfires, leaving only a disgruntled few who thought that they were wasting their time with raw trainees. But I continued with this sergeant until one day I was taken up by the chief instructor, a flight lieutenant aged about forty, and learned more from him in about an hour than in all my previous flights.

By that time I had flown for a total of about nine hours and went solo. Training then continued on intermittent days with the sergeant but then I was called to an interview with the chief instructor and some of his colleagues.

The author in a de Havilland Tiger Moth later in the war, at Mkomo airstrip near Salisbury in Southern Rhodesia (now Harare in Zimbabwe). (Author's collection)

They gently suggested that I transfer to training as an air observer, after which I could resume training as a pilot if I wished. The thought of escaping from that hectoring sergeant was appealing, and I joined a group of trainees who had received similar advice – all of whom, perhaps unsurprisingly, had previously achieved good results with the ground subjects.

Then events moved quickly. For some unexplained reason, we were all sent down to Babbacombe, near Torquay in Devon. Trains did not run on time in those days, being subject to military requirements, and the journey was lengthy. We were told that we were to become service policemen, but did not fulfil this role. After a few days, we were all sent back to Prestwick, where we arrived on 11 August to join No 1 Air Observers Navigation School.

By comparison with the haphazard nature of our pilot training, this air observers' course proved extremely efficient. It lasted for twelve weeks, with a mixture of work on the ground and in the air. There was a very high standard of instruction. The hours were long and the pace was fast, but this was welcomed by almost all the trainees. Most of these were young and had formerly been pupil pilots but some were older volunteers who had chosen this category of aircrew since it required a different academic standard.

This Fokker F.XXXI was a four-engined passenger airliner built in Holland, sold to a British company in 1939 and given the serial letters G-AFZR. It was acquired by the RAF and sent to No 1 Air Observers Navigation School at RAF Prestwick in Ayrshire, where it became a 'flying classroom' for initial navigation training. (Aeroplane Monthly)

On the ground, lectures covered the subjects of 'dead-reckoning' navigation, aircraft compasses, meteorology, maps and charts, direction-finding instruments, air reconnaissance and air photography. There were frequent written tests and a few trainees who failed to reach the required standards were weeded out. I applied myself diligently to all these subjects and vied for the top marks with a new friend named Charles McLean (inevitably known as 'Jock'). One study which particularly interested me was astro-navigation, coupled with recognition of the major stars and planets; unfortunately, we did not practice this in the air, since we flew only in daylight. These lectures were interspersed with flying, which began a couple of days after our arrival. We boarded a four-engined Fokker airliner which had been acquired by the RAF from Dutch Air Lines and converted to a type of flying classroom. There were tables on which we pinned charts for navigation plotting and windows through which we could practice map-reading. Instructors flew with us and were most helpful and encouraging. We flew over the islands and indented coastlines of western Scotland, finding this an unexpected and novel experience, although quite hard work. It became evident that navigators in the RAF had little time

The Avro Anson first entered service as a reconnaissance aircraft with Coastal Command in March 1936. Powered by two 350hp Armstrong Siddeley Cheetah IX engines, it had a range of only 700 miles and could carry only 480lbs of bombs. Armament consisted of a single machine-gun firing forward and another in a manually-operated dorsal turret. This example was on the strength of 502 Squadron at Aldergrove in Northern Ireland. The Anson also became a standard trainer for RAF navigators, wireless operators and air gunners from the spring of 1939. It was highly reliable, served in the RAF for thirty-two years and became known as 'Faithful Annie'. (Author's collection)

The Course and Speed Calculator (CSC) Mark II was the standard instrument employed by RAF navigators at the beginning of the Second World War for solving the 'triangle of velocities' (direction and speed of wind, course and speed of aircraft through the air, and track and speed of aircraft over the ground). For instance, the navigator usually knew before take-off the required track and airspeed as well as the forecast wind speed and direction. He set these on the CSC and rotated the disk until the course to fly appeared against a pointer. The CSC could then be used to ascertain the actual wind speed and direction when a ground position was identified. (Author's collection)

to relax in flight and were constantly at work with calculations, map-reading and writing logs.

After about twenty of these flights in the Fokker we graduated to the Avro Anson, a highly reliable twin-engined monoplane which had become a standard trainer in the RAF. Only two trainees flew with an experienced pilot in each aircraft, one plotting on his chart and the other map-reading. The aircraft was fitted with a 'course-setting bombsight' in the nose, enabling a trainee to find the drift, i.e. the angle between the heading of the aircraft through the air and that over the ground or sea, providing part of the means of calculating wind speed and direction, an all-important factor.

An unusual feature of the admirable Anson was its undercarriage, which was retractable but had no automatic mechanism, having to be wound up and lowered by a handle. This took 156 turns and was quite exhausting when winding up but much easier when lowering – although one had to be sure that the undercarriage clicked into place and did not collapse on landing.

At the end of September, when halfway through this course, we were all given leave for a long weekend. This had also happened at Cambridge, when I could reach home in Woodford Green quite easily by train. The journey from Glasgow was much longer and the train was also delayed. On the approach to St Pancras station in the evening, there was a fiery glow ahead, together with vivid flashes and searchlights. It was obviously one of the raids, at a time when Hitler had ordered the Luftwaffe to bomb central London instead of the airfields of Fighter Command.

The all-clear sirens had sounded by the time we reached the station and I found a taxi driver prepared to take me to Liverpool Street station on the other side of London. We got as far as the City when he had to stop, being unable to drive over hosepipes in use by firemen. I paid him with thanks and began to walk, knowing the way but having to skirt around buildings where firemen, wardens and medical staff were trying to put out flames and rescue civilians. The calm resolution of these heroic people amazed me, but I was worried about my father who worked in the City during daytime as well as the possibility that some bombs might have fallen around my home area.

Nevertheless, the local trains were still running and I reached home. It was a relief to find that my two younger brothers had built a splendid air raid shelter in the garden lawn, clear of the house, using timber and corrugated iron provided by one of our uncles. This was deep and commodious, with the earth piled in a large mound on top, a heavy entrance trapdoor, wooden bunks inside and an

London during the Blitz at night, with firemen tackling the effect of bombs and incendiaries. (Author's collection)

emergency exit. The family seemed unafraid of the bombing and my father dismissed talk about damage in the City.

Another raid was in progress during the evening of the return journey, and I met some of our other trainees at St Pancras station. We had to take shelter for a while in the vaults of the station, listening through grills to bomb explosions and the pattering of shards of exploded anti-aircraft shells on the roads outside. The experience of these raids strengthened our resolve to serve on air operations against Germany.

Back at Prestwick, the training continued at its usual fast pace. We were in B Flight, while other trainees had arrived after us and entered A Flight. Our course finished on 6 November and I passed with high marks, recorded in my Flying Log Book together with an 'Above average' rating.

Our next move was to No 7 Bombing & Gunnery School at RAF Porthcawl in Mid-Glamorganshire, South Wales, close to the grass airfield of RAF Stormy Down from where flying training took place. In those early days of the war, qualified navigators had to train additionally as air gunners and bomb aimers, after which they were rated as air observers. There were already air gunners in the RAF but sometimes the air observer had a machine-gun in his position. When the larger four-engined aircraft came into service in Bomber Command, the classes of navigator and bomb aimer became separated while that of air observer was discontinued.

As usual, our training consisted of a combination of ground subjects and air exercises. We already had a good knowledge of the Browning and Vickers machine-guns but had never fired either in practice. At first, we fired them on a range, which I found pleasurable since my left-handedness was no handicap. Short bursts of guns firing at over 1,000 rounds per minute was highly satisfactory. This was followed by more ground practice, in a moveable gun turret mounted within a black dome. From this, the gun provided a light which shone at the interior and enabled us to practise deflection aiming at a model aircraft moving at different angles, using the ring and bead sight of the machine-gun. It was an effective method of practice without firing bursts of bullets.

In the air, practice took place in the obsolescent Fairey Battle monoplane and the twin-engined Armstrong Whitworth Whitley bomber. Both of these were

This apparatus was developed for training student air gunners in deflection shooting from a moving platform. A model aircraft (named an 'electric hare' after those employed in greyhound racing) was run at high speed round a track while a mobile turret, equipped with four Browning .303in machine-guns, was also set in motion. Both were stationary when this photograph was taken. (Author's collection)

An air gunner in a Fairey Battle aiming a Lewis gun. When these machines were transferred to Bombing and Gunnery Schools, the Lewis gun had been replaced with the more modern Vickers K gun. (Aeroplane Monthly)

usually flown by Polish pilots who had somehow managed to reach England after their country had been divided and occupied by German and Soviet forces. The trainee stood behind a single drum-fed Vickers in the rear cockpit of the Battle, or sat in the rear turret of the Whitley with four belt-fed Brownings. Short bursts, constantly adjusting the aim, were fired at a drogue towed by another aircraft simulating an attack from various angles. On the ground, the bullet holes in the drogue were counted and the trainee was assessed accordingly.

Bombing practice took place with course-setting bombsights in Fairey Battles flying over bright yellow rafts moored in the sea. To achieve accurate results it was first necessary to find the wind speed and direction which would affect the bomb during the period of fall. This was obtained by first flying on three courses and obtaining the angles of drift, then plotting them on a chart. As a rough measure, the time a streamlined bomb takes to fall in seconds is the square root of the height in feet of the aircraft. For example, a bomb dropped from 10,000 feet would fall for about twenty-five seconds. Thus an error of 5mph in wind speed alone would create an error of nearly 200 feet.

On approaching the target, the aimer levelled the bombsight with its spirit levels and set on it the wind speed and direction, the aircraft's height and airspeed, and the terminal velocity of the bomb. He then gave the pilot directions, such as 'left-left', 'right' and 'steady'. When the target passed down

The sting in the tail of an Armstrong-Whitworth Whitley was a turret equipped with four Browning .303in machine-guns. (Author's collection)

The Fairey Battle light bomber entered service with the RAF in May 1937 but suffered such heavy losses in the German Blitzkrieg of May 1940 that it was soon withdrawn from front-line service and turned over to training duties. This example is serial K7639 of 63 Squadron, the first to be equipped with Battles. (*Aeroplane Monthly*)

The 'Course Setting' bombsight was in general use by the RAF at the beginning of the Second World War. It was levelled by the bomb aimer, who set the wind speed and direction, the altitude in feet, the true airspeed and the terminal velocity of the bombs carried. On the final run-up to the target, he guided the pilot visually, while turning the milled knob at the bottom of the instrument until the target appeared along the drift wires and was lined up with the sights, when the bombs were released. The instrument could also be used to find the aircraft's drift when navigating. (Author's collection)

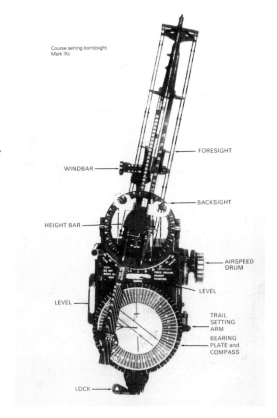

the drift wires of the bombsight and appeared in the ring sight, he pressed a release button and said 'bomb gone'.

When the practice bomb, coloured white and weighing 10lbs, hit the sea and exploded with a puff of smoke, its exact position was plotted by watchers on the shore. I had hoped to obtain a direct hit on the tiny raft but this proved impossible from 10,000 feet, although the explosions were always nearby. My results in a succession of these air tests were satisfactorily high, as were my marks in the written examinations and in Morse Code.

The course lasted for about eight weeks, bringing us to 11 January 1941. Towards the end of this period, we left our reasonably comfortable billets, presumably to make way for the next trainee course, and were housed in a former amusement arcade on Porthcawl pier. As usual this was unheated, and we wrapped ourselves in blankets and newspapers when on our bunks, awaiting our results and fates. We had expected to be promoted to sergeants and posted to Operational Training Units (OTUs), before joining squadrons.

Jock McLean came top of the course, beating me into second place by a few marks. Most unexpectedly, six of us were commissioned as Pilot Officers (General Duties). All the others became Sergeants. I was one of those commissioned, backdated to 12 January 1941, and my Flying Log Book was endorsed 'With Credit Class A. Above average – a sound Air Observer'.

Even more surprising, six of us were posted directly to an operational squadron. These were three commissioned officers, Jock McLean, myself, an older married man known as 'Monk' Matthews, and three sergeants. Our destination was 217 Squadron, based at St Eval in Cornwall. We made some enquiries and learned that St

The badge of 217 Squadron, RAF Coastal Command.

Eval was near Newquay on the north coast of Cornwall and that No 217 was a reconnaissance squadron of Coastal Command. Its badge showed a shark's head protruding from sea, with the motto 'Woe to the Unwary'.

Observer's badge (left) and Navigator's badge (right). Even in the RAF, the authorities did not make a clear distinction between these two badges. At the time the author qualified in January 1941, all navigators wore the Observer's badge, which had been introduced by Army Order No 327 of September 1915 and was worn by those qualified as navigators, bomb aimers and air gunners. In September 1942, Air Ministry Order No N1019/42 introduced the Navigator's badge with the letter N instead of the O and twelve feathers instead of the previous fourteen. This was devised for those becoming qualified solely as navigators but was also intended to be retrospective for those who had qualified as Observers from the beginning of the Second World War. However, those who already wore the Observer's badge did not make the change.

Chapter 2

South-Western Approaches

Unknown to the six newly-qualified air observers, RAF St Eval had only a very short history. Its construction had been proposed after the area five miles north of Newquay in Cornwall had been surveyed in early 1938 on behalf of RAF Coastal Command. At this time, the Air Officer Commanding-in-Chief of this Command was Air Chief Marshal Sir Frederick W. Bowhill. The headquarters were at Lee-on-Sea in Hampshire, although on 7 August in that year they were transferred to a more suitable location at Eastbury Park, Northwood in Middlesex.

Air Chief Marshal Sir Frederick W. Bowhill, the Air Officer Commanding-in-Chief of Coastal Command from 18 August 1937 to 14 June 1941. (Author's collection)

Coastal Command was considered to be the 'Cinderella' of the RAF in terms of new equipment, since priority in manufacture had been allocated to Fighter and Bomber Commands, perhaps with some justification. Nevertheless, the Command was well-organised with the resources available and forward-thinking with its projects. It consisted of three Groups, Nos 15, 16 and 18, covering the north-western and south-western sea approaches, the North Sea and the English Channel.

It was recognised that, in the event of war, co-operation with the Royal Navy would be vital. Naval liaison officers

The station badge of RAF St Eval, with St Eval Church as its emblem.

Roy Dunstan in 1937 at the age of twelve, in the garden of Trevisker Farmhouse. He watched the construction of RAF St Eval in 1938, saw the later arrival of aircraft and was sometimes allowed to board them by the ground crews. (The late H. Roy Dunstan)

were attached to all Coastal Command headquarters and plans were made for air protection of sea convoys approaching British waters. It was anticipated that many of these convoys would sail from the USA, bringing war materials and other supplies. Long-range flying boats such as Short Sunderlands, Saro Londons and Supermarine Stranraers were available for this purpose, but airfields were necessary for the land-based aircraft such as the Avro Anson, the Lockheed Hudson and the Vickers Vildebeest torpedo bomber. There were insufficient airfields near the north coast of Cornwall and RAF St Eval was planned to remedy this defect.

The people living in the area of the proposed airfield were aware that the survey had taken place but did not know the outcome. During the summer of 1938, farmers in the locality had gathered in their wheat crops and ploughed their fields ready for the next season. Visitors were expected for the shooting season and tourists for beach holidays. But on 22 November 1938 the Clerk of Works from the Air Ministry, Bill Plester, arrived on a Brough Superior motorbike to deliver news of compulsory purchases and the construction of a new airfield. He stayed overnight in Trevisker Farmhouse. This was close to St Eval Church, with its twenty-foot bell tower which for centuries had provided a landmark for mariners sailing along the rocky coast to and from Bristol.

The son of the owner of Trevisker Farm, Roy Dunstan, was thirteen years of age at this time. He rode with Bill Plester on the following day, witnessing him hiring lorries and engaging manpower. Five houses were to be demolished, one farm was to disappear entirely while Trevisker Farm lost all its ground save about 35 acres. A bulldozer and levelling machines arrived. Work soon began on demolishing some of the country lanes, as well as their high hedges which were built partly of feldspar.

This work went on apace, the only redeeming feature being increased employment for local residents. Other residents had to sell up and move out of the area. The airfield began to take shape during the following spring, when barracks, hangars, a control tower, a canteen and even a small cinema were being built. Roy Dunstan could see the appearance of all these new buildings as he cycled to and from school. On one day he saw a small monoplane and recognised it as a Miles Magister, presumably having brought an official to examine progress. More developments took place, continuing to the time when war was declared on 3 September. Then, exactly a month later, he counted nine Avro Ansons which had arrived. These proved to be on the strength of No 217 Squadron, RAF Coastal Command.

A tractor hauling stones from hedges in late 1938, during clearance of lanes and farmland in preparation for the building of RAF St Eval airfield. (The late H. Roy Dunstan)

RAF St Eval, six miles north-west of Newquay in Cornwall, was opened in 1939 as part of Coastal Command's No 19 Group. When this aerial photograph looking towards the coast was taken in 1940, there was a single camouflaged runway available for take-offs and landings. St Eval Church, with a tower 100 feet high, was on the northern boundary outside this photograph. A lighthouse on Trevose Head, five miles to the north-west, was another landmark. (Author's collection)

The history of 217 Squadron went back to 1 April 1918 when it was formed at Dunkirk with De Havilland D.H.4s. As. It operated with these long-range day bombers until the end of the Great War, and then for a while in a transport role until being disbanded back in the UK on 19 October 1919.

With the growing crisis in Europe, 217 Squadron was re-formed on 15 March 1937 and equipped with Avro Ansons as a general reconnaissance squadron of Coastal Command. In the absence of any suitable land base near the coast, it was first stationed at the training station of RAF Boscombe Down in Wiltshire. However, in the following June it moved to the fighter station of RAF Tangmere, which at least was nearer the coast.

During this period, the crews specialised in ceremonial flying in close formation. There two pilots in each aircraft, both of whom were also qualified in air navigation. Most of these were commissioned officers in the regular RAF or held 'short-service' commissions lasting for four years. The other pilots were sergeants who had originally passed through intensive technical training at RAF Halton in Buckinghamshire and later moved on to training as pilots; men such as these could eventually obtain permanent commissions and rise to high ranks in the RAF. The other aircrew members were usually junior NCOs, wireless operators capable of maintaining their equipment and ground staff such as fitters who had volunteered to train and fly as air gunners.

The ceremonial flying took place in the massed Air Display at Hendon in August 1938 and on several occasions as air escorts to royalty on sea crossings over British coastal waters. The latter included a visit by King George VI to France and another to Canada, a visit to Britain by the King of Belgium and another by the King of Romania. These official occasions were considered to give 217 Squadron the accolade of a VIP squadron. When flying, the pilots sometimes wore white overalls with badges of rank to indicate their special status.

This pleasant life, rather akin to that of a club for skilled gentlemen, could not last indefinitely. In August 1939, the squadron had to leave the comfortable conditions at RAF Tangmere and move to RAF Warmwell, near Dorchester in Dorset, where facilities were less favourable. Then war against Germany was declared on 3 September and the crews soon learnt that they would be operational from the newly-built station of RAF St Eval.

Wing Commander A.P. Revington had commanded 217 Squadron since May 1939. He had a rather fiery disposition and was a stickler for high standards of serviceability as well as good performance in the air, but he was well-liked

On 19 July 1938, King George VI and Queen Elizabeth sailed in the Royal Yacht Victoria and Albert *on a state visit to Paris, returning three days later. No 217 Squadron, based at Tangmere in Sussex, provided an air escort of fifteen Avro Ansons for both the outward and return journeys.* (Author's collection)

by his men and certainly the right person to lead them in operational work. However, conditions at RAF St Eval were less than perfect in these early days. Living accommodation was very poor, especially for the ground crews, but these maintained high spirits and worked for long hours to keep the Ansons in top flying condition. The grass airfield was not completely level and parts of it soon became muddy. Meteorological 'warm fronts' rolled in, over the sea from the west, the air rose over the coastal cliffs of north Cornwall and heavy rain fell on the airfield. Strong wire mesh had to be laid on the ground in servicing points and dispersal areas.

The crewroom for 217 Squadron was situated close to St Eval Church on the northern perimeter of the airfield. As with all others in the country, its bell tower was silenced after the outbreak of war – although it was eventually rung with all other church bells in Britain, on Winston Churchill's orders of 15 November 1942, in celebration of the defeat of the Afrika Korps by the British Eighth

The crewroom of 217 Squadron at RAF St Eval was situated near the perimeter of the airfield, close to St Eval Church. This was originally Norman, built in the thirteenth century. It fell down in 1700 but was restored by Bristol merchants. It deteriorated once more but was restored in in the 1890s and has remained as a landmark since then. (St Eval Church)

Army in the Western Desert. The young Roy Dunstan soon became friendly with the airmen working on the Ansons, and was sometimes allowed to sit in the pilot's cockpit when they were testing the engines. Airmen used to call at nearby Trevisker Farm asking for cups of tea, since their NAAFI was a long walk away. Some even enjoyed meals there, for the farm provided its own food supplies, and brought tea and coffee in return.

Meanwhile, 217 Squadron began flying operations almost immediately after its arrival. The term 'Phoney War' was not relevant to the war at sea. A few hours after Neville Chamberlain's declaration of war at 11.00 hours on 3 September, the Type VII *U-30* under Leutnant zur See Fritz-Julius Lemp had sunk the passenger liner *Athenia* of 13,581 tons, about 250 miles north-west of Ireland. This was sailing singly, before the convoy system could be introduced, and 112 lives were lost, including some Americans. Within the first month of war, U-boats operating mostly from their home ports of Kiel and Wilhelmshaven had sunk forty-one ships totalling about 153,000 tons. Moreover, the modern and formidable fleet of German capital ships posed the threat of breaking out

The coastline at Newquay in Cornwall, close to RAF St Eval, photographed in 1941. (Author's collection)

into the Atlantic and destroying entire convoys. The Royal Navy was forced to maintain many of its capital ships in home waters to counter this huge menace.

The primary role of 217 Squadron was to meet incoming convoys and to provide air escorts for as long as possible, as some deterrent against the deadly U-boats. However, the maximum endurance of the Anson, which by that time was obsolescent in front-line service, was only six hours. Thus the time the aircraft could spend over the convoys was very limited, since these were met far out to sea, and a succession of Ansons had to meet each convoy. The bombload carried by the Anson was merely two 250lb anti-submarine bombs. These were effective against the hull of a U-boat only if they exploded with six feet, an accuracy which was extremely difficult to achieve. A 'stick' of six bombs timed to drop in rapid sequence athwart the hull would have been required for better results, but the Anson did not have the capacity or means to carry that number or weight. All the pilots could do was to fly at about 1,200 feet, which was believed to be the height that U-boat periscopes were set when sweeping to sky. The sight of an RAF aircraft might deter a U-boat.

Of course, the crews would have attacked a U-boat if they had spotted one, and then alerted the escorting vessels in Morse with the Aldis Lamp. Other than that, they carried bundles of newspapers which they attempted to drop on the decks of the vessels, to welcome the crews back to England, but these often missed and fell into the sea.

These sorties required precise flying over the sea and there were no special navigation aids. The navigator could find the wind velocity by taking drifts with the bombsight plus compass bearings of the 'wind lanes' (streaks in the sea at right angles to the waves). These wind velocities enabled him to calculate a succession of 'dead reckoning' positions of the aircraft on his Mercator chart, before heading back to St Eval. The main danger occurred if bad weather clamped down the airfield and a diversion was required, while limited fuel remained in the tanks. However, the crews became familiar with the headlands and bays of the coastline and usually managed to find a visual 'pinpoint' by flying under the cloud base.

Living conditions gradually improved at St Eval. Married personnel were able to rent holiday bungalows at Mawgan Porth, about two miles distant from the airfield. Detachments from other Coastal Command squadrons sometimes arrived, such as Lockheed Hudsons from 220 Squadron and Bristol Blenheim IVs from 236 Squadron. There was a strange period from November 1939 when the Germans began depositing magnetic mines around the coasts of Britain, dropping then from aircraft or laying them from U-boats. In return, the RAF formed 'Coastal Patrol Flights' (CPFs) of Tiger Moth and Hornet Moth biplanes to keep watch. Two of these CPFs came under 217 Squadron, No 6 at St Eval and No 5 at Carew Cheriton in Pembrokeshire. They duly went into action, with the biplanes flying in pairs, but nothing was spotted.

The convoy escorts continued through the autumn and then the winter. These were mostly without incident but occasionally an Anson crew saw a torpedoed ship sinking and photographed it. On 6 February 1940, an Anson flown by Flying Officer John White and Pilot Officer Arthur Wright came down

A tanker sinking in late 1940, probably photographed from an Anson of 217 Squadron on convoy escort from RAF St Eval. (Author's collection)

when circling a convoy. A single survivor of the crew was picked up from the sea. All he could say was that something unknown went wrong with the aircraft when it was turning and that control was lost. The bodies of the other three men were not recovered. On 7 April, an Anson flown by Flying Officer Fenton bombed a U-boat and claimed a 'probable', but this cannot be confirmed by a post-war analysis of U-boat losses. No doubt the 250lb bombs fell very close but not within the necessary six feet.

In May 1940 there occurred the beginnings of two events which would change 217 Squadron's operations from 'general reconnaissance' to those which statistics showed were the most dangerous carried out by the RAF in the course of the Second World War.

The first began the early morning of the 10th when the 'Phoney War' suddenly came to an end and the Germans suddenly invaded Belgium and Holland. In response the British Expeditionary Force advanced into Belgium but the enemy made an additional and unexpected thrust through the Ardennes, between the British and French lines. These attacks were preceded by Ju 87 Stuka dive-bombers fitted with screamers and delivering their loads with pinpoint accuracy. Then came armoured divisions headed by Panzerkampfwagen III tanks and followed by motorised infantry, covered by swarms of Luftwaffe fighters and bombers.

The British divisions were completely outclassed and began a fighting retreat towards Dunkirk. On 16 May the Germans also broke through the Maginot Line and sent the French reeling back. The only manoeuvre which caused the Germans any major problem occurred three days later when Colonel Charles de Gaulle led three battalions of tanks round the rear of their forces in the region of Laon, about sixty miles north-east of Paris, and inflicted heavy casualties. These tanks had to retreat when bombed from the air, but the action vindicated de Gaulle's belief that this war would not be fought by opposing static lines but

A Panzerkampfwagen IIIE tank, together with German soldiers, on arrival in front of the church in the Saint-Pierre-Quilbignon district of Brest. About 350 of these tanks had formed the spearhead of the Blitzkrieg which began in May 1940 against the French and British forces. Each weighed 15 tons, had an output of 300hp and was armed with a 3.7cm gun in the turret. (Archives Municipales de Brest, ref: 2Fi 10520, via Geneviève Moulard)

Military vehicles abandoned in May 1940 by retreating British forces on a road near Brest, from where they were evacuated by ships to England. (Archives Municipales de Brest, ref: 2Fi 10510, via Geneviève Moulard)

Three leaders in front of a Cruiser tank on 15 February 1941. General Wladyslaw Sikorski, leader of the Free Polish Forces; Mr Winston Churchill, Prime Minister; General Charles de Gaulle, leader of the Free French Forces. (Author's collection)

Churchill's Flights to France, May–June 1940

Winston Churchill had replaced Neville Chamberlain as Prime Minister on the day the German Blitzkrieg began on 10 May 1940. He witnessed with increasing dismay the disintegration of the Allied forces and decided that something must be done to bolster the morale of the French government.

He had at his disposal three de Havilland D.H.95 Flamingo airliners, converted to VIP transports and with yellow livery, forming part of the RAF's 24 (Communication) Squadron at Hendon in Middlesex. Escorted by Hurricane fighters, he flew to Paris in one of these on three occasions between 16 and 30 May, meeting the French Premier Paul Reynaud and his military commander Marshal Phillipe Pétain. He tried to persuade them to mount counter-attacks and offered to land British and Canadian divisions at French ports, replacing the men bottled up at Dunkirk. Their response was entirely negative and defeatist. Meanwhile the Royal Navy's evacuation of troops from Dunkirk began on 26 May and continued until 4 June, by which time all the troops save a gallant rearguard had been landed at home ports.

On 10 June, Mussolini (termed 'Hitler's jackal' by Churchill), declared war on France and Britain. Churchill made another flight to France on that day, this time to Briare, about 100 miles south of Paris, to which the French government had fled to avoid advancing German troops. He offered once more to send troops to France but returned with no response.

Churchill's last flight to France took place late on 12 June, further south and landing on a bomb-pitted runway at Tours, near to where the French government had retreated. On the next day he found that the morale of the French had completely collapsed. They talked of evacuating to Bordeaux and seeking an armistice. Churchill flew home.

The de Havilland D.H.95 Flamingo was an all-metal, high-wing, civil airliner powered by two 800hp Bristol Perseus XIIC radial engines. The prototype first flew on 22 December 1938. It carried a captain, first officer and wireless operator, together with up to seventeen passengers. Two aircraft were placed on order. After the outbreak of war these two, together with the prototype, became VIP transports with the RAF's 24 (Communication) Squadron at Hendon. They were at the disposal of Winston Churchill in the period when he made flights to France before the evacuation from Dunkirk. (Mark Postlethwaite WW2images.com)

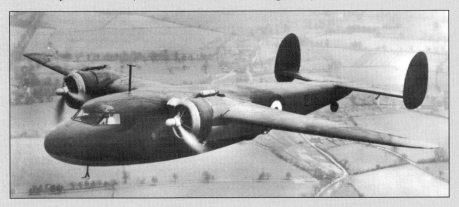

be one of movement. He was promoted to Brigadier-General and appointed as Under-Secretary of State for National Defence.

De Gaulle flew to London on 9 June and met Churchill for the first time, primarily to ask for RAF fighters to help in the struggle against the Wehrmacht invaders. Churchill was unable to help, since the RAF had lost many aircraft in the Blitzkrieg and he needed to build up RAF Fighter Command for the Battle of Britain which was already beginning.

De Gaulle returned empty-handed. However, the two men had recognised in each other great qualities of leadership and determination, although they were different in one major respect. Churchill was a Francophile, admiring the people and speaking French quite fluently, although sometimes making up his own versions of certain nouns and verbs. De Gaulle was Anglophobic, steeped in the history of past conflicts and deeply auspicious of the British Secret Service; to him, England was 'perfidious Albion'.

On 14 June, the French government carried out its intention of moving to Bordeaux. It seemed that military collapse was inevitable and de Gaulle believed that a further evacuation to the French colony of Algeria might be necessary, carrying on the war from there. He decided to discuss this project with Churchill and drove to Brest, from where he left on the French destroyer *Milan* to Britain. Churchill was contemplating a possible political union with France, which was soon abandoned. He wisely lent de Gaulle one of his airliners to fly back to Bordeaux. On landing there on 16 June, after a circuitous route over the sea, de Gaulle learnt that Paul Reynaud, the prime minister, had resigned and that Marshal Pétain was about to form a government and sign an armistice. He refused to admit defeat and, with his own life possibly in danger, flew back to London in his borrowed airliner on the following day. From there, on 18 June, he made his famous broadcast on the BBC, exhorting the French people to continue the fight, alongside the entire British Commonwealth and supported by the vast production facilities of the USA.

The Armistice was signed on 22 June but the terms were not announced until the following day. The north of France, including Paris, came under German control, as well as a tract in the west of the country with its coast down to the Spanish border. The rest of the country, as far as the Mediterranean, became the so-called 'Free Zone' under Marshal Pétain, based on the new capital of Vichy. This French government lost no time in sentencing de Gaulle to death *in absentia*, a move that the prosecutors came to regret about four years later when he returned in triumph to Paris and its ecstatic population. This division

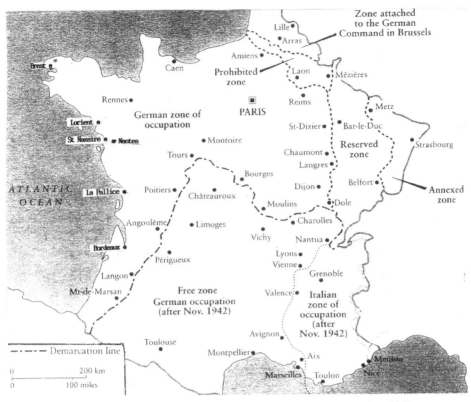

Lille•
•Arras
Amiens •
Zone attached
to the German
Command in Brussels
Brest •
Caen
Prohibited
zone
•Laon
•Mézières
Rennes •
German zone of
occupation
PARIS
Reims
Metz
Lorient •
St-Dizier •
Bar-le-Duc
St Nazaire • • Nantes
• Montoire
Chaumont •
Reserved
zone
Strasbourg
Tours •
Langres •
Bourges
ATLANTIC
OCEAN
La Pallice •
Poitiers •
Châteauroux
Dijon •
Belfort •
Annexed
zone
Moulins •
•Dole
Angoulême•
• Limoges
• Charolles
Vichy
Nantua •
Bordeaux •
Lyons •
Vienne•
Périgueux
Langon•
Grenoble
•
Mt-de-Marsan •
Free zone
German occupation
(after Nov. 1942)
Valence•
Italian
zone of
occupation
(after
Nov. 1942)
Toulouse
•
Avignon•
Montpellier•
Aix
Menton
Marseilles
Toulon
Nice
–•–•– Demarcation line
0   200 km
0   100 miles

Stages of France's partition, after her surrender to Germany was signed on 22 June 1940.

of France lasted until November 1942 when Germany occupied the 'Free Zone', while handing over to Italy an area in the south-east.

For 217 Squadron at St Eval, the German occupation of the ports along the west coast of France would define most of its activities in the latter months of 1940 and the whole of 1941. German troops reached Brest on 19 June and Lorient two days later, to be greeted by burning oil tanks set on fire by the local garrison. Saint-Nazaire was also reached on 21 June, this having been the scene of a major tragedy for Allied troops four days earlier. Soon after mid-day on 17 June, a flight of Ju 87 Stuka dive-bombers had arrived, escorted by fighters. Several bombs scored direct hits on the Cunard White Star liner *Lancastria* of 13,000 tons which was in course of embarking about 5,300 British, Czechoslovakian and Polish troops. The liner turned turtle and slowly sank in the oily sea while the German aircraft made several more passes and fired their machine-guns. When these left, small boats tried to rescue survivors but with little success. Over 3,000 bodies were washed

German soldiers checking a map on the road to Brest in June 1940, probably drivers of vehicles. The photograph was taken by another German soldier. (Archives Municipales de Brest, ref: 2Fi 10033, via Geneviève Moulard)

A huge cloud of smoke rising from a fuel oil depot at Brest, blown up by the French shortly before the arrival of the German occupation forces on 19 June 1940. The photograph was taken by one of the German soldiers. (Archives Municipale de Brest, ref: 2Fi 10515, via Geneviève Moulard)

ashore. La Pallice was occupied by German troops on 23 June but Bordeaux was given a few days extra for the former French government to sort out its affairs.

The commander of the Kriegsmarine's U-boat arm, Admiral Karl Dönitz, arrived at Lorient on 23 June 1940. On his instructions, his staff officers had spent about three weeks surveying the five major ports of western France to assess their suitability as bases for U-boats. All were admirable, but Lorient topped the list. Dönitz was exultant when he examined the facilities of its docks and shipyards. Normally pessimistic, he became convinced that Germany could now defeat Britain. No longer would his U-boats have to return to Germany for supplies of food, fuel and armaments. Moreover, they could range much further across the Atlantic. He returned to Berlin to explain a new-found optimism to Hitler. The Führer was captivated by his arguments and put into force a huge increase in production of U-boats, partly at the expense of surface warships.

Admiral Karl Dönitz opening six bunkers of the Torpedo Arsenal constructed in Lorient, named Jaguar, Polecat, Leopard, Lynx, Tiger and Wolf. Staff members of the Todt Organisation, wearing paramilitary uniforms, are standing to attention. This organisation controlled about 65,000 forced labourers working on huge concrete bunkers in the port. (The late Fregattenkapitän a.d. Günther Heinrich)

The personnel of 217 Squadron lined up in front of a Beaufort I at RAF St Eval in Cornwall in late 1940. (Author's collection)

The other event which would change the character of 217 Squadron's wartime operations began on 24 May 1940 with the arrival at St Eval of three Bristol Beaufort Mk Is, the first of several intended to replace the Avro Ansons. These new and robust aircraft, fitted with 1,330hp Bristol Taurus engines, were designed for a crew of four, had an endurance of six hours, and were armed with a single Browning .303in machine-gun in the port wing and a Vickers K machine-gun in a mid-upper turret. They were intended primarily as torpedo bombers, carrying a single torpedo, but could also be employed as medium bombers carrying a bombload of about 2,000lbs.

Two other Coastal Command squadrons had already received Beauforts and were busy training in the torpedo role. These were 22 Squadron, which had taken its first deliveries in November 1939 when based at RAF Thorney Island in Hampshire but had since moved to RAF North Coates in Lincolnshire, and 42 Squadron at Thorney Island which had received its first aircraft in April 1940.

The pilots in 217 Squadron needed to convert on to these new Beauforts and two of the most experienced were immediately sent to the windswept training station of RAF Silloth in Cumberland (after the war part of the new county of Cumbria). They began training on Beauforts three days later and the course lasted for four weeks, following which they became qualified to instruct the other pilots on these new machines.

The Bristol Beaufort I first entered service in November 1939 as a replacement for the Vickers Vildebeest biplane. Initially powered by two 1,010hp Taurus II engines, it carried a crew of pilot, air observer, wireless operator and air gunner. It was armed with a single Browning .303in machine-gun firing forward in the port wing and a Vickers .303in machine-gun in the mid-upper turret. Carrying a single torpedo or a bombload of up to 2,000lbs, it was considered the fastest torpedo bomber in the world. This example is serial N1041 of 217 Squadron, photographed off the north coast of Cornwall in mid-1941. (Author's collection)

Other events took place at St Eval during this period. On 1 July, Wing Commander A.P. Revington was promoted to Group Captain and took over command of the station, while handing over command of 217 Squadron to Wing Commander L.H. Anderson. The squadron also implemented the RAF's new regulation of increasing the ranks of all junior NCO aircrews to that of sergeant, a change which was beneficial to many of the wireless operators and air gunners.

The Battle of Britain had begun in the skies about England and, although 217 Squadron was still operating with Ansons, it was expected to assume a more aggressive role. This became evident in daylight near Guernsey on 11 July when Sergeant Nelson H. Webb shot down a Heinkel He 59 floatplane with Red Cross markings. The Channel Islands had been occupied by the Germans and British intelligence had reported that these aircraft were being employed in the role of reconnaissance rather than air-sea rescue.

The conversion to Beauforts proved lengthy. The aircraft was far more difficult to handle than the docile Anson, there were problems with the engines, while new machines were delivered and then taken away for various reasons. The squadron was still operating with Ansons in mid-July 1940 when Wing

This Heinkel He 59 floatplane serial D-AGIO of Seenotflugkommando 1 *was on reconnaissance while masquerading as a Red Cross aircraft. It was shot down near Guernsey on 11 July 1940 by an Anson of 217 Squadron flown by Sergeant Nelson H. Webb. The three crew members got into a dinghy and were picked up by a German rescue launch.* (Mrs E. Godfrey collection)

Commander Anderson was ordered to send them at full strength on a daylight attack against the docks at Brest. This seemed to be a pointless suicide mission, for the port was known to be strongly defended with flak and, more significantly, two *Staffeln* (Squadrons) of Messerschmitt Bf 109Es. An Anson would have stood no chance against the twin 20mm cannons and twin 7.9mm machine-guns of the latter.

Anderson appealed against this order, while offering to fly himself with a volunteer crew against the port. His appeal was dismissed and he was faced with an impossible dilemma, for he was not prepared to sacrifice his squadron on a useless mission. He refused to obey the order, lost his command, was reduced in rank to Squadron Leader, and told that he faced a court martial. The squadron was taken over on a temporary basis by one of the Flight Commanders, Squadron Leader L.B. King, and continued to fly patrols and convoy escorts.

Soon after midday on 11 August, an Anson flown by Pilot Officer Anthony Gordon-Peiniger took off on one of these operations. Some time afterwards it sent out an SOS. A search was mounted but nothing was found and all crew members lost their lives. The reason was never discovered but it must have been something unexpected and violent, for the wireless operator had only enough time to send the aircraft's call-sign and the SOS.

Three days later, Wing Commander Guy A. Bolland arrived at RAF St Eval to take over command of 217 Squadron. He was a very capable and popular officer, commissioned in 1931 and with experience of various squadrons at home and abroad. He had also commanded a Coastal Command station. In his own words, he rated the Ansons as 'quite useless in any wartime role except a limited anti-submarine patrol to protect shipping'. To increase their defensive capability, he had each fitted with a Vickers K machine-gun in a waist position. When Group Headquarters heard of this, they ordered the guns removed, but Bolland quietly chose to ignore their order.

September was the month when the Battle of Britain reached its climax, with the Luftwaffe defeated by a narrow margin. It was also the month when the activities of 217 Squadron ceased as general reconnaissance and began on night bombing. The Ansons were employed with other Coastal Command squadrons and several of Bomber Command in attacking enemy ports, primarily those along the north coast of France, where barges had been gathered to transport troops and armaments for Hitler's invasion of Britain. Usually six Ansons were dispatched on nights when the weather was suitable, with each aircraft carrying two 250lb or four 120lb bombs.

Numerous barges and dock installations were destroyed in these raids, but the Germans effected quick repairs and brought up more barges from the inland waterways. Nevertheless, if the vessels had put to sea without the Luftwaffe's control of the air, they would have been obliterated by the guns of the Royal Navy and the bombs of the RAF. On 17 September, Hitler was forced to postpone his invasion 'indefinitely'.

The Ansons then switched to night attacks on the military port of Brest, at the request of the Admiralty. Between 23 and 27 September, twenty Ansons were dispatched on sorties, each carrying up to 500lbs of bombs which usually included incendiaries. The crews flew these sorties with great determination, remembering the fate of their commanding officer during the previous month. Beauforts of 217 Squadron made their first operational sorties on the night of 26 September, when two were dispatched to Brest, each carrying four 250lb bombs.

One surprising outcome of these September operations, which numbered almost 200 sorties, is that not a single Anson was lost. There was plenty of

Warships of the Home Fleet in the English Channel, ready to resist any attempt at invasion after the fall of France. Some of them flew balloons to snare Junkers Ju 87 Stuka dive-bombers. An Avro Anson is on patrol above them, probably carrying two anti-submarine bombs. (Author's collection)

flak but the crews reported that it always burst *ahead* of them. It seems that the German gunners did not realise that they were being attacked at night by venerable aircraft with cruising and maximum speeds about 50mph less than the average for RAF bombers, and did not adjust their deflection shooting accordingly.

By October, the Luftwaffe had switched almost entirely to night bombing of Britain. It was the beginning of the 'Blitz' against cities, towns and ports. The area around RAF St Eval also had to endure numerous attacks, when the German bombers seemed to drop their bombs on ETA (Expected Time of Arrival) after obtaining a visual 'fix' on the coastline. Most of these bombs missed their main target and fell in the surrounding countryside, especially when a dummy airfield was lit up about two miles to the east. Many of these raids took place when the dockyards of Plymouth were being bombed and a fiery glow could be seen low on the horizon.

This Heinkel He 111 which tried to approach the south-west coast of England was shot down into the sea with its starboard engine on fire by a Lockheed Hudson of Coastal Command. The photograph is undated but the incident probably occurred when a detachment of Hudson Is operated from St Eval in Cornwall from 6 November 1940 to 28 April 1941, sent from their base of Thornaby in Yorkshire. (Author's collection)

The siren sounded almost every night during the winter months and some families in the area moved away, especially those with children. Aircrews were billeted several miles distant from RAF St Eval, in hotels requisitioned for that purpose. One German bomber was shot down, and the crew members were buried in St Eval Churchyard, with shots fired over their graves. The crew of another bomber baled out and became prisoners.

On 17 October, Squadron Leader L.H. Anderson was tried at a court martial at Coastal Command's Headquarters in Northwood, where he was 'severely reprimanded'.[1] This sentence blighted his career, for he remained in the same rank for the remainder of the war, but at least he was regarded as a saviour by the members of his former squadron.

---

1. The National Archives: AIR 21/3 General Courts Martial, home, June 1918–December 1960.

Apart from the first day of the month, when six Ansons were sent out on a sortie over north-east France, the activities of the aircrews of 217 Squadron in October were confined to converting on to the new Beauforts and testing them for carrying various bombloads.

However, ominous events took place during the month in the ports in western France. On 3 October, the first Italian submarines arrived in Bordeaux to join the U-boats in attacking British convoys. These were large long-range vessels and they formed a flotilla named Betasom, with 'Beta' for the letter 'B' and 'som' for 'sommergibili' (submarines).

Even more threatening was the arrival on 16 October of Admiral Karl Dönitz at Lorient, to form his operational headquarters in a large requisitioned mansion near the waterfront of Kernéval. By this time, his U-boats were using French ports for refuelling, rearmament and maintenance. The first to do so had been the Type VIIA *U-30* at Lorient on 7 July, under the command of Käpitanleutnant Fritz-Julius Lemp.

The headquarters of Admiral Karl Dönitz at Lorient, situated at Larmor-Plage near the dry dock of Kernével and only a short distance from the U-boat bunkers. The ground floor was protected by a thick concrete fortification and there were blockhouses in the grounds. It was known as the 'House of Sardines' by the U-boat crews. (The late Fregattenkapitän a.d. Günther Heinrich)

Dönitz held daily conferences with his staff in these headquarters. Its walls were covered with maritime charts on which little flags were pinned showing positions of U-boats and whatever was known of enemy vessels and their probable courses. There were also drawings and charts showing differences in time zones, daily meteorological reports, conditions of ice and fog, daily updates of the times U-boats could remain at sea and the facilities available for them in the various ports. There was also a huge globe which gave accurate distances.

One of the first visitors to Lorient was Dr Fritz Todt, the engineer who headed the huge Todt Organisation which had built the German autobahns and the Siegfried Line. With the authority of Hitler, Todt and Dönitz devised a colossal plan for building massive shelters for the U-boats, their crews and stores in the French ports.

German officers with civilians (possibly from the Todt Organisation) in front of the U-boat bunkers known as Keroman I and Keroman II in Lorient. The two bunkers faced each other across a slipway which had direct access to the sea. Keroman I was 120 metres in width, 85 metres in length and 18.5 metres in height; it contained five chambers, entitled K1 to K5. Keroman II was 180 metres in width, 138 metres in length and 18.5 metres in height; it contained seven chambers, numbered K6 to K12. All the chambers in both bunkers had facilities for hauling U-boats up into dry dock. This complex was completed in October 1941. (Bundesarchiv Koblenz, ref: 10111-MW-3936-01A, via Tim Carroll)

The U-boat bunker at Saint-Nazaire was built on the northern side of the rectangular dock named the Bassin de Saint-Nazaire. It was 295 metres in width, 130 metres in depth and 18 metres in height. There were fourteen chambers with eight each housing a single U-boat and capable of hauling it up into dry dock, while six could house two U-boats. An underground railway ran along the rear of the bunker, giving access to all chambers. The roof was protected with gun emplacements armed with 20mm cannon. This photograph of part of the bunker was taken in April 1942, when construction was nearing completion. (Bundesarchiv Koblenz, ref: 10111-MW-3747-30,via Tim Carroll)

The Type XI U-67 photographed in 1942 on the flat surface of a wedge-shaped 'chariot', partly in one of the dry dock chambers of bunker Keroman II in Lorient. After its initial war cruise from Wilhelmshaven, this U-boat made seven more from Lorient. It was sunk on 16 July 1943 when returning from Bermuda by a Grumman TBF Avenger operating from the aircraft carrier USS Core. There were no survivors. By this time, it had sunk fourteen Allied vessels. (The late Fregattenkapitän a.d. Günther Heinrich)

The U-boat bunker in Brest was situated in the far west of the dockyard, covering an area 300 metres in length and 177 metres in depth. The height was 18 metres, which included a reinforced concrete roof with an average thickness of 4 metres. There were fifteen chambers, lettered A to E and then numbered 1 to 10. These were of different lengths. A to C could each house three U-boats while D to E could each house two. All the numbered chambers housed only a single U-boat but this could be hauled up a slipway into dry dock. This photograph of part of the bunker was taken in September 1941 while construction was still in progress. When the bunker was complete, three gun emplacements were situated on the roof, each armed with 20mm cannon against low-flying aircraft. There was also a radar station. (Bundesarchiv Koblenz, ref: 10111-MW-2849-03, via Tim Carroll)

A later stage of the construction of the U-boat bunker at La Pallice. When completed, the bunker was 195 metres in length, 165 metres in depth and 19 metres in height. There were ten chambers for U-boats, each protected by a reinforced concrete roof over 4 metres thick. (Bundesarchiv, Koblenz, ref: 10111-MW-6863-23, via Tim Carroll)

The U-boat bunker at La Pallice under construction at the east end of the dock basin, showing a swarm of forced labourers of the Todt Organisation. Cofferdams in front of the bunker held back the sea during most of this work. (Archives départmentales de la Charente-Maritime, ref: 62 Fi 76, via Geneviève Moulard)

Together with the huge increase in production of U-boats, these plans were intended to defeat Britain, which seemed to be happening already. In October and November 1940, the Kriegsmarine sank about 830,000 tons of shipping, about 80 per cent of which was by U-boats. This rate of attrition was far greater than could be made good by the British shipbuilding industry. These months were called 'The Happy Time' by the U-boat men. It is no wonder that Winston Churchill said years later: 'The only thing that ever frightened me during the war was the U-boat peril.'

In November, the aircrews of 217 Squadron were still occupied with testing their new Beauforts, but operational sorties took place in daylight on a couple of days. On the 10th, a Beaufort made an unsuccessful hunt for a reported U-boat. On the 29th, three Beauforts hunted without success for a reported enemy destroyer but instead were tackled by Messerschmitt Bf 109s. Fortunately they were still over the sea and were able to escape by skimming over the surface at extreme low level, at which the RAF pilots were adept and which thwarted the diving tactics of the Germans. All the Beauforts escaped with little damage. By the end of November, most of the Ansons in 217 Squadron had disappeared and the aircrews were ready to fly operationally in Beauforts. Their main initial target was to be Brest, aiming at the military port and its power station, but sometimes including the nearby airfield of Lanvéoc. The bombloads were either a single Time Impact Mine (TIM), an adapted sea mine which weighed about 1,700lbs and descended with a parachute which kept it in an upright attitude, or a mixture of 250lb general-purpose bombs together with clusters of 4lb or 25lb incendiaries.

The Beauforts usually took off in the evenings, during darkness. Six sorties against Brest were flown on 1 December and all aircraft returned safely. Nine took off on 7 December and the squadron suffered its first loss with Beauforts when one, flown by Flying Officer Hugh Mussenden, was brought down by flak; all four men were killed and given a military funeral by the Germans. Six other Beauforts attacked on 8 December, five more on 10 December, six more on 11 December and seven more on 14 December; all returned from these sorties.

There was a change of target on 16 December, when six Beauforts took off before midnight to attack the docks at Bordeaux, possibly to give the Italian submariners an unpleasant surprise. Four were loaded with TIMs and two carried eight 250lb general-purpose bombs. The target was at the extremity of their range and they were routed over the French mainland. One carrying a TIM ran into bad weather and turned back. Four reached the target and caused damage to a shipyard, a factory and a sluice bridge.

The remaining Beaufort, carrying bombs and flown by Sergeant Douglas Matthews, was hit by flak, probably near Nantes, and had to turn back with an engine which soon failed completely. Matthews managed to nurse the Beaufort to the north coast of France and then attempted to force-land on a beach, but hit a slope and was killed. The gunner, Sergeant Charles Ayres, and the wireless operator, Sergeant Archibald Hastie, were injured and soon captured.

The second pilot, Sergeant John Roy Massey, was unharmed and tried to evade capture. He made his way down to Marseille in Vichy France, probably with the help of an escape line set up by Captain Ian Garrow of the Highland Division, who had reached this port after Dunkirk. Massey's family were notified that he was safe. From there, he gradually followed another escape line via Barcelona, Madrid and Lisbon to Gibraltar. On 23 May he boarded Catalina AH560, being ferried from the Middle East back to Mount Batten in Cornwall, but this was lost for no known reason and there were no survivors.

One the night of 9/10 December 1940, RAF Bomber Command despatched ninety aircraft to bomb airfields and other targets at Düsseldorf, Lorient and Bordeaux. Some bombs at Bordeaux caused considerable damage to vessels and the docks, but others fell in residential areas. The Stock Exchange and the Hotel Fronfède were among those damaged, as shown here. Sixteen civilians were killed and sixty-seven injured.
(Archives de Bordeaux, via Geneviève Moulard)

An Italian submarine (left) alongside a German U-boat, moored in La Pallice harbour. (Archives départmentales de la Charente-Maritime, ref: 62 Fi789, via Geneviève Moulard)

Meanwhile, 217 Squadron continued its night bombing attacks against the French ports. On 18 December, another long-range attack was attempted against the docks at Bordeaux. One of the Beauforts, flown by Flight Sergeant N.S. Petch, ran out of fuel shortly before reaching the English coast on the return flight. Petch made a successful ditching near The Needles off the Isle of Wight, but the 'Mae West' lifejacket worn by the wireless operator, Sergeant Henry E. Postill, failed to inflate and he was lost. The other three men were picked up by an air-sea rescue launch.

On the next night bombing attack, 20 December, Brest was again the choice, but with Lorient as a secondary target. Five Beauforts carrying TIMs took off, but the winter weather was poor and Brest was covered with low cloud. Only one Beaufort dropped its mine, without visible result. Two turned back to St Eval, still carrying their mines. One flew on to Lorient, found it covered with cloud, and then turned back to St Eval with its mine. The fifth Beaufort, flown by Pilot Officer Nelson Webb, who had been awarded a DFM and also commissioned, also tackled Lorient. Webb seems to have come down through cloud and found the target, but his Beaufort was shot down by flak and there were no survivors.

Two views of Beaufort I serial L4463 of 217 Squadron, which crashed near Vannes in Western France on the night of 16/17 December 1940, after being hit by flak on the outward flight for an attack on the docks at Bordeaux. (Archiv Petrick)

Sergeant John Roy Massey of 217 Squadron, a pilot who flew as navigator in Beaufort L4463 over France on the night of 16/17 December 1940. He survived when the aircraft crashed but evaded capture and eventually reached Gibraltar via Spain and Portugal, only to lose his life on 23 Kay 1941 in Catalina AH560 en route to England. (Tom Massey)

The weather inhibited flying for the next few nights, but on 24 December Flying Officer Robert Robertson took off from St Eval on an air test. The Beaufort stalled, crashed and burst into flames, killing him immediately. This was not the end of the calamities in December. Another long-distance raid against Bordeaux took place on the 26th, but one Beaufort flown by Flying Officer John H.D. Tilson did not return, for an unknown reason. All four crew members lost their lives.

Thus December 1940, the first month when 217 Squadron had been mainly involved with night bombing in Beauforts, had resulted in the loss of six aircraft and eighteen crew members, Of the latter, seven were pilots although two of them had been flying as navigators. The nominal strength of the squadron was eighteen aircraft and crews. The Beauforts could be replaced but it was difficult to find fully-trained and experienced crew members.

These war graves of the crew of Beaufort serial L4474 of 217 Squadron were discovered unexpectedly by Air Commodore Graham R. Pitchfork when passing through Lorient. He laid some flowers on the plot. The Beaufort was shot down on 20 December 1940 during a bombing raid on the docks. Right to left: Pilot Officer Nelson H. Webb (pilot); Sergeant C.H. Tiplady (air observer); Sergeant P. Milligan (wireless operator); Sergeant H. Plant (air gunner). (Air Commodore G.R. Pitchfork, MBE, RAF (Ret'd))

Chapter 3

Operational Beginnings

My promotion from Leading Aircraftman to the commissioned rank of Pilot Officer was very gratifying but completely unexpected. I had expected to become a Sergeant when qualifying as an air observer but obtaining a commission was only a vague possibility in the distant future, dependent on proven merit and a certain amount of good luck. One immediate problem was that I did not have a uniform, for my airman's kit had to be handed in at RAF Stormy Down. This was in the days before all RAF aircrew members were provided with battledress on which they wore their badges of rank with wings or brevets.

I was given a grant to purchase my new uniform as well as leave for a few days, plus first-class rail travel warrants as befitted my new status as an RAF officer, wearing civilian clothes that I had always carried in my kitbag, I returned home to Woodford Green where my father recommended a military tailor in the West End of London. Some items such as peaked cap, forage cap, gloves, greatcoat, shirts, black tie, shoes and socks, could be purchased immediately. However, the uniform jacket (with its single narrow stripe on each sleeve, brass VR badges for each lapel and air observer badge on the left breast) had to be made to measure, as did the trousers.

My written orders were to report to 217 Squadron at RAF St Eval in Cornwall on 25 January 1941, but the tailor could not provide the uniform jacket and trousers until a couple of days after that date. It seemed best to arrive on the correct date, wearing a civilian suit and carrying those items of clothing already purchased. I took a train to Padstow, the nearest railway station, on the appointed day and arrived in the evening. Taxis were available and I took one to the airfield, about five miles away. There were brilliant flashes ahead as we neared the airfield, obviously from an air raid. The driver stopped and I walked to the guardroom, carrying my kit.

The guard examined my orders and pointed out the Officers' Mess, a short distance away, while an ambulance and fire engine dashed past from right to left. I walked to the Mess, where I was given a room for the night. It seemed that a

Two Beaufort Is of 217 Squadron with the squadron letters MW, carrying torpedoes. Both survived their operational careers. Beaufort letter E serial L4487 was 'struck off charge' with No 6 Operational Training Unit on 27 July 1944. Beaufort letter E serial N1019 was 'struck off charge' with No 5 Operational Training Unit on 15 November 1944. (Author's collection)

German parachute mine had fallen on an air raid shelter and that there had been many killed, perhaps including airwomen.

Records show that twenty-two airmen were killed by this parachute mine, one of whom died on the following day. All were ground staff and five were aircraftmen serving in 217 Squadron. It seems that no airwomen were in the shelter. One of the remaining Ansons on the strength of 217 Squadron was destroyed by the blast. This loss of life among ground staff on 25 January 1941 was by far the worst suffered at RAF St Eval during the war.

On the following day, I needed to report to 217 Squadron and was advised to head for the crewroom, on the other side of the airfield alongside St Eval Church. Before this, I went to station stores and drew out a sheepskin Irvin jacket, a flying helmet and goggles, flying boots and a 'Mae West' lifejacket. Then I went to the armoury and collected a Smith & Wesson .38in revolver, which was the standard issue for RAF officers. Lastly I visited the parachute

Ground crews of 217 Squadron at RAF St Eval in Cornwall, enjoying a tea break on the arrival of the NAAFI's 'Char Waggon'. (Author's collection)

section and collected a parachute pack with its separate harness. Navigational instruments such as parallel rules, dividers and a course and speed calculator were already in my possession. All these items remained RAF property and were 'on my charge', so I had to keep a list of them.

Wearing the Irvin jacket over my civilian suit, flying boots on my feet and peaked cap on my head, I walked over the muddy airfield to the crewroom. There were several aircraft on the hardstanding, recognisable as Bristol Beauforts, although I had never seen one before. The crewroom was empty apart from three sergeants, members of a crew who by coincidence were worried since their air gunner had reported sick and they were due to take off on a daylight reconnaissance patrol. I eagerly explained that I was a qualified air gunner in addition to being a navigator and bomb aimer, and they accepted my services.

We duly took off and headed over the sea towards the south coast of Eire. I entered the turret, which was equipped with a single Vickers K gun. My job

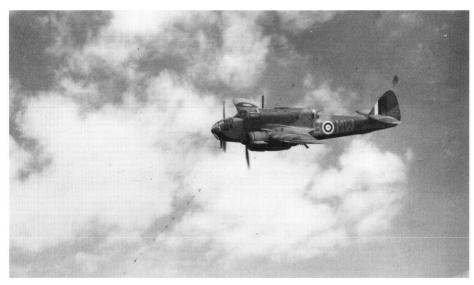

A Beaufort I of 217 Squadron photographed in 1941. (Author's collection)

The pilot's controls in a Beaufort. There was another seat on his right, where the navigator sat on take-off and landing, or when he was not occupied in the nose of the aircraft (shown here on the right). (Author's collection)

was to scan the sea for any U-boat periscope and the sky for any enemy aircraft. The turret seemed to have a minor fault, for it would not traverse fully to port, but this did not seem to be serious enough to abort the flight. I hoped that there would be some excitement which would enable me to demonstrate my skill with a machine-gun, but the sortie was completely uneventful and we eventually landed back at base.

After the landing, I reported the minor turret defect to the pilot and made my way back to the officers' mess. I did not enter the sortie in my flying log book, for fear of getting in trouble for flying while still in civilian clothes, but

A pilot in a Beaufort looking towards a sergeant navigator seated by his chart table in the nose. The aircraft was so noisy that they had to use the intercom, even at this short distance. (Author's collection)

The navigator's position in a Beaufort, looking forward from the right of the pilot's seat. Chart table and swivel seat are on the left, a 'course-setting' bombsight is in the nose and the instrument panel is on the right. This Beaufort is also fitted with a rearward-firing blister gun in the floor, aimed through a mirror and designed as protection against enemy fighters making belly attacks. (Author's collection)

at least I had had the useful experience of examining the navigator's position in the nose of a Beaufort. This had a revolving seat, with a chart table on the left and an adjustable light above it, A course-setting bombsight was fitted forward, through which there was a good view of the ground or sea. There were also clear views through the Perspex above and to the sides. Various gadgets were fitted on the right, such an automatic bomb distributor (nicknamed a Mickey Mouse), the bomb fuser, catches holding a bearing compass and an Aldis Lamp, There was no machine-gun, but a single .303in Browning was fitted in the port wing, from where it was fired by the pilot. The Beaufort could carry about 2,000lbs of bombs, which was considerable for a machine of its size. It all seemed very impressive to me, apart from the fact that there was no astrodome and thus no possibility of astro-navigation in flight.

Sitting alone in the officers' mess, as a teenager wearing civilian clothes who was being eyed suspiciously by other officers, was very embarrassing. It was therefore a great relief on the following day when the tailor turned up with my uniform, having patriotically made a special journey from London. In addition my fellow air observers McLean and Matthews arrived, presumably having been delayed by similar difficulties. We were billeted with other officers in the Watergate Hotel on the coast north of Newquay, partly since there was insufficient accommodation on the airfield and partly as shelter from the enemy bombing. Matthews was an older married man and set about finding a cottage for himself and his wife. The sergeant aircrew members had their own mess on the station and were billeted further down the coast at Treyarnon Bay. We had little contact with them, apart from the occasions when we were being briefed for flying or when we were in the same aircraft.

The six newly-arrived air observers, officers and sergeants, soon realised that they were not welcome at 217 Squadron. There was no personal animosity but the problem was two-fold. Firstly, they had been picked out while at Bombing & Gunnery School to replace pilots who were acting as navigators and enable these to fly as first pilots. But each crew were already a smooth-running team dependent on each other for efficiency and perhaps preservation of their lives.

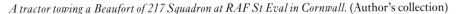

A tractor towing a Beaufort of 217 Squadron at RAF St Eval in Cornwall. (Author's collection)

Secondly, the new air observers had not passed through an Operational Training School (OTS) and were not qualified to fly operationally.

Thus 217 Squadron was expected to provide operational training for the newly-arrived air observers, and this presented considerable difficulties. The nominal strength of the squadron was eighteen aircraft and aircrews, but these had been depleted by the losses in December. New Beauforts had arrived but the remaining aircrews were fully occupied with urgent operational work. Among these was the Squadron Navigation Officer, Pilot Officer Jack E. Gibson, an air observer who normally flew with Pilot Officer Kenneth J. Holmes. For the time being, the six new air observers were left to pick up whatever information they could, by examining the Beauforts and discussing matters with experienced aircrew members in the messes and squadron crewroom.

Despite the usual meteorological difficulties of flying in January, 217 Squadron had made huge efforts in its role of bombing enemy targets in Brittany. One of these was the heavy cruiser *Admiral Hipper* which had passed, initially

The 12,900-ton heavy cruiser Admiral Hipper *in dry dock at Brest, photographed on 20 January 1941 by a Spitfire PR1 of No 1 Photographic Reconnaissance Unit flown from RAF St Eval by Pilot Officer J.D. Chandler.* (Author's collection)

undetected, from German waters into the North Atlantic. The cruiser HMS *Berwick* had been detached from duties in the Mediterranean and exchanged gunfire with this formidable enemy, but she had slipped into Brest on 4 January for refuelling, re-arming and servicing. Her presence caused alarm in the Admiralty, for she was quite capable of wiping out an entire convoy as well as its escorting destroyers. The RAF was called upon to deal with this menace. Attacks had been made during January by Whitleys, Hampdens and Wellingtons of Bomber Command, and by Beauforts and Blenheims of Coastal Command. In spite of these the warship remained unscathed.

In total during January, the Beauforts of 217 Squadron had made thirty-three sorties against Brest, seventeen against Lorient and six against other mainland targets, in addition to other sorties hunting for enemy surface vessels off France. Somewhat miraculously, no Beauforts had been lost to enemy fire but there had been a serious accident on 17 January when Flying Officer Forward returned in very bad weather to St Eval from an attack on Brest. He flattened out too high over the airfield, stalled and dropped about fifty feet on to the runway. The Beaufort was destroyed and all four crewmen were taken into hospital with spinal injuries. There was a change in command structure for RAF St Eval on 5 February 1941 when No 15 Group was moved from Plymouth to Liverpool, taking with it the responsibilities for protecting the south-western approaches. The new No 19 Group under Air Commodore G.R. Bromet was formed at Plymouth in its place, with the task of increasing operations against the enemy ports in France.

Meanwhile, on 1 February 217 Squadron lost two Beauforts on a daylight attack against the *Admiral Hipper* in Brest. They were flown by Flight Lieutenant R.A. Oakley and Sergeant J.B. Rutherford, and all eight men were killed. This was followed by a loss on 12 February, when Flight Lieutenant A.V. Hunter was sent on a patrol in the Bay of Biscay, but was shot down by a flak ship off Brest; the four crewmen were picked up but a passenger from 19 Group, Flying Officer Wybrant, was lost. Then, on 15 February, three more Beauforts were sent out on another attack against the *Admiral Hipper*, flown by Pilot Officer F.B. Tams, Flying Officer R.W. Gair and Sergeant C.G.L Williams. All were shot down by enemy fighters, with the loss of ten lives.

Wing Commander Guy Bolland visited 19 Group to protest against the orders to send his aircraft over Brest in daylight, but the only response was to select him for replacement. Some explanation of the background to the orders came to me many years later when I received a letter from Squadron Leader Gilbert

Group Captain Guy A. Bolland CBE. As a Wing Commander, he commanded 217 Squadron at RAF St Eval from July 1940 to March 1941. He was relieved of this command when he protested about the futility of sending Beauforts on suicidal daylight missions against the heavily defended port of Brest. (Author's collection)

Hayworth, DFC, DFM. At the time, he had been a pilot of one of three Handley Page Hampden Is of 50 Squadron, Bomber Command, detached to RAF St Eval from their base of RAF Lindholme in Yorkshire. Winston Churchill had personally demanded action against the *Admiral Hipper*, which was reported to have sunk seven from a convoy of nineteen merchant ships. Gilbert Hayworth was ordered to carry a load of two 2,000lb and two 500lb bombs, the heaviest possible for a Hampden I, and dive-bomb the cruiser in daylight while in dock at Brest. The dive had to be made from above 4,500 feet, in order to give the bombs sufficient velocity to penetrate the armoured deck of the cruiser. But at the last moment the operation was cancelled, since the cloud base over Brest was believed to be too low. The three Beauforts were sent as an alternative, I passed this information to Wing Commander Frank A.B. Tams, one of the few survivors of the Beauforts sent out on that day, and the two veterans communicated with each other. Frank eventually wrote a book about his own experiences in RAF service and this included a description of being shot down by a Messerschmitt

Pilot Officer Frank Tams of 217 Squadron, wearing an Irvin flying jacket, photographed for publicity purposes as 'A typical Coastal Command pilot'. His Beaufort was shot down by a Messerschmitt Bf 109 on 15 February 1941 during a daylight raid on Brest. He was wounded but managed to bale out. He then spent the remainder of the war as a PoW in German prison camps. (The late Wing Commander Francis A.B. Tams, OBE)

Bf 109 over France on that day.[2] He was able to amplify this from a meeting with the German pilot involved and an eyewitness from the French Resistance. The German pilot, who visited him in the Kriegsmarine hospital in Brest, said that he had put his first burst into the turret, the second into the port engine and the third into the cabin. Frank gave the order to bale out but the gunner, Sergeant James F.J. Sheridan, had already been killed. The navigator, Flying Officer A.H. Stratford (who was a pilot acting in that capacity) and the wireless operator, Sergeant C.W.D. Cannon, left by the top hatch and parachuted to the ground where they were captured.

Frank had been wounded in the legs and one wrist. He had difficulty extricating himself from the diving aircraft but was eventually pulled out by the slipstream. When floating down by parachute, he was perturbed to see the Messerschmitt circling round him, wondering if the pilot intended to shoot him. But the German pilot who, like most of those who flew in the RAF and the Luftwaffe, had an affinity with their opponents. He told Frank that he was merely indicating his descent to the troops on the ground.

---

2. F.A.B. Tams, *A Trenchard 'Brat'*. Bishop Auckland, The Pentland Press Limited, 2000.

After the war, the French witness told Frank that he saw two RAF aircraft shot down and three men parachute from one of them before it exploded. The German pilot then made a 'few somersaults in the sky to show his triumph'. Researches made by French air historians show that all three Beauforts were shot down by Messerschmitt Bf 109s from Jagdgeschwader 77. Seven of the eight men in the other two Beauforts were killed instantly but the navigator of one of them, Sergeant Joseph R.H. Webster, died of his injuries two days later.

Despite their losses, the crews of 217 Squadron carried out their attacks at night against Brest. On 21 February, six Beauforts carrying full bomb loads made a combined attack with six Blenheim IVs of 59 Squadron, the latter being on detachment at St Eval from their base at Thorney Island, In total, the aircraft carried twenty-two semi-armour-piercing (SAP) bombs of 500lbs and ten of 250lbs. They attacked from high level and the *Admiral Hipper* was not damaged hut a gasworks near the docks was hit.[3] All twelve aircraft returned safely.

Other efforts were made on 24 February. A single Beaufort flown by Flying Officer John Welsh was despatched in daylight to intercept two German destroyers which had been reported sailing along the north coast of France from Le Vierge. The Beaufort was escorted by two Blenheim IVFs (the fighter version of this machine) of Coastal Command's 236 Squadron, which was based at St Eval at this time. The formation came across the destroyers when they were about eighteen miles east of Ile Brehat and Welsh dropped two 500lb bombs, which were seen to explode but evidently caused no damage. There was then an encounter with a Messerschmitt Bf 109 of II Jagdgeschwader 77 which damaged the Beaufort, but all three RAF aircraft returned to St Eval. However, an engine in one of the Blenheims cut out when it was landing, resulting in a crash in which the three crewmen suffered slight injuries. A night attack against Brest by five Beauforts was made in the evening of the same day. Four of these dropped a total of sixteen 500lb SAP bombs but none of these damaged the *Admiral Hipper*. However, a gasworks was hit and a gasometer destroyed. Unfortunately several houses were destroyed or damaged, resulting in one civilian dead and three injured. All the Beauforts returned, evidently with one still carrying bombs.

---

3. Details of bomb damage in these raids are taken from extremely detailed researches carried out by French air historians and contained in the books written by Roland Bohn and entitled *Raids Aériens sur La Bretagne durant La Seconde Guerre Mondiale*.

Two members of the Women's Royal Naval Air Force putting an F2A air camera in a Fairey Swordfish of the Fleet Air Arm (FAA) before going on a training exercise. They are wearing flying helmets with goggles as well as Sidcot flying suits. These young ladies also tested wireless sets and other equipment in aircraft. (Author's collection)

The six air observers who had arrived in 217 Squadron towards the end of January took no part in the operations in February, perhaps fortunately for them. However, within a few days of my arrival I was appointed as the Squadron Photography Officer. This seemed to be no more than a nominal position that someone had to fulfil, for it did not include any special duties. Nevertheless it seemed interesting and I visited the Station Photography Section and introduced myself.

The airmen photographers seemed very proud of their collection and showed them to me enthusiastically. There were many photographs taken by F24 cameras of Beauforts in the air and on the ground, as well as some of St Eval airfield and the surrounding countryside. There were also some taken of ships sinking after attacks against convoys and, most interesting of all, others of

A tanker on fire, somewhat larger than the one seen on 19 March 1941 off the south-west coast of Wales by Flying Officer D. Levin-Raw and his crew in Beaufort N1018 of 217 Squadron. (Author's collection)

enemy ports taken in daylight by the photo-reconnaissance Spitfires of B Flight, No 1 Photographic Reconnaissance Unit, which was based at St Eval. Some of the latter had enlarged and photostat copies taken of them.

I picked out a number of these photographs and asked if I could have copies. These were provided and I took them away for further perusal. Not being sure whether such action was permissible, I said nothing to anyone else in the squadron, kept them safely in my locker and never took them in the air.

All six air observers were issued with 1:1,000,000 scale Mercator plotting charts covering the area over which 217 Squadron was operating. There were two of these charts, which was awkward when transferring one plot to the other, but I cut up mine with a razor blade and a ruler, stuck them together and then trimmed them, making a convenient single chart. There were also Ordnance Survey coloured topographical maps on a scale of 1:250,000, used for map-reading. I studied these intently and was pleased to see that most of the west coast of France was very indented and that there were many small islands offshore, making for easy identification.

The chart table in the nose of a Beaufort, showing a chart pinned to the table with a plotting arm over it, a heavy ruler alongside and a Course and Speed Calculator. (Author's collection)

We were required to take eye tests, which included night vision. The latter was carried out in the dark, looking at a screen in which black drawings of aircraft and ships were slid while a light behind them was progressively dimmed. I managed to identify these for an unusually long period, causing the medical attendant to call for a colleague to see the result. It seemed that my night vision was exceptional, a matter of which I was completely unaware but was gratifying to know.

Apart from such matters in this period when we were not allowed to fly, I drew a Mark IX bubble sextant from Station Stores, as well as an air almanac for 1941, Air Publication 1528 *Astronomical Navigation Tables* for our latitudes, and an astro-navigation wristwatch which gave the time to the second provided one checked it daily with the last of 'the six pips' on the wireless. Using my copy of Air Publication 1234 *Air Navigation*, which included star charts, I practised taking shots of the planets, moon and major stars at night, then plotted the position lines on my chart. All this was of no use in an aircraft without an astrodome, but I thought that all RAF navigators should have this ability.

Moreover a knowledge of the heavens could be of use if I was ever shot down over France and was 'on the run' at night down to the non-occupied zone.

On 24 February, I had my first opportunity to fly as a navigator in a Beaufort. It was a non-operational navigation exercise, evidently to test my ability. My pilot was Pilot Officer Tom Kitching who (I learnt much later) had joined the RAF in 1931 as a clerk and had progressed to flying training and eventually became qualified. Like all the pre-war pilots in 217 Squadron, he was highly skilled and meticulous, as well as a very pleasant person. The navigator sat on a seat beside the plot for take-offs and landings but otherwise occupied his swivel seat in the nose. We flew on a series of legs across the country to RAF Squires Gate, near Blackpool, in Lancashire, and then returned by a different route. I did my best to perform exactly, giving small alterations of course so to fly precisely over the turning points. All seemed to go well. Two days later I was sent

The blister gun in a Beaufort of 42 Squadron at RAF Leuchars in Fifeshire. This was intended to protect the aircraft from a belly attack but the cartridge belt of the Browning .303in gun frequently jammed in its chute. The central figure in the photograph is Flight Lieutenant A.H. 'Junior' Simmonds, who became a Flight Commander in 217 Squadron. (The late Wing Commander A.H. Simmonds DFC)

up with Pilot Officer Spencer-Schrader, another pre-war pilot, for a gun-firing exercise over rocks in the sea off nearby Trevose Head. Spencer-Schrader tested his front gun and I tried to fire another .303in Browning fitted in a blister under the navigator's position. This pointed backwards against a possible belly attack and the navigator lay prone looking through a mirror, somewhat awkwardly. The gun was not successful, for the ammunition belt was fed through a convoluted chute and invariably jammed after a few shots. These blisters were fitted in a few of our Beauforts but eventually all were removed. A more effective additional gun was a drum-fed Vickers K mounted in the entrance door and fired by the wireless operator against an enemy attack. This gun behaved correctly but there was a danger that its bullets might hit the Beaufort's port wing or tailplane in any excitement.

I had hoped to be crewed up on a more permanent basis after these tests but this did not happen for a few days. Instead, on 1 March eight of our aircrews and

The mid-upper turret in a Beaufort I, fitted with a single drum-fed Vickers K machine-gun, with another free-handling Vickers K in the port waist hatch, which could be fired in an emergency by the wireless operator. (Author's collection)

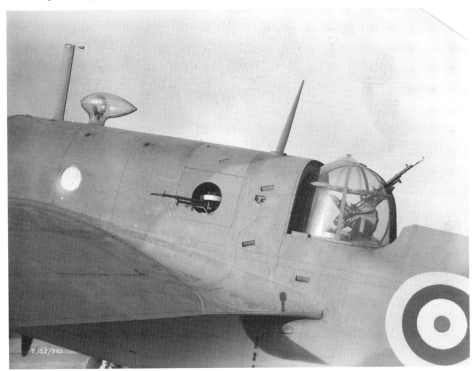

Beauforts were detached to RAF Limavady in County Londonderry, Northern Ireland, where their temporary duties were to provide convoy escorts under the direction of Coastal Command's No 15 Group in Liverpool.

After our squadron's losses in February, only a handful of aircrews were left at St Eval. Thus 217 Squadron was unable to respond immediately to Winston Churchill's directive of 6 March to the RAF, giving full priority to the Battle of the Atlantic. Heavy and medium bombers of Bomber Command and various squadrons from Coastal Command intensified their attacks against Brest and Lorient, but still the *Admiral Hipper* remained unscathed.

At last, on 3 March, I was crewed with another pre-war pilot, Flying Officer Douglas E.H. Levin-Raw, together with an air gunner, Sergeant Kenneth Reeves, and a wireless operator, Sergeant 'Davy' Davis. I was destined to fly with those two sergeants for many months and they were both highly competent, invariably cheerful and seemingly unaffected by the frequent losses suffered by the squadron. But our flight on that day was merely a cross-country exercise, getting accustomed to flying together. We then awaited further orders.

The next flight was in my capacity of Squadron Photography Officer, with Spencer-Schrader flying the Beaufort. An F24 camera had been fitted vertically in the machine and we flew over the locality of St Eval on a series of parallel tracks close to each other. The camera was automatic and took a series of photographs which partly overlapped each other, so that the result could be formed into a mosaic. The flight seemed to be successful but I never saw the mosaic, which was probably prepared for No 19 Group.

The weather was consistently bad in this period. Weather fronts came in from the Atlantic, bringing clouds and rain. Sometimes one could stand on a cliff and see a mist rolling in over the sea before covering us. This weather ruined my first operational flight, which took place in daylight on 11 March with Levin-Raw. We had been ordered to escort a convoy and went out over the Atlantic to hunt for it, but the visibility was so poor that we returned after more than four hours of fruitless search.

On the evening of the same day, the depleted 217 Squadron made a token effort to join in the bombing of the *Admiral Hipper*, by sending a single Beaufort to accompany eight Blenheim IVs of 59 Squadron over Brest. The visibility was so bad that the Beaufort and two Blenheims returned with their bombs. Five of the other Blenheims dropped their bombs but did not see any explosions. The other Blenheim, flown by Pilot Officer D.K. Plumb, was shot down and all three crew members were killed.

On the following day, 12 March, Wing Commander Leslie W.C. Bower arrived at St Eval to take over command of 217 Squadron from Wing Commander Guy A. Bolland. His arrival was not greeted with any enthusiasm by members of the squadron, who resented losing their very popular commander, but Bower was not responsible for the move and was well qualified for the position. He was a regular officer who had joined the RAF in 1929 and passed through RAF College Cranwell and then served in bomber squadrons in the UK and India. He had then qualified as an instructor at the Central Flying School and taught undergraduate pilots in the Cambridge University Air Squadron. Following this, he had served with 202 Squadron in the Mediterranean at a time when it was equipped with Saro London flying boats. On the outbreak of war he was a staff officer in Air Headquarters Malta. Lastly, he had commanded the flying-boat base of RAF Felixstowe in Suffolk.

On 15 March, the *Admiral Hipper* slipped out of the much-bombed port of Brest and began making her way back to German-controlled waters. British intelligence was immediately made aware of this move from an informant in the port, and the attentions of the RAF were switched to Lorient. However, the depleted aircrews and Beauforts of 217 Squadron did not participate in these operations, although some of the eight crews detached to Limavady in Northern Ireland were beginning to return to their home station. The weather over North Cornwall remained a mixture of cloud and rain, making conditions difficult for operational flying, especially at night.

On one of these days, we were sitting in our 217 Squadron crewroom near St Eval Church when we were asked to help the ground crews push a Beaufort out of the muddy ground. We trooped out and began the work when an aircraft suddenly appeared below the cloud. Somebody asked if it was one of the new Beaufighters but another shouted 'Heinkel!'. We all turned to look and then bolted for the airfield perimeter, where we jumped into a wet drainage ditch, on top of each other. The Heinkel He 111 swooped down and there was a rattle from a machine-gun, but this may have come from the ground defences since nobody was hit. The German crew may have been on a daring daylight photo-reconnaissance mission.

The weather on 19 March cleared sufficiently for daylight flying. Three Beauforts, including one flown by Levin-Raw, were sent out to investigate a report that merchant ships sailing from the west had passed round the south of Ireland and were being attacked by German aircraft while heading up to Liverpool. We were not given any precise positions and each Beaufort flew individually. In our aircraft, we flew on a series of courses until we passed the approaches to the Bristol Canal, where we came across a tanker on fire. Obviously this required a report and to obtain an exact position we headed a short distance southwards to the south-west tip of Wales. With careful timing, this would enable us to send a signal, giving precise information.

After a few minutes we reached Smalls Lighthouse, on rocks in the sea to the west of Pembroke. Then we saw two dinghies in the sea and a small merchant ship nearby. Circling low, we could see that these dinghies were not the RAF's round and yellow type but a darker colour and more rectangular. I looked carefully through my binoculars. The dinghies were tied together and five men were aboard, seemingly German and possibly the crew of a Heinkel He 111. I flashed the Aldis lamp to them but they made no response. We then approached the merchant ship and I flashed in Morse 'Please pick up men in life raft!.' The response in Morse was 'No bloody fear'. Obviously the rocks were too dangerous for them to lower a boat and make an approach.

We flew back to the dinghies and resumed circling. By then these were being swept up against the rocks under the lighthouse. They suddenly reared up and then reappeared with only three men aboard. Then they were swept up again and again until these three men had disappeared. We could only watch helplessly before turning back to base.

Soon after we left the second Beaufort, flown by Pilot Officer Dunn, arrived and the crew saw the empty dinghies and a body floating in the water. They tried to attract two nearby naval launches to the scene but without success. Then three Heinkel He 111s arrived and Dunn tried to fire at them, but two disappeared into cloud while the other flew low over the sea to escape. The Germans possibly thought that the Beaufort was the far more deadly Beaufighter.

On the way back, we saw smoke rising from Lundy Island in the distance but did not investigate. The third Beaufort, flown by Sergeant Routledge, was able to report that this came from a Heinkel He 111, crashed and burning. Thus ended my first day when I saw action when flying in 217 Squadron.

The respite at Brest did not last long. Before dawn on 22 March, the battlecruisers *Scharnhorst* and *Gneisenau* entered the roads of Brest and then moored in the docks, having reportedly sunk twenty-two merchant vessels sailing singly in the Atlantic instead of in convoy. These German warships were monsters, each of 31,850 tons displacement and classed at battleships by the Kriegsmarine. They were to cause the Royal Navy and the RAF a great deal of worry and expenditure of effort. By the end of March the last of the eight

Beauforts detached to Limavady had returned to St Eval. This detachment had carried out thirty-one sorties on behalf of No 15 Group, without loss. The squadron was also expecting new aircrews to arrive from No 3 OTU at RAF Chivenor in North Devon. These would be qualified in Beauforts and bring the squadron back up to strength after the losses sustained during February.

The Gneisenau *viewed from the starboard side. She was recorded as a battlecruiser by the British but classified as a battleship by the Germans. She was 771 feet long and displaced 31,850 tons. The main armament consisted of nine 28cm and twelve 15cm guns. Anti-aircraft armament included fourteen 10.5cm, sixteen 37mm and twelve 20mm guns. She could achieve a speed of 32 knots.* (The late Chris Davies collection)

Chapter 4

The German Battlecruisers

On the night of 4/5 April 1941, RAF Bomber Command made one of its raids on the port of Brest. This action followed a directive of 9 March from the Air Ministry, to the effect that it was to concentrate temporarily on enemy targets which posed a threat to British shipping.

On this occasion, fifty-seven bombers were despatched. The main force consisted of thirty-seven Vickers Wellingtons carrying 500lb general-purpose or armour-piercing bombs. Then there were eleven Handley Page Hampdens carrying a variety of bombs – 1,900lb general-purpose, 2,000lb general-purpose,

A firing party in Brest at the military funeral of German sailors killed by RAF bombing, probably when a reception for the Kriegsmarine was held at the Continental Hotel on the night of 4/5 April 1941 and this was hit by Bomber Command, causing much loss of life. (Jean-Louis Roba collection)

A photographic mosaic of Brest, used by the author in 1941 as a target map for bombing attacks and mine-laying sorties. (Author's collection)

500lb SAP and 250lb SAP. Lastly, there were four Avro Manchesters carrying 2,000lb armour-piercing bombs.

The attacks took place from high level and produced significant results. By coincidence, the Kriegsmarine was holding a reception at the Continental Hotel in Brest and this received direct hits. The number of German casualties is not recorded but almost certainly would have included officers from the recently-arrived *Scharnhorst* and *Gneisenau*. French civilian casualties are recorded as four killed and thirteen injured. One Hampden was shot down by flak, flown by the Commanding Officer of 106 Squadron, Wing Commander P.J. Polglase.

One of the 500lb SAP bombs carried by the Hampdens fell into the dry dock where the *Gneisenau* was berthed, but failed to explode. This was obviously a major hazard and in the early morning the battlecruiser was towed to the outer harbour and anchored. Two hours later, a Spitfire from No. 1 Photographic Reconnaissance Unit at St Eval flew over Brest on a routine mission. The negatives from its F24 camera were developed and printed immediately after it landed. The alarm was raised.

The most effective weapon for sinking a battlecruiser was the torpedo, and nine Beauforts capable of carrying this weapon had arrived at St Eval a week before. These were part of 22 Squadron, based at North Coates in Lincolnshire. This squadron normally operated over the North Sea but the nine had been sent on detachment after the arrival of the battlecruisers at Brest. Our pilots in 217 Squadron were not trained in torpedo-dropping nor were our aircraft fitted for that purpose. On the other hand, 22 Squadron had become operational with torpedo-carrying Beauforts in April 1940, in addition to their conventional functions of low-level bombing and mine-laying. All operational work in Beauforts was highly dangerous and the squadron had lost thirty of these aircraft in the previous twelve months.

In the afternoon of 5 April, twenty-four aircrew members of 22 Squadron were sitting around the table in 217 Squadron's crewroom at St Eval. Some were examining maps and charts but others were writing farewell letters in the belief that they had been ordered to fly on a suicide mission. Six Beauforts were to take off on an attack against the *Gneisenau* at anchor in Brest harbour. These were timed to arrive over the target at 'first light', when the rising sun was just below the horizon but providing a narrow band of light above it.

Three of these Beauforts were to carry TIMs. These mines were intended to blow gaps in torpedo nets suspended on timber baulks, which RAF intelligence officers believed the Germans would have placed around the battlecruiser. Each of the other three Beauforts was to carry a torpedo to be aimed at one of the gaps caused by the TIMs.

Such a plan would have been difficult to achieve in practice, with each of the two flights of Beauforts flying in formation, in broad daylight and without enemy opposition. It proved impossible in the weather conditions prevailing at the time, for there was low cloud with steady rain over south-west England and north-west France. Bomber Command despatched seventy-seven bombers against Brest during the night and these were ineffective but suffered no losses. At St Eval, two of 22 Squadron's Beauforts carrying TIMs became stuck in the rain-soaked and boggy grass airfield and could not be moved, let alone take off. The third, flown by Flight Sergeant Menary, managed to take off and hunted fruitlessly for the target, finally dropping it over some vessels spotted off the north coast of France. In the event, however, these TIMs were not required, for the Germans were not able to provide torpedo nets to protect the battlecruiser.

The three torpedo-carrying Beauforts managed to take off on time, although the crews were not aware that two carrying mines had failed to do so. One of these was Beaufort I serial N1016 flown by a Scotsman, Flying Officer Kenneth Campbell, taking off at 03.22 hours GMT. The fate of this aircraft is described

Flying Officer Kenneth Campbell of 22 Squadron was awarded a posthumous Victoria Cross after torpedoing and severely damaging the battlecruiser Gneisenau *in the outer harbour of Brest in the early morning of 6 April 1941. His aircraft, Beaufort I serial N1016, was shot down immediately after the torpedo was released and all four members of the crew were killed.* (Author's collection)

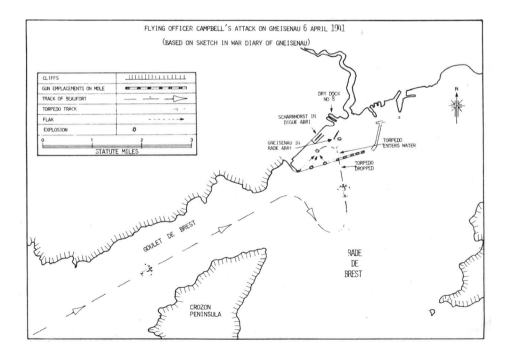

in German records. It appeared over Brest harbour at low level under heavy cloud and turned south. It then came down lower, to about fifty feet, turned back northwards and released a torpedo. Both aircraft and torpedo flew over the outer mole. The torpedo struck the hull of the *Gneisenau* on the starboard side and exploded, blasting a huge hole.

At the same time, intense fire was opened up on the Beaufort from a flak gun mounted on the end of the outer mole. This was probably a deadly 'quad gun', with all four barrels pouring out 20mm explosive shells. The Beaufort was hit and turned to port before crashing into the outer harbour, killing all four crew members.

The time of this crash was 05.16 hours, almost two hours after take-off from St Eval. The normal time from St Eval to the target of Brest via Land's End was an hour and a half. It is likely that the additional time was spent in finding a way underneath the low cloud, after ETA (expected time of arrival) over the French coast. This would entail flying back over the sea for a few minutes, descending safely and then turning back at low level to the coast. The navigator could then identify the position and guide the pilot through Brest estuary to the target. Possibly Campbell thought that, by this time, the mine-carrying Beauforts had done their work and that he should attack.

The other two torpedo-carrying Beauforts flew above cloud to the target. One was flown by an Australian, Flight Lieutenant James R. Hyde. It was hit by flak over the island of Ushant (Ile d'Ouessant) off the north-west corner of France but the damage was not serious and Hyde continued to the target. The other was flown by Sergeant Alan Camp, who reported that it was daylight by the time he arrived and that he could see flak. The target was covered with cloud and they were expecting a signal from the mine-carrying Beauforts, which of course did not happen. Both returned to St Eval with their torpedoes.

German records show that the *Gneisenau* was very badly hit. There was extensive damage to the bottom plating, the starboard propeller-shaft tunnel and several fire-control positions and magazines. Numbers 1 and 3 turbine compartments and the base of 'C' turret were flooded. The battlecruiser might have sunk if help had not been on hand to effect temporary repairs and tow her back to dry dock, where she remained out of commission.

With regard to the crew of the Beaufort, the Germans found the bodies of the wireless operator Sergeant William Cecil Mulliss and the air gunner Sergeant Ralph Walter Hillman floating in the harbour. Perhaps they had managed to take up their ditching positions and inflate their lifejackets, in a few seconds before the Beaufort hit the water. Divers then went down and recovered the bodies of Flying Officer Kenneth Campbell and the Canadian air observer Sergeant James Phillip Scott, who were seated alongside each other. They thought at first that Scott was the pilot, since he was on the right-hand seat, the position for German pilots. The Germans admired their bravery, and all four men were given a full military funeral.

An extremely courageous worker for the French Resistance at Brest, in communication by wireless with British intelligence under the codename 'Hilarion', was Lieutenant de Vaisseau Jean Phillipon. He managed to send a message on 8 April, reporting the condition of the *Gneisenau*. In general terms, this information must have percolated down to the Intelligence Officers at RAF St Eval. A few days later, I was sitting in the Officers' Mess with a small group of junior officers from 22 and 217 Squadron. A somewhat agitated young pilot from 22 Squadron came in and approached us. He said to his friends: 'Do you know what happened to Campbell? He went into Brest and torpedoed the *Gneisenau*! Of course, they blew him out of the sky! Now they'll expect all of us to do the

The graves in Brest Cemetery of two of the crew of Beaufort serial N1016 flown by Flying Officer Kenneth Campbell on 6 April 1941. Left to right: Sergeant James Phillip Scott, the Canadian air observer; Sergeant William Cecil Mulliss, the wireless operator/air gunner. (Jacques Ilias collection)

The battlecruiser Gneisenau *in dry dock in 1941, following the damage caused by the torpedo dropped by Flying Officer Kenneth Campbell of 22 Squadron on the night of 6/7 April 1941. Flood water is being pumped out of her starboard quarter.* (Jean-Louis Roba collection)

same thing!' Nevertheless, British Intelligence seems to have been sceptical of the facts passed from Jean Phillipon. It was not until 13 March 1942 that the posthumous award of the Victoria Cross appeared in the London Gazette.[4] The *Gneisenau* seems to have been an unlucky warship, for her problems intensified shortly after the strike from Campbell's torpedo. On the night of 10/11 April, Bomber Command despatched thirty-six Wellingtons, twelve Blenheims and four Manchesters on another raid over Brest. One Wellington was shot down but the others reported good bombing. Four bombs fell directly on the *Gneisenau*, killing fifty of her crew, wounding ninety others and causing more damage. The battlecruiser would be out of commission for eight months, causing considerable concern to the Kriegsmarine and Adolf Hitler.

While the unlucky *Gneisenau* was suffering these disasters in early April, 217 Squadron was still trying to arrange its aircrews into regular four-man teams

---

4. See Appendix B for an account of the presentation of this Victoria Cross by Kenneth Campbell's brother to the Commanding Officer of 22 Squadron.

and to carry out a diversity of roles. These were medium-level bombing of French ports, 'Armed Rovers' (hunting for enemy shipping off France), convoy escorts, reconnaissance patrols and – towards the end of the month – dropping sea mines in the approaches to French ports. It was also rumoured that the squadron would have to convert to torpedo-dropping, and thus become the same as the other RAF squadrons equipped with Beauforts.

On 6 April, two Beauforts were despatched in daylight to attack two large merchant vessels about twenty miles south-south-west of Ushant. These were located and five 250lb bombs were dropped but no results were seen.

During this period, I navigated on a couple of non-operational flights and one convoy escort, all of which were uneventful. Then, on 11 May, I was detailed to fly on my first night operation with another pilot, Flying Officer Dunn. This was a 'Stopper' patrol off Brest, carrying bombs and hunting for any German warship that might have broken out. Presumably this possibility was the *Scharnhorst*, since British Intelligence knew that the *Gneisenau* was damaged.

The battlecruiser Scharnhorst, *viewed from her bow. Her displacement was 31,850 tons and she was armed with nine 28cm and twelve 15cm guns, as well as numerous anti-aircraft guns. She was sunk near Bear Island and the North Cape of Norway on 25 December 1942 by the Royal Navy, while attempting to intercept an Arctic convoy. Only thirty-six of her crew were picked up, 1,803 others being lost.* (The late Chris Davies collection)

We took off at 20.45 hours and headed for Land's End and then Ushant, flying at 1,200 feet in reasonably clear weather. The eastern side of the island showed up at the right time, but I suddenly saw tracer fire coming up directly towards us and shouted a warning to Dunn. He banked and turned to starboard. Fiery yellow shells, seemingly the size of golf balls, flashed past our port wing. They were my first experience of 20mm cannon fire and were enough to confirm my suspicions that the offshore French islands contained flak emplacements. The islands were very useful for identifying 'pinpoint' navigational positions but we should avoid flying over them.

From the vicinity of Ushant, we patrolled the mouth of Brest Estuary, our other turning point being the Ile de Sein, a tiny island with a lighthouse, in which the men were always either fishermen or sailors. Unknown to us, this island was already a source of Gallic pride, for after of General de Gaulle's 'Call to Arms' of 18 June 1940 on the BBC, every man on the island had sailed to England to enlist in the Free French Forces. Moreover, they had been followed via this island by almost 3,000 French soldiers and sailors.[5]

We patrolled for over an hour but saw no vessels in the sea below, despite clear visibility. There was occasionally a searchlight in the direction of Brest and what appeared to be a gunflash, but records show that neither Bomber Command nor Coastal Command made attacks on the port during the night. The time came to head back to base and I gave Dunn a course to fly from Ushant to Penzance. About halfway along this course, Dunn's wireless operator, Sergeant James, handed a note to me: 'Divert at Boscombe Down.'

I hunted in my map and found this airfield, close to Salisbury in Wiltshire, then worked out another course and handed it to Dunn. All seemed to go well until we suddenly found ourselves flying past barrage balloons, when on course over Plymouth. Fortunately we were able to climb rapidly above these, but Dunn was furious, shouting at me that this was a 'prohibited area'. I could only apologise, for I had never been told that such areas existed, not having been to an OTU.

Then we received another wireless message, telling us to resume flying to St Eval. In this period, our airfield was undergoing enemy air attacks almost nightly, principally by Heinkel He 111s from Kampfgruppe 100 based at Vannes in northern France, and one of these was probably the reason for the initial

---

5. In 1946, General de Gaulle visited the Ile de Sein to award it the Liberation Cross.

A balloon barrage, with cumulus clouds. (Author's collection)

A diagram showing the peril of flying into a balloon barrage. If the Beaufort had struck one of the cables, the latter would have parted at top and bottom, and two parachutes would have opened at each end. The drag would have brought the aircraft crashing to the ground while the balloon would have deflated and descended slowly. (*Aeroplane Monthly*)

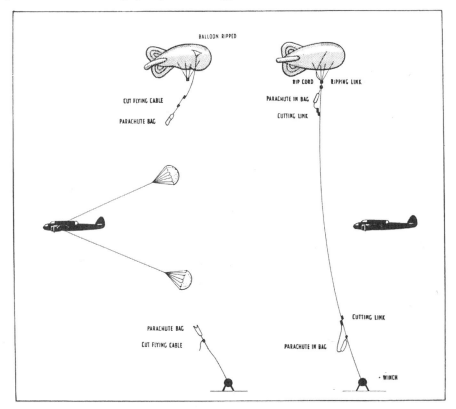

diversion. All was clear when we arrived and landed safely.[6] I spent some of the next few days enquiring about other prohibited areas and marking them in red on my chart.

Evidently I was not in disgrace after making this navigational error for two days later I was detailed to navigate our Commanding Officer, Wing Commander Leslie Bower, on a special operation. Sergeants Davies and Reeves were to be the other crew members. The objective was to make a night attack on the docks at Granville, near the south-west corner of the Cherbourg Peninsula. This port had had little attention from the RAF, but perhaps our CO had knowledge of some circumstances which he did divulge.

We took off at 01.15 hours on 15 April, carrying a full load of 2,000lbs of general-purpose bombs. The night was clear, the sky cloudless and there was a bright moon. Our course was south-east to Dodman Point on the south coast of Cornwall and then across the English Channel towards Granville. We passed Guernsey, exactly on course, flying at about 1,000 feet, but then entered a layer of sea mist as we approached the French coast.

I could still see the sea below and assumed that we would attack from about 500 feet with our bombs, which were fitted with delayed-action fuses. However, Bower decided to climb above this mist. The moon then shone on the upper surface so that it became a completely opaque white and I could not see the sea, the coast or the target. I suggested that we cut across France to Lorient, where perhaps there would be no mist, but Bower rejected this idea and ordered a course to our secondary target, the docks at St Malo along the coast to the west.

This was only a short flight, and on ETA at this height we found that our target was also covered with the sea mist. For over an hour, we then patrolled to and fro along the north coast of France, looking for a likely target such as a naval vessel. The sea mist was patchy to the west, but we saw nothing and had to return to return to base after a total of five hours flying. Bower was disgruntled, probably having hoped to establish himself as an aggressive pilot with the members of his 217 Squadron, and I was very disappointed.

---

6. The Operations Record Book (ORB) for 217 Squadron (AIR 27/1341) at The National Archives incorrectly lists Sergeant Whitehouse as the navigator on this sortie, whereas it is entered in my Flying Log Book with date, times, aircraft number and signature. It seems that there must have been a switch of navigators and the information was not passed to the writer of this entry.

Two days later I flew as navigator with yet another pilot, Flying Officer John Welsh, on one of the many daylight operations known as 'Armed Rovers' being carried out in this period by 217 Squadron over the Bay of Biscay. The purpose of these solo flights was to hunt for enemy shipping, such as a blockade runner, and make low-level attacks on it with a full load of bombs. We took off at 10.10 hours and made 'Cross Over Patrols' in clear weather – over the sea west of Brest and Lorient, but saw no enemy ships. The sortie lasted for five hours, being perhaps interesting as a 'dead-reckoning' navigational exercise over the sea without any special aids, and we returned safely back to St Eval.

The attacks against the docks at Brest continued. Before midnight on 18 April, two Beauforts of 217 Squadron and two Blenheims of 53 Squadron took off from St Eval for this familiar target. One Blenheim carried four 250lb bombs and the other two 500lb bombs. The two Beauforts, flown by Flying Officer Douglas Levin-Raw and Pilot Officer Kenneth Holmes, each carried a 2,000lb 'Magnum' land mine. Levin-Raw was attacked by a Messerschmitt Bf 110 night-fighter and had to jettison his land mine in order to avoid the tracer fire. The Messerschmitt disappeared into cloud but then came out for a frontal attack, during which the two pilots fired at each other and the Beaufort was slightly damaged. The Messerschmitt then disappeared once more. Meanwhile, Holmes dropped his Magnum and the resulting explosion was seen. The two Blenheims also bombed, from lower level, and all four aircraft returned to St Eval.[7]

This raid on Brest was followed by another during the next evening. Four Beauforts of 217 Squadron each carried a Magnum, while six Blenheims of 53 Squadron each carried four 250lb SAP bombs. The three Beauforts dropped their mines but only one explosion was seen, on the torpedo sheds near the dry dock. Three of the Blenheims did not bomb, presumably because the weather conditions were unfavourable, and the bombs dropped by the other three seem to have been widely scattered. All aircraft returned safely. By this time I was feeling somewhat frustrated, having been in the squadron for almost two months without dropping a single bomb on enemy positions.

It was therefore with a mixture of eagerness and apprehension that on 20 April I received orders to fly on a night attack against Brest, in a crew with Levin-Raw, Davies and Reeves. By then, this target had a fearsome reputation,

---

7. The Operations Record Book for 217 Squadron lists me as flying with Levin-Raw, but it is not included in my Flying Log Book, I have no recollection of it and no navigator's log written in the air.

The 8.8cm flak gun was the standard heavy weapon employed by the Flak Arm of the Luftwaffe. The earliest version fired shells weighing 19.8lbs at the rate of fifteen rounds per minute and had an effective ceiling of 26,250 feet. (Author's collection)

being ringed with about 250 medium and heavy flak guns, in addition to the numerous machine-guns and cannon ready to greet raiders prepared to fly in at low level. Our Beaufort was to be one of four in 217 Squadron to attack on that night, together with six Blenheims of 53 Squadron, with the latter to precede us by a few minutes. Each Beaufort carried a 2,000lb Magnum mine, while each Blenheim carried two SAP bombs.

We took off at 20.35 hours and flew in reasonable weather to Dodman Point on the south coast and then to a position near Ushant before eastwards towards the target. There was no mistaking this, for the sky was already full of exploding shells, tracer and searchlights, probably directed at the Blenheims which had arrived a few minutes before.

This was my first experience of intense flak, but I was more interested than scared when viewing it from my grandstand position in the Perspex nose of the Beaufort. I had no prior knowledge of the fact that it could be multi-coloured and only later learned that German gunners used different chemicals

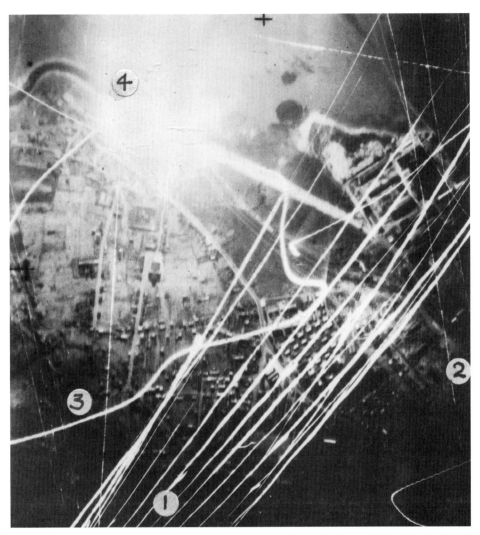

Flak at night in 1941 over the port of Saint-Nazaire during low-level attacks by aircraft of RAF Coastal Command, analysed by photo-interpreters. (1) Intense light flak. (2) Tracer bullets. (3) Searchlight beams hunting the bombers. (4) Fire in the dock area. (Author's collection)

to distinguish the trajectory of their own shells. Strontium nitrate produced a red trace, copper a shade of green, cobalt a bright blue, sodium the more normal orange and potassium a mauve hue. Of course the explosions were all bright yellow-orange flashes.

Fortunately we flew through this spectacle without any damage and I was able to pick out our target, the Port de Lannion, from our height of about 2,000

The vivid effect of an 8.8cm shell exploding at high level after being fired from a German anti-aircraft gun. (Author's collection)

feet. We turned towards it, I gave small alterations of course over the intercom to Levin-Raw, and pressed the bomb release switch at precisely 22.00 hours. We then turned away, heading out of the maelstrom. From the rear turret, Reeves reported a large explosion in the dock area some seconds later. In the words of Winston Churchill, probably from his experiences in the Boer War. 'There is nothing more exhilarating than being shot at without result.' This describes my feelings on that occasion, mixed with relief.

With our mine duly delivered, we turned and flew back over the estuary and then towards Penzance and St Eval, where we landed at 23.35 hours. I sat beside

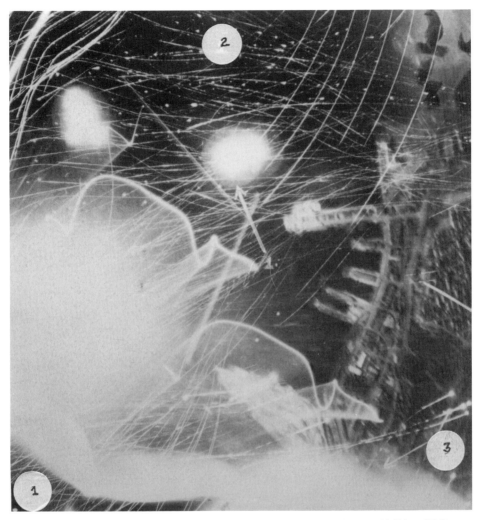

Flak over Brest photographed with a short time exposure on the night of 4/5 May 1941 by a Wellington IC of No 115 Squadron based at Marham in Norfolk. Photo-interpreters identified (1) a Flak battery; (2) tracer from light flak; (3) fogging caused by searchlights. At the time, Brest was the most heavily defended place on mainland Europe. (Author's collection)

Levin-Raw while he taxied to dispersal and then switched off the engines, and went into the nose to pack my maps and instruments in the canvas bag issued to all navigators. Suddenly and unexpectedly, a stick of about six bombs fell across the nose of the Beaufort, two of them close enough to rock the aircraft violently and spatter it with earth.

My reaction to this intrusion was a mixture of indignation and a desire to hit back. I headed back to the turret, in time to see Levin-Raw's boots disappearing through the top hatch. There was no sign of Davies and Reeves, who had already left by the port entrance door. I went into the turret and tried to turn it to starboard and have a shot at the intruder, but of course it would not rotate since the power had been switched off. In any case, the German aircraft was no longer in sight.

Feeling somewhat stupid, I made my way to the Operations Room. Davies and Reeves also arrived but Levin-Raw had not yet appeared. Our Station Commander, Group Captain Revington, stood by and listened while I described to a staff member the near-miss by enemy bombs and my futile action. Revington came up to me, yanked open my Irvin jacket, looked at my brevet, grunted and walked away. Then Levin-Raw turned up. He had raced to the airfield perimeter, where he had found several cylinders sticking out of the ground and wondered what they were. They turned out to be a 'secret weapon' named Parachute and Cable Armament. Each cylinder contained a rocket fired by remote control, carrying a small parachute from which cables hang in the hope that they would become entangled in propellers or cause some sort of damage. They had not been fired, nor had there been any anti-aircraft fire against this sneak raider.

All of the four Beauforts and the six Blenheims returned from this operation. One of the Beaufort pilots had to jettison his mine over the sea when tackled by a German night-fighter. The other two had dropped their mines but no resulting explosions were seen. All the six Blenheims had dropped their bombs, some of which were reported as having exploded in some torpedo sheds near the dry dock.

Thinking about this sortie after the event, it seemed to me that, from the navigational point of view, there were two matters worthy of further consideration. One of these was our direction when bombing the French ports. That German bomber had approached St Eval from the land and then disappeared over the sea. Our airfield defences had not been alerted, possibly because the British radar system was directed solely over the sea. Perhaps the same circumstances existed with the German defences in the French ports.

The other matter concerned our return flights from the French ports. We usually headed for Penzance, which was the shortest route, and during this leg the wireless operator was often asked to obtain a W/T bearing from base, the result being transmitted 'in clear'. This could be dangerous if passed by German Intelligence to a prowling night-fighter.

Coupled with this problem, there could be a danger if cloud covered the rocky coastline of Penzance or the hills inland. It was well known that about 10 per cent of RAF casualties occurred in accidents, and descending through cloud overland could be extremely dangerous. Topographical maps were small scale and did not always show up high ground, while altimeters were set to estimated barometric pressure which could be wrong or have changed while in flight. Perhaps it would be more prudent to head for the Scilly Islands in cloudy weather, for these were quite extensive, conveniently flat and easily recognisable. One could come down through cloud over the sea in advance. Each crew was allowed discretion in matters such as these, and I expected to discuss my thoughts with Levin-Raw. But after this flight he was posted away from the squadron, having served his allotted time on operations. He left to take a course as an instructor, in a School of General Reconnaissance, Thus Davies, Reeves and I were left once more without a regular pilot.

The three of us were put on standby while 217 Squadron and 53 Squadron intensified their combined attacks at night on Brest. These underwent a change of tactics, with the Beauforts carrying four 500lb SAP bombs and the Blenheims carrying two of these. Perhaps it was realised that conventional bombs could be aimed more accurately than the Magnums, or perhaps the latter could not be supplied. The timing was also changed, the attacks taking place after midnight and before dawn. Four Beauforts and five Blenheims set out on 23 April, three Beauforts and four Blenheims on 24 April, four Beauforts and four Blenheims on 25 April, and two Beauforts and two Blenheims on 28 April. No aircraft were lost on these operations and most of the crews reported accurate bombing.

These attacks by Coastal Command were interspersed with others by Bomber Command, on different days, with greater numbers, heavier bombers and thus more bombs, dropped from higher level. The aiming point for all bombers was usually the docks, on the east of the point where the Penfeld river flowed south into the estuary. To the north and east of this military objective was a suburban area, partly built in squares in the usual French architectural style

It was perhaps inevitable that some of these bombs fell into this suburban area, especially those dropped from higher level. When the bombing began, arrangements had been made by the French authorities for the orderly evacuation of some civilians, particularly children, into the surrounding countryside. However, the whole of Brest was under German control and this evacuation was not permitted. Probably some was carried out surreptitiously, but there were heavy casualties among the majority who remained. Exact numbers are not available for the period up to the end of April but they certainly amounted to several hundred killed or injured.

The attack of 28 April was the last occasion when 217 Squadron was ordered to join in the bombing of Brest harbour. Thereafter, we were directed to other targets and began the additional function of minelaying. The mine carried was similar in appearance to the Magnum but was electro-magnetic, being activated by the magnetic field of a vessel passing over it. It was dropped from low level close to the approaches of enemy harbours and, like the Magnum, was kept upright while in the air with the aid of a parachute. Resting on the sea bottom, it could then be activated by the magnetic field of a vessel passing above. These mines were believed to remain active for about six months and caused a great deal of trouble to the Germans, being extremely dangerous to warships, U-boats and merchant vessels.

The first mining operation took place on 29 April when three Beauforts were sent out, each carrying a mine to be dropped in Brest Estuary. Davies, Reeves and I were part of one of these crews, our pilot for the occasion being the highly-experienced Pilot Officer Tom Kitching. We took off at 03.15 hours and made our way down the familiar route via Land's End and Ushant to Brest Estuary. The mine was duly dropped, in circumstances which were far less dramatic than the bombing attacks on the port. The return journey was similarly uneventful, for the other two Beauforts as well as us. After this operation, we waited once more to be crewed up with a pilot on a more regular basis.

Underside of a Beaufort in flight, carrying a parachute mine of about 1,850lb in the open bomb bay. These mines were employed against enemy dock areas but others of the same weight and appearance were magnetic mines dropped near harbours, resting on the sea bed but exploding when vessels passed above them. (Author's collection)

Chapter 5

Bombing, Mining, Patrolling and on Standby

In early May 1941, 217 Squadron was mainly involved with dropping mines and carrying out patrols in case the *Scharnhorst* attempted to break out of Brest and make for home waters, to escape the relentless attacks by Bomber Command. Two mines were dropped in Brest Estuary before dawn on the 2nd, two on the 4th/5th and three more on the 6th/7th. This procedure was codenamed 'Gardening' while the mines themselves were 'Cucumbers'. The various dropping areas were also given codenames, such as 'Jellyfish'. The aircrews seldom bothered to remember these names and it is unlikely that they confused the Germans, who were probably well aware of the operations.

An oblique reconnaissance photograph taken from low level of the port of Saint-Nazaire. This great port, used before the war by transatlantic liners, was also the home of a large shipbuilding industry. Other than Brest, it was the only port on the west coast of France capable of accommodating and servicing the huge battleships Bismarck *and* Tirpitz. *(Author's collection)*

With the docks of Brest no longer a target for 217 Squadron, the number of bombing sorties declined. However, attention was turned to the docks at Saint-Nazaire. Six Beauforts and several Blenheims attacked this new target on the night of 5/6 May. Some accurate results were claimed and all the aircraft returned safely.

At this time, I was introduced to a recently-arrived pilot from No 3 Training Unit, who was to form a Beaufort crew with Davies, Reeves and myself. He was Flying Officer John F. Percival and, unlike other new arrivals, was already highly experienced operationally. He was a Canadian from Vancouver, aged 25, and had entered the RAF before the war with a short-service commission. He had a ready grin, a rather sardonic manner, and it soon transpired that his opinion of senior RAF officers was less than respectful. He told me that he had flown in a Blenheim squadron, but the only other detail was that his navigator used to shout 'Jink!' at him in an annoying way when they came under fire. I hastened to inform him that this word was not in my vocabulary and that I preferred to remain calm in action.

Long after the war, I found Percival's prior operations in the Public Record Office. He had joined 62 Squadron on 27 May 1940 and had gone into action two days later. This squadron was based at Watton in Norfolk, part of Bomber Command's No 2 Group, and was equipped with the fighter-bomber Blenheim IV. It was mainly engaged in bombing German troop concentrations, tanks and gun emplacements during the Blitzkrieg through Belgium and France, usually despatching twelve aircraft every day. After Dunkirk, it turned to bombing French airfields and even industrial targets in the Ruhr. Percival had participated in these highly dangerous daylight operations until 8 July 1940. On one occasion on 10 June he had shot down a Henschel He 125, a two-seater monoplane employed on army reconnaissance.

A series of night-bombing attacks on St Eval began on 10 May, apparently delivered by the Heinkel He 111s of the pathfinder unit Kampfgeschwader 100 based at Valines in western France. Four RAF aircraft were destroyed (including two Beauforts of 217 Squadron) and twenty-four others damaged. An even heavier raid took place on 12 May, when fifteen Heinkels attacked, damaging more aircraft and hangars as well as living quarters. These attacks continued until 17 May, when fifteen more Heinkels dropped about 100 bombs. They then ceased, perhaps since many of the Luftwaffe's aircraft were being withdrawn from France in preparation for Germany's assault on Russia which began on 22 June under the name of Operation 'Barbarossa'.

Refuelling a Beaufort of 217 Squadron at RAF St Eval in Cornwall. (Author's collection)

The aircrews of 217 Squadron were not affected by these attacks, unless they happened to be on night operations, since they were billeted some miles away in their requisitioned hotels on the coast. The ground staff on the station, normally unrecognised by the public or in histories of the RAF, worked miracles by restoring the damage to buildings and repairing aircraft. They managed to keep the RAF squadrons flying.

One of the Beauforts of 217 Squadron which took off on 12 May failed to return. It was flown by Sergeant Dermot E.R. Ellwood, the air observer was Sergeant Gerald T. Hardwick; the wireless operator Sergeant William Bennett and the air gunner Sergeant George A.D. Ritchie. Six crews had been briefed to attack ships in the Penouet Basin of Saint-Nazaire, carrying general-purpose and incendiary bombs, from a height of 9,000 feet. This was an unusual height for a Beaufort, the normal being low level or sometimes medium level, but it was known that the Germans had begun to fly balloons over Brest. This was one of reasons why 217 Squadron and 53 Squadron had ceased flying over Brest, and it seemed possible that the danger might also exist over Saint-Nazaire.

What happened to Ellwood's aircraft and crew can be related in some detail, mainly from evidence provided by one of the survivors. The time of take-off should have been 22.40 hours, but the Beaufort allocated to the crew proved to be unserviceable – possibly as a result of the enemy bombing – and they had to change to another, serial W6494. Thus they took off late, before climbing to their operating level *en route* to the target. They were above cloud, with a bright moon casting their shadow on the cloud below, when a night-fighter attacked. Ellwood took avoiding action and descended into the cloud. Flying on instruments, he continued towards their target.

The cloud began to clear as they flew southwards, and they saw ground below, partially covered with mist. Ellwood, who had previously flown as second pilot/ navigator, thought they were near Lorient but was probably mistaken. They continued further south and came across another port, which was probably La Pallice. Ellwood was uncertain of the position and wished to avoid the wrong target, with the danger of killing French civilians. They had been ordered to land back at RAF Thorney Island, near Chichester, and they turned in that direction, still carrying their bombload. Another night-fighter spotted them, and once more Ellwood took successful avoiding action.

By this time, they had not made a positive landfall since leaving St Eval, they had been chased over the sky and fuel was running low. Bennett suggested obtaining a W/T bearing, hut Ellwood refused in case it alerted another night-fighter. They continued until he thought they were somewhere over the south of England. Then they saw a flarepath, with an aircraft landing. Ellwood circled, put on the landing lights and made an approach. The flarepath went out, searchlights were switched on, and flak poured up at them. They were over the Luftwaffe base of Carpiquet, near Caen in France. The Beaufort was hit but still flying, and Bennett managed to send out three SOS messages, which were picked up in England at 04.06 hours. Then the Beaufort crashed.

Fortunately the bombs did not explode, but Sergeants Ellwood and Hardwick were killed in the crash and given military funerals by the Germans, attended by many French people from Caen. Bennett and Ritchie were badly injured, the former with both legs dislocated and flak wounds in his back, one leg and throat, while Ritchie had other wounds and a broken femur. They were kept under sedation in hospital, unconscious for several days and attended by Sister Cecilia Mehl, a German lady in the International Red Cross. It was not until next

Two views of Beaufort I serial W6494 of 217 Squadron, shot down on 13 May 1941 by flak from Carpiquet airfield, near Caen in northern France, during an operation at night to attack shipping at Saint-Nazaire. The pilot, Sergeant Dermot R. Ellwood, and the navigator, Sergeant Gerald T. Hardwick were killed instantly. The wireless operator, Sergeant George Richie, and the air gunner, Sergeant William Bennett, were badly injured and became PoWs. (Archiv Petrick)

June when they were fit enough to be transported to Dulag Luft, the German interrogation centre for RAF prisoners.[8]

In the afternoon of this loss, 13 May, Flying Officer Percival took off with Davies, Reeves and myself on his first operational flight in 217 Squadron. It promised to be an exciting occasion, for we were one of three Beauforts ordered to attack an enemy convoy off Guernsey, escorted by Spitfires. We left St Eval at 17.05 hours and headed for the target area but the Spitfires did not appear and, when we were about halfway along our course, instructions to abort the raid came over the W/T. We headed back to St Eval, where no explanation for the change in instructions was provided. Perhaps it had been discovered that the 'enemy convoy' was no more than a line of small tunny boats, with the Breton fishermen trying to earn a living in extremely difficult circumstances. A few days later, one of these small boats was sunk in error by a Beaufort from our squadron, the crew having believed that it was a German vessel gathering intelligence.

We were sent off the following afternoon, 14 May, on a single sortie called a 'Bust Patrol'. This was in daylight along the north coast of France from Paimpol to Ushant, carrying a full load of bombs and flying at 500 feet under patchy cloud but in clear visibility. Our targets were possible enemy coastal shipping, but we saw nothing except some small vessels which were probably those Breton tunny boats. Suddenly there were two large crashes underneath the fuselage and the Beaufort buffeted upwards. It seemed at first that gunfire had exploded underneath us, but then Reeves reported six splashes in the sea below. Four bombs had fallen off the wings while two had crashed through the closed bomb-bay doors. Of course, they were not fused and there must have been some sort of electrical fault. All we could do was return to base and report the problem.

Then, on the night of 16/17 May, we were one of four crews sent out to drop sea mines in Brest Estuary. This was completely uneventful and we plonked the weapon down in the approved place, by then quite familiar to me, and returned safely. By then, we seemed to be working smoothly as a team and certainly had confidence in our respective abilities. The first occasion when we made a

8. In December 1959 Sister Mehl, who lived in Hanover, contacted the local British authorities in order to find out what happened to her former patients, give them her Christian greetings, and present to them some German photographs of their crashed aircraft. William Bennett was found but George Ritchie could not be located. Bill Bennett later became a member of the Beaufort Aircrews Association.

A dummy Al Mark I mine, nominal weight 1,500lbs, fitted to a Hampden by the Royal Aircraft Establishment. Sea mines were dropped by Coastal Command off the shores of France, Belgium and Holland, and by Bomber Command off the shores of Germany and Denmark, as well as in the Baltic. (Roger Hayward collection)

An electro-magnetic sea mine, weighing about 2,000lbs, dropped from a Beaufort and descending by parachute to the sea. The light spots are reflections from the surface of the sea. (The late Jack Gibson)

Bombs on trolleys being towed by a tractor to a Beaufort I. (Author's collection)

bombing attack on an enemy position took place on the night of 20/21 May, when we were one of eight crews ordered to take off for the German airfield of Lanvéoc. This was situated close to the north shore of the Crozon Peninsula, about six miles south of Brest across the estuary. It was the base of the Heinkel He 111s of I/Kampfgeschwader 40, which had probably participated in the bombing of St Eval.

We took off in our Beaufort at 23.20 hours. Percival was content to leave the direction of approach to me. I navigated the aircraft so as to cross the French coast south of the target, and then headed north-west to the airfield, thus attacking the target from land to sea. I could see the airfield buildings, although there were no aircraft visible near the runway. We dropped our load, on this occasion consisting of two 250lb general-purpose and twenty-four 40lb fragmentation bombs. There was no flak, so perhaps we took the defences by surprise. All eight Beauforts returned safely. German records of the effect of our attack do not seem to exist.

Percival was very pleased with the way his crew had settled down, but he asked if I could provide more of a running commentary of events over the intercom, especially on the run-up to the target. He also wanted me to use the American expression 'Bingo!' when the bombs fell, instead of the RAF 'Bombs gone!'

In some respects, I had the most diverse duties in the crew. My first duty was to get the others to synchronise their watches with mine. Then I had to work out the compass courses to fly, tell the pilot and also pass notes for him to prop up behind his P4 compass. Then I had to take drifts over land and sea with the bombsight, work out geometric problems with my Course and Speed Calculator, plot the results on my Mercator chart, identify landfalls with topographical maps, and write up my navigator's log for the purpose of debriefing. I also had to fuse, aim and drop the bombs. Apart from all this, it was necessary to keep a lookout for any night-fighters above, below and sideways. Nevertheless it would

An anti-submarine bomb being fitted under the starboard wing of a Beaufort. The aircraft could carry up to 2,000lbs of bombs or a single torpedo. (Author's collection)

A deadly weapon against low-flying aircraft was the 'quad gun', consisting of 20mm guns rapidly firing explosive shells weighing 4oz, fed by magazines each containing twenty rounds. It could be mounted on special vehicles as well as stationed in a static position. (Author's collection)

be beneficial to keep the whole crew informed of progress and I agreed to do my best, apart from sticking to the RAF 'Bombs gone!'.

On 23 May, our squadron suffered the loss of another aircraft and crew, in daylight. Sergeant C.W. Harper was the pilot of a Beaufort sent off to locate a U-boat off the coast of La Pallice. He came across it and made a dive-bombing attack, opening fire and releasing four of his six bombs. Return fire from machine-guns and cannon damaged the Beaufort, but Harper made a second attack with the other two bombs. Return fire caused further damage, including a leak to a fuel tank. Nevertheless, Harper made a third attack with machine-guns and then turned for home. The fuel finally ran out by the time the Beaufort reached the coast but Harper glided down and crash-landed about two miles inland from Penzance. All four crewmen were badly injured and the aircraft was written off. This extremely gallant action was not rewarded.

On the same day as this episode there was a sudden scramble in 217 Squadron to collect enough crews to make a night attack on the docks at Saint-Nazaire. Although we were not told the reason, the emergency was probably connected with

The battleship Bismarck *and supporting vessels, photographed on 21 May 1941 at Grimstadtfjord in Norway by Flying Officer Michael F. Suckling in a Spitfire PR IC of No 1 Photographic Reconnaissance Unit from RAF Wick in Caithness.* (Author's collection)

information from air reconnaissance by the Fleet Air Arm over Bergen in Norway. The battleship *Bismarck* and the heavy cruiser *Prinz Eugen* were no longer in this port, having left about two days before. They might be heading to the Denmark Strait, between Iceland and Greenland, from where they could enter the North Atlantic and create havoc with British convoys. After that catastrophe, they would probably head for either Brest or Saint-Nazaire, the only two ports in western France with docks that accommodate the colossal *Bismarck*.

With Percival at the controls, our Beaufort took off at 21.45 hours. We headed on a series of courses which took us around the coast of France before we turned east for the target. Our landfall was made off the northern tip of Noirmoutier Island, near the south of the Loire Estuary. From there, we flew down the Loire and then turned north-north-west towards the docks at Saint-Nazaire, thus approaching from inland.

My log, written in the air, lists the height of 500 feet and includes the note 'tracer, Bofors, searchlights' on the run-up to the target, meaning that we

A 'time-exposure' photograph showing the effect of German light flak at night during low-level attacks made by Beauforts against ports in western France. (Author's collection)

experienced machine-gun and 20mm cannon fire. This seemed at first to be curving towards us but then it whipped past the wings. The searchlights probed but did not catch us. The threat of balloons, which had dogged our squadron's previous attack, seemed to be unfounded.

I could see the docks clearly from 500 feet and released our load of two 500lb and four 250lb general-purpose bombs at 23.54 hours. These were fitted with seven-second delay fuses to avoid blowing up ourselves, but the quick succession of explosions which followed still jolted the Beaufort. We did not have a full load of fuel and cut straight across land to the north coast of France, then headed for St Eval and landed at 01.40 hours. It had been a most satisfactory sortie.

The Admiralty's assumption of the course of the two German warships was proved correct later in that morning, 24 May, when they were encountered west-south-west of Iceland by the battleship HMS *Prince of Wales* and the battlecruiser HMS *Hood*. In the ensuing gun battle the *Hood*, which was not fitted with a heavy armoured deck, blew up with terrible loss of life. The *Prince*

The battleship Bismarck, *41,700 tons displacement, photographed from the heavy cruiser* Prinz Eugen *before sailing from Korsfjord in Norway for the North Atlantic. Her heavy armament consisted of eight 38cm and twelve 15cm guns, and she could achieve a speed of 29 knots.* (Author's collection)

of Wales was badly damaged but remained seaworthy. However, the *Bismarck* did not escape damage. A shell had passed through her forward hull, causing her to lose fuel and ship tons of water. Together with the *Prinz Eugen*, she headed south, tracked.by the cruisers HMS *Suffolk* and HMS *Norfolk*, which had reached the area.

The captain of the *Bismarck* was Kapitän zur See Ernst Lindemann, but also on board was Admiral Günther Lütjens. The latter decided to detach the *Prinz Eugen* for commerce raiding, while the *Bismarck* would sail towards Saint-Nazaire for repair and refuelling. The two vessels parted company but then, about twenty hours after HMS *Hood* was sunk, the *Bismarck* came under attack by the Fleet Air Arm.

Another Royal Navy force had left Scapa Flow and was speeding towards the German warships. This consisted of the battleship HMS *King George V* (with the commander of the Home Fleet, Admiral John C. Tovey on board), the aircraft carrier HMS *Victorious* and the battlecruiser HMS *Repulse*. The carrier

A pre-war photograph of the battlecruiser HMS Hood, *42,000 tons displacement. She was completed in 1920 and for many years remained a symbol of Britain's sea power. Her main armament consisted of eight 15in guns and twelve 5.5in guns. However, the latter were eventually replaced by an anti-aircraft battery which included seven twin 4in guns and three eight-barrelled pompoms. She lacked heavy armour plating and was sunk in the Denmark Strait by 38cm gunfire from the battleship* Bismarck *in the early morning of 24 May 1941.* (The late Dorothy Peacock via Mrs Nina Stimson)

King George VI reviewing the ship's company of HMS Hood. *There were only three survivors from over 1,400 men on board when the battlecruiser was sunk by the* Bismarck. (The late Dorothy Peacock via Mrs Nina Stimson)

Admiral Günther Lütjens was born in 1890 and entered the Imperial German Navy in 1907. He served in torpedo boats in the First World War. By the outbreak of the Second World War he was Vice Admiral in charge of reconnaissance forces in the North Sea. He was promoted to Admiral in September 1940 and gained operational experience in his flagship Scharnhorst. *Although intelligent and courageous, he had a reserved and forbidding manner. He was killed on the* Bismarck, *shortly before she sank on 28 May 1941.* (Author's collection)

had flown off nine Fairey Swordfish torpedo bombers of 825 Squadron and six Fairey Fulmar fighters of 802 Squadron.

Eight of the Swordfish, led by Lieutenant-Commander Eugene Esmond, came in at low level against the port side of the *Bismarck*, under intense anti-aircraft fire and even spouts of water from heavy guns. They dropped their torpedoes but Lindemann skilfully manoeuvred his battleship to 'comb the tracks' of these. However, the ninth Swordfish had slipped unseen round to the starboard side and scored a hit with its torpedo. This exploded against the armoured belt, killing one seaman but not penetrating the hull. The Germans claimed five Swordfish shot down but all returned to their carrier. Possibly the violent manoeuvring had upset the aim of the gunners. Two of the Fulmars were forced to ditch but their crews were picked up.

Lindemann turned east after this attack, realising that he was being tracked, before heading south-east to Saint-Nazaire. The radar on the shadowing HMS *Suffolk* lost its blip, so that Admiral Tovey no longer knew the position of his

The 36,700-ton battleship HMS King George V, *ploughing through heavy seas in the North Atlantic. She was armed with ten 14in and sixteen 5.25in guns and could achieve a speed of 28 knots.* (Author's collection)

Admiral Sir John C. Tovey, Commander-in-Chief of the Home Fleet from 22 December 1940 to 14 April 1943. (Author's collection)

Quadruple 0.5in anti-aircraft guns on the 9,800-ton Kent *class cruiser HMS* Suffolk, *on patrol in the Arctic as part of the 1st Cruiser Squadron, with two ice floes in the background. She was armed with eight 8in guns and could achieve 31 knots. At 19.22 hours on 23 May 1941, a lookout on this warship was the first seaman of the Royal Navy to spot the battleship* Bismarck *at sea, about 55 miles north-west of Iceland's North Cape.* (Author's collection)

enemy. The German crew was jubilant at this stage. They had sunk a major warship, escaped an aerial attack, believed they had shot down five aircraft, and were heading to a destination in Occupied France which was popular with crews of the Kriegsmarine.

At St Eval, an entry dated 25 May in 217 Squadron's Operations Record Book read 'A terrific flap was going on all evening because it was believed that *Bismarck* was heading this way. All available crews were kept standing by, and as soon as she came within range, the Squadron would have gone out with 500lb SAP bombs.'

This information regarding the *Bismarck* must have been transmitted to the Admiralty by Admiral Tovey and then passed down the RAF's chain of command to our Intelligence Officers at St Eval. Bomber Command was also involved, for on that night, 25/26 May, No 5 Group sent out forty-eight Hampdens on minelaying operations off Brest and Saint-Nazaire. Only twenty-seven aircraft were successful in the prevailing weather conditions. The others probably flew above cloud and could not locate the target areas.

Four Beauforts of 217 Squadron were also sent out minelaying on that night, two to Brest and two to Saint-Nazaire. All flew at low level and were successful. Percival was one of those sent to Saint-Nazaire, the area being code-named 'Beach'. We took off at 21.00 hours and dropped our mine close to the dock entrance, then landing back at St Eval at 01.05 hours.

The normal procedure for aircrews of 217 Squadron after a night operation was release to our hotel billets for some sleep, but on this occasion Davies, Reeves and I were sent to our respective Messes and told to await further orders. The Officers' Mess was crowded with aircrew from 217 Squadron sitting in chairs and sleep was almost impossible, apart from short periods of dozing.

We spent the remainder of the night and the whole of the next day in those chairs, unaware of the events at sea but told of our forthcoming sortie. The latter was recorded in our Operations Record Book as 'The CO has organised a dive-

Kapitän zur See Ernst Lindemann, commander of the battleship Bismarck. *Born in 1894 in Altenkirchen/Westerwald, he joined the Imperial German Navy on 1 April 1918 and rose to become Chief of the Training Section of the Kriegsmarine in 1938. He was appointed to command the* Bismarck *in the spring of 1940. He was last seen by survivors, standing to attention on the sinking battleship, saluting with his hand to his white cap.* (Author's collection)

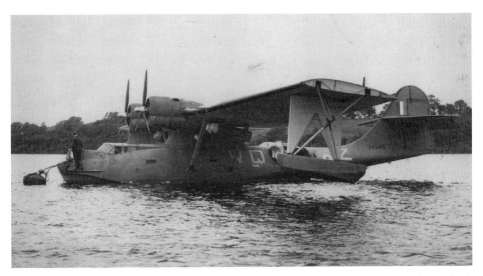

Catalina I letter Z serial AB545 of 209 Squadron, at her moorings in Lough Erne, Northern Island. This was the flying boat in which Flying Officer Dennis A. Briggs located the battleship Bismarck *on 26 May 1941 in the North Atlantic about 690 miles west-north-west of Brest.* (Author's collection)

Flying Officer Dennis A. Briggs, the captain of Catalina I letter Z serial AB545 of 209 Squadron, based at Lough Erne in Northern Island, which located the battleship Bismarck *in the North Atlantic at 10.30 hours on 26 May 1941. He was photographed during a BBC broadcast to the British public.* (Author's collection)

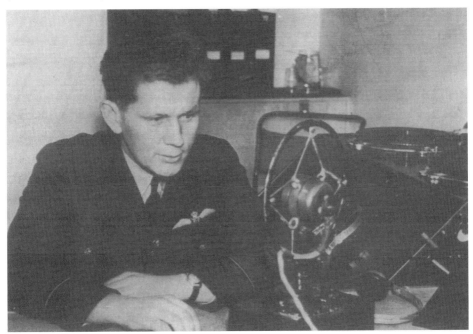

bombing attack of seven aircraft, led by himself, which will attempt to worry the battleship's upper works and more lightly armoured parts . . .' There was no mention of any fighter escort, but we were ordered to circle the *Bismarck* in 'Indian file' and then dive in simultaneously so as to spread the anti-aircraft fire, when the CO fired his Very pistol. Davies, Reeves and I were to be his crew on the operation.

In the *Bismarck* on that day, 26 May, Lütjens had dampened the enthusiasm of his crew by correctly forecasting an impending sea battle and ending his address with 'Victory or Death!'. Later in the day, at 10.30 hours, the battleship was located about 600 miles west of Brest by a Catalina of 209 Squadron flown from RAF Lough Erne in Northern Ireland by Flying Officer Dennis A. Briggs. Thereafter, its progress was monitored by other RAF flying boats and Fleet Air Arm aircraft flown from an approaching aircraft carrier.

The battleship HMS *King George V*, with Admiral John Tovey on board, and the cruiser HMS *Norfolk* were in pursuit of the *Bismarck*, but the aircraft carrier HMS *Victorious* and the battlecruiser HMS *Repulse* had dropped out. However, the battleship HMS *Rodney* had left her escort duty off the west coast of Scotland was racing west to join up with the two pursuers. Also, the cruiser HMS *Dorsetshire* was approaching from the west, likewise having been detached from escort duties. Destroyers from Britain were also racing westwards, to deal with any U-boats which might enter the conflict. The two battleships could tackle the *Bismarck* but their fuel was running low and the maximum speeds of these three major warships were roughly the same. The only hope of reaching their quarry was by crippling her with an air strike.

The best hope lay with Force H from Gibraltar under Vice-Admiral Sir James Somerville, which was sailing northwards on an intercept course with the *Bismarck*. This consisted of the aircraft carrier HMS *Ark Royal*, with a full complement of Swordfish torpedo bombers, the battlecruiser HMS *Renown* and the cruiser HMS *Sheffield*.

In the early afternoon of 26 April, Force H had reached a position about forty miles south-east of the *Bismarck*. At 13.40 hours, Vice-Admiral Somerville ordered HMS *Sheffield* to close with their quarry and shadow her. The cruiser was equipped with radar and was able to carry out this duty. Then, at 14.50 hours, fifteen Swordfish were launched from HMS *Ark Royal* to attack the enemy battleship. By some extraordinary oversight, the pilots had not been told about HMS *Sheffield* and, at 15.50 hours, mistook the cruiser for their target. They all dived down, then flew at low level and dropped their torpedoes from

Two major warships which were part of Force H from Gibraltar ordered to intercept the Bismarck. *The battlecruiser HMS* Renown *(left), 30,750 tons displacement, was armed with six 15in guns and could achieve a speed of 32 knots. The aircraft carrier HMS* Ark Royal *astern of her had a displacement of 22,000 tons, could carry up to sixty aircraft and had a maximum speed of 30 knots.* (Author's collection)

the usual distance about 1,000 yards. Three of these exploded on hitting the water, owing to a fault in the magnetic detonators in the warheads, and HMS *Sheffield* managed to evade the others. The pilots were dismayed by this error, but at least the warheads of other torpedoes were exchanged for the contact variety.

By the early evening of the same day, the crew of the *Bismarck* had become optimistic about their chances of reaching safety. The sky was darkening and by the following morning they would be nearing Saint-Nazaire, protected by an umbrella of fighters and bombers of the Luftwaffe as well as a screen of U-boats. Then, at 21.30 hours, fifteen Swordfish from HMS *Ark Royal* dived out of the clouds and began their low-level approach.

Of course, Lindemann put his battleship into violent turns to evade the torpedo tracks, while anti-aircraft guns blazed at the Swordfish and heavy and medium guns raised waterspouts in front of them. But on this occasion there

The Ark Royal *at Portsmouth, after crossing the South Atlantic from Cape Town to Rio de Janeiro at the time of the sinking of the 'pocket battleship'* Admiral Graf Spee. (Author's collection)

A Fairey Swordfish with wings folded being lowered by lift to one of the two hangars of Ark Royal. *(Author's collection)*

The pilot of a Fairey Swordfish practising a torpedo drop. Aircrews of the Fleet Air Arm achieved some remarkable successes against enemy warships in these biplanes during the early stages of the Second World War. (Author's collection)

were too many torpedoes dropped at the same time. Two of them exploded against the armoured belt forward, without piercing the hull. A third hit a vulnerable part of the hull, blowing a large hole in the steering compartment aft. Seawater poured in and the twin rudders became jammed, registering 'port 12 degrees'. The crew believed they had shot down seven Swordfish but all returned to the carrier.

By then, the *Bismarck* was about 450 miles west of Brest, but she could only steam in circles. Darkness fell, and for several hours she was harried by five destroyers, sending up starshells and firing more torpedoes. Her crew became exhausted and some fell asleep at their stations. Divers went down into the steering compartment but could not budge the jammed rudders. Lindemann realised that the end was inevitable and decided to send the ship's War Diary to safety in one of her Arado Ar 196A floatplanes, but the launching catapult did not function, possibly after damage from one of the torpedoes.

Meanwhile, the strange movements of the *Bismarck* were monitored by HMS *Sheffield* and passed to Admiral Tovey, who realised that his quarry was crippled.

The Bismarck *carried four of these Arado Ar 196A floatplanes for reconnaissance, liaison with other warships and fighter protection with their pair of 20mm cannon and two machine-guns. They were housed in hangars near the mainmast and launched by means of a catapult. Powered by a 970hp BMK 132K radial engine, the Ar 196A had a range of about 650 miles. On 26 May 1941, when warships of the Royal Navy were closing in on the* Bismarck, *one attempted to take off with the battleship's War Diary, but the catapult was found to have been damaged.* (Georges Van Acker collection)

At this time, the wind was strong and the sea heavy, making night firing difficult. He decided to wait for daybreak before closing in with two battleships and two cruisers for the final kill.

These events were not known to the aircrews still sitting in their Messes in St Eval during the night of 26/27 May, awaiting orders. We continued to believe that the *Bismarck* was heading for Brest but was not yet within our range. Evidently this view was also held by Bomber Command, which despatched thirty-eight Hampdens on that night, mostly to drop mines near Brest and only a few off Saint-Nazaire. However, we knew that aircraft were pouring into St Eval, mainly Wellingtons, for their aircrews had joined our vigil. It was a comfort to know that others would join our squadron in the attack, but we were spending another sleepless night. Although not keen on the prospect of circling the *Bismarck* while her gunners fired at us, I was even more worried about the

The battleship HMS King George V *firing her after turret's quadruple 14in guns.* (Author's collection)

The Nelson *class battleship HMS* Rodney, *36,000 tons displacement, firing a broadside from her nine 16in turret guns. In addition to this armament, she had twelve 6in guns. She could achieve a speed of 23 knots.* (Author's collection)

problem of navigating after two nights with almost no sleep. An interception course followed by a possible search pattern after ETA required a clear head, not one dulled by lack of sleep.

The battleships HMS *Rodney* and HMS *King George V* began to close with the *Bismarck* in the early morning of 28 May. At 08.47 hours they opened fire against the enemy's port side from a range of about 20,000 yards, the former with her nine 16in guns and the latter with her ten 14in guns. This combination was far heavier than the eight 15in guns of the *Bismarck*, while Lindemann had the additional problem of being unable to manoeuvre. Enemy fire fell short or over the British battleships, which closed up further and added their secondary armament to the engagement. Twelve Swordfish arrived from HMS *Ark Royal* but the pilots could not dive down to 50 feet to make their attack in the middle of a sea battle. They returned to the carrier with their torpedoes.

By 09.10 hours the jammed rudders of the *Bismarck* caused her to begin turning away to port while she was being straddled by British gunfire. Direct hits were observed, principally from HMS *Rodney*, causing fires to break out both forward and aft. The cruisers HMS *Suffolk* and HMS *Devonshire* joined in the bombardment with their 8in guns. The *Bismarck* was hit again and again. By 09.46 hours she could no longer defend herself, with all her fire-control instruments and her four gun turrets out of action. Her deck was a smoking shambles and littered with dead and wounded, but she was still afloat and under continuous fire. HMS *Devonshire* struck her with three torpedoes and she began to sink by the stern, according to one survivor when a party of her crew scuttled her. She rolled over and went down at 10.36 hours. Only 110 men were saved from her complement of 2,200. Lindemann and Lütjens were among those lost. Admiral Tovey commented on the sinking, 'She put up a most gallant fight against impossible odds'.

The news came through to us at St Eval a few hours later and we dispersed thankfully. I was due for five days of leave from the next day, the first since joining 217 Squadron four months before. A break was welcome, since we were always on duty every day of every week. In the early morning, I boarded a train at Padstow and found an empty first-class compartment. Still feeling tired, I tipped up the arm rests, lay down and went to sleep. Shortly afterwards, the train jolted and I woke up to see passengers sitting opposite and others standing in the corridor. Nobody had woken me. It was very embarrassing and I jumped up and apologised, but they just smiled and sat down. The RAF was very high in public esteem, a matter which was always a boost to our morale.

The events at St Eval relating to the *Bismarck* soon went out of my mind, but they returned about fifty years later when the Public Record Office (now renamed The National Archives) passed on to me a request for some details of the air operations from the senior survivor of the battleship.[9] This was Baron Burkard von Mullenheim-Rechberg, who had been the fourth gunnery officer as well as the adjutant to Kapitän zur See Ernst Lindemann, with the rank of Kapitänleutnant (Lieutenant-Commander). He had already written a book on the subject, entitled *Battleship Bismarck*, but wanted more information.

I was able to answer his various questions, which were written in clear longhand and perfect English, and I also described the build-up of aircraft at St Eval awaiting the *Bismarck* when it came within our range. The latter added to his despondency at what seemed to be, in retrospect, an unwise decision to send the battleship and the *Prinz Eugen* on the operation. It might have been better to wait until the two battlecruisers *Scharnhorst* and *Gneisenau* in Brest were ready to join them.

There was one matter which did not enter our correspondence. In his book, Baron Burkard described how eighty-five men wearing lifejackets were rescued from the oily sea by HMS *Dorsetshire*, with her crew throwing ropes over the side and then hauling survivors aboard. These were given excellent care, with injuries tended while clean clothes, cigarettes, hot tea and meals were provided. But the cruiser moved away from the area while there were still some survivors in the water. The Baron protested to the ship's captain, Captain Benjamin C.S. Martin, and was told there was a danger from U-boats, He did not accept this but, unknown to him at the time, the Government Code and Cipher School at Bletchley Park was routinely decrypting U-boat signals. In the National Archives, there is a German signal sent to all U-boats, decrypted at 16.58 hours on 26 May 1941, 'AT 1820 BISMARCK IN SQUARE BE 53, COURSE 115 DEGREES, 24 KNOTS. CRUISER OF SHEFFIELD CLASS SHADOWING'.[10] A warning would have been sent to the Royal Navy warships.

For those of us who served in 217 Squadron, the most astonishing revelation about the *Bismarck* occurred on 7 March 2001 when an obituary of our former commanding officer, Group Captain Guy Bolland, appeared in *The Daily*

---

9. At this time, I had been invited by the Public Record Office to utilise their staff sections in order to research and write illustrated books based on the large collection of RAF photographs in their Image Library.
10. The National Archives ref: DEFE 3/1, p 985.

Survivors from the Bismarck *being rescued by the cruiser HMS* Dorsetshire *on 27 May 1941. Only 115 men were saved from her complement of over 2,200.* (Author's collection)

Telegraph[11] after he had died at the age of 91. Unknown to us, after he had been removed from his command in March 1941 when protesting to No 19 Group about the folly of sending young men on fruitless suicide missions in Beauforts, he had been appointed as Fleet Aviation Officer to Admiral John Tovey, who commanded the Home Fleet.

This had taken him to Scapa Flow and then to service on the battleship HMS *King George V*, which left the port on 23 May to hunt for the *Bismarck*. Thus he was the officer who consulted with the Admiral during the air operations which followed and eventually resulted in the crippling of the enemy battleship. Had we known this during the two nights we were waiting for orders to take off and make an attack, it would have given a tremendous boost to our morale.

---

11. Researched and written by Air Commodore Graham R. Pitchfork MDE, RAF (Ret'd).

Chapter 6

French Ports Under Occupation

On return to St Eval in early June 1941, I learnt that the *Prinz Eugen* had arrived in Brest. Bomber Command had dispatched fifty-two Wellingtons and twelve Stirlings on 27 May to hunt over a wide area of the Atlantic for the missing cruiser, but without success. Perhaps she had been sailing under cloud cover, but four days later she slipped into Brest harbour with engine trouble, presumably preceded by minesweepers. Thus she joined the *Scharnhorst* and *Gneisenau* to form a major threat to Britain's Atlantic lifelines. Bomber Command had the duty of continuing frequent attacks against the port, only to find that the dock area was usually covered by ground haze and smokescreens.

Our squadron was engaged primarily on a mixture of daylight anti-shipping sorties and night-time mining operations, the latter being almost entirely within Brest Estuary. Percival had not yet returned, for he was due for a long leave after his longer period of operational flying. In fact, unknown to us he was using the opportunity to marry his fiancée. In the meantime, Davies, Reeves and I were crewed up with an experienced pilot in 217 Squadron, Flight Sergeant Wood.

Flying Officer John F. 'Jack' Percival and his wife Peggy, who were married in a parish church in Oxford on 21 June 1941 when he was on leave from 217 Squadron at RAF St Eval in Cornwall. (Mrs Peggy Connell-McDowell)

All our flights with Wood were daylight anti-shipping sorties. The first took place on 4 June and four more followed during the next twelve days. Nothing remarkable happened on any of them, but the weather was unfavourable and on one occasion St

Eval was covered with fog and we had to land at RAF Perranporth, down the coast about eight miles south-west of Newquay. On 22 June, we made a daylight sortie with another pilot, Sergeant Banning, which was similarly uneventful.

Although we had no serious problems in any of these operations, 217 Squadron lost four Beauforts in the same period. The first happened on 10 June, after Flight Sergeant Peter F. Hollely had returned to RAF Chivenor from a minelaying operation during which his mine had 'hung up' and he had been forced to bring it back. He took off for St Eval later in the day but one of his engines caught fire and the Beaufort came down in the sea. The mine exploded and all four men were killed. Hollely's body was the only one recovered.

The next happened on 17 June when Flying Officer John A. Eyre took off from St Eval on his first solo circuit but an engine stalled and he crashed near Padstow, resulting in his death. On the following day, Sergeant Anthony Gosden took off from RAF Thorney Island for a minelaying sortie in the Brest Estuary but the Beaufort was shot down, probably by a flak ship, and all four crew members were killed. Then, on 22 June, Pilot Officer John Welsh took off from St Eval on another minelaying sortie in Brest Estuary and was also shot down. The only survivor was the wireless operator, Sergeant H.E.C. Young, who was picked up and became a PoW.

In April 2000, the Beaufort Aircrews Association received a request from John Welsh's son, also named John, for further details of the loss of his father. It was found from German records that the Beaufort had been shot down by *Sperrbrecher 16* of the Kriegsmarine. This type of vessel was one of the German answers to the problem of the RAF's minelaying campaign. They were converted merchant ships with the bottoms of their hulls reinforced with layers of concrete, so that they could safely explode magnetic mines. Their decks were packed with anti-aircraft weapons, making them very formidable adversaries to low-flying aircraft. Apart from these monsters, there were also smaller flak ships plus the ever-present danger of night-fighters. Thus minelaying could be very dangerous, and for the aircrews it was less satisfying than low-level bombing of ports, for there was no obvious result from plonking a mine down in the sea.

There was also a change in top command in this period. On 15 June, Air Marshal Sir Philip B. Joubert de la Ferté took over Coastal Command from Air Chief Marshal Sir Frederick W. Bowhill. He brought with him a knowledge of technical advances which were to be introduced into the Command, but he had less experience of operational matters.

Another change took place, on 16 June, for the commissioned officers of 217 Squadron. We were moved from the Watergate Hotel a short distance up the coast to the Waterbeach Hotel, which had been acquired by the RAF. This resulted in a considerable improvement in our living conditions, for we were each allocated a separate room instead of the former dormitories. Moreover there were batmen to clean our rooms and look after our uniforms. The Mess Hall was far more agreeable and there was a bar, although it served little more than beer. There was also a lounge where we could read newspapers and magazines, as well as listen to the wireless. The beach below was attractive, with rocks which formed a sort of swimming pool. However, we could seldom enjoy this since trucks took us every day to St Eval for standby duties or operational flying.

Air Chief Marshal Sir Philip B. Joubert de la Ferté, the Air Officer Commanding-in-Chief of Coastal Command from 14 June 1941 to 4 February 1943. (Author's collection)

On 21 June, John F. Percival married Peggy Trumble in Oxford and brought his bride to St Eval where they found accommodation in one of the nearby cottages available as married quarters. However, their honeymoon lasted only a few days, for on 24 June he was ordered to fly with Davies, Reeves and myself on a minelaying sortie in Brest Estuary. There was nothing remarkable about the flight. My navigator's log records 'intense flak and searchlights' in the distance, probably from a bombing operation over the port. We were one of six Beauforts which flew on this minelaying operation and all returned safely.

We were glad to be flying once more in a regular crew and made five more minelaying sorties in the next eleven days, being diverted to land at RAF Boscombe Down on one occasion. When landing at St Eval, we always seemed to take a long time in the circuit and I assumed there was a build-up of aircraft before we were given a green landing light. Long after the war, Peggy told me that her husband took a wide sweep over their cottage and roared the engines.

The crew of a Bristol Beaufort I of No 217 Squadron at RAF St Eval in mid-1941. Left to right: Sergeant Davies, wireless operator; Flying Officer Jack Percival, pilot (Canadian); Sergeant Kenneth Reeves, air gunner; Pilot Officer Roy C. Nesbit, navigator and bomb aimer (Squadron Navigation Officer). (Author's collection)

The port wing of a Beaufort I of 217 Squadron at RAF St Eval. The aircraft had returned safely from a minelaying operation near Brest harbour, taken place shortly before dawn on 26 June 1941. The shell was probably fired from a harbour defence vessel or a Sperrbrecher *(a mine-exploding vessel heavily armed with anti-aircraft guns).* (Author's collection)

She always remained awake, waiting for this noise and thus knowing he would be home within about an hour, after our de-briefing.

Our next flight, on 10 July, came very close to disaster. We took off from St Eval at 22.45 hours on a minelaying sortie to Saint-Nazaire. All went well on the outward and return flights but, when we approached base, the land was completely covered with mist. The beacon at St Eval was flashing its identification letters in Morse and we could see these when directly over the airfield but nothing when circling to make an approach. This difficulty persisted for about forty minutes, when we were ordered to fly to Dodman Point on the south coast and circle again to await further orders.

Eventually we were diverted to RAF Boscombe Down, but on ETA there was also thick mist and we could see nothing. Our fuel gauges were registering zero and a crash-landing through fog would have been suicidal. We prepared to bale out but then, providentially, the fog began to clear and I saw a beacon flashing 'V–L', the letters for RAF Andover, not far from our objective. Percival managed to land but our engines stopped when taxying to dispersal. We were quickly refuelled and took off for the short flight to Boscombe Down. This was an experimental station and it put on amazing display for our landing at about 04.00 hours, with a circle of perimeter lights and blue 'funnel lights' leading to a brilliantly-lit runway. We learnt that this was the new 'Drem lighting system'.

After our landing, we reported to the control tower and Percival was able to make a reassuring telephone call to his wife. We had a few hours' sleep and then I was able to look around the airfield before clearance arrived from St Eval. A peculiar aircraft was flying, a Westland Lysander fitted with a rear turret. It was not until after the war that I discovered it was designed to strafe German troops if they landed on English beaches. Another aircraft was on the ground, a huge bomber in black livery, with somebody guarding it. He was Joe Rickard, an air observer with whom I had trained. Joe did not allow me to board the aircraft but told me that it was named a Lancaster and gave me some details of its performance and bombload. It seems probable that this was the second prototype, serial DC 595, of the magnificent aircraft which first entered RAF squadron service in December 1941.

Back at St Eval and throughout the month, our crew was detailed to carry out minelaying sorties at night, while other crews were selected for daylight anti-shipping operations. Among the latter was a newly-arrived crew with Pilot Officer Peter Graham as pilot and Pilot Officer John Stockley as air observer. During a flight on 9 July they had found what appeared to be a U-boat on the

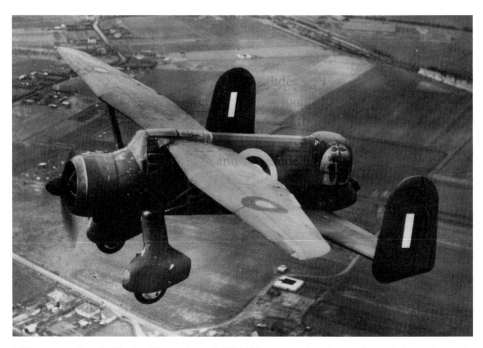

This strange aircraft, Westland Lysander serial K6127, was fitted with twin fins and the mock-up of a four-gun turret. It was tested at the RAF's Aeroplane and Armament Experimental Establishment at Boscombe Down in Wiltshire, and was intended to strafe German troops on the beaches in the event of an invasion. (Author's collection)

The second prototype of the Avro Lancaster, serial DG595, which first flew on 13 May 1941. It made a series of tests at RAF Boscombe Down in Wiltshire. (Author's collection)

surface and attacked it with bombs, depth-charges and machine-gunfire. It later turned out to be HM Submarine *Tuna*, which managed to limp home despite damage.

Stockley told me that they intended to seek out targets closer to enemy shores than their patrol lines. They produced a result at about 09.00 hours on 16 July after an early morning sortie, when they diverted to the mouth of Brest Estuary and found a large ship near the Ile de Sein. Graham dived down out of the sun and straddled the stern with his stick of general-purpose bombs. It was identified after war as *Sperrbrecher 4*, a mine-exploding vessel of 6,757 tons. She was very badly damaged but did not sink. On the following day, Graham chased and fired his front gun at an Arado Ar 196 (the type of floatplane which *Bismarck* had carried), but the engagement was broken off without result.

In the week following these episodes, 217 Squadron suffered the loss of three more Beauforts. The first took place on 18 July when a Canadian pilot, Flying Officer Thomas E. Kerr, was flying one of several Beauforts attacking shipping close to Saint-Nazaire. His aircraft was shot down by flak and all four crew members were killed, although their bodies were recovered and interred by the Germans. In daylight two days later, a Beaufort flown by a New Zealander in the RAF, Sergeant Sidney W. Jarvis, was shot down during daylight in the Bay of Biscay. The exact circumstances are not known but all crew members were picked up

Sergeant Sidney W. Jarvis, a New Zealander in the RAF, was the pilot of Beaufort I serial L9970 of 217 Squadron at RAF St Eval which took off at 12.55 hours on 20 July 1941 for a daylight 'Rover Patrol' over the Bay of Biscay. The other crew members were Sergeant M. Gillies of the RCAF (air observer), Sergeant R.S.C.T. Griffin (wireless operator) and Sergeant G. Goodwin (air gunner). The Beaufort did not return and the circumstances of its loss are not known, but all four men became PoWs. Jarvis is still wearing the blue serge uniform of a sergeant in this post-war photograph but the forage cap in his shoulder tab is that of a warrant officer, a rank he would have attained while in captivity. He has since died and the photograph was provided by his nephew. (Charles Hamlin)

The attack on 24 July 1941 by fifteen Handley Page Hampdens of Bomber Command on the battlecruiser Scharnhorst *at La Pallice when she was hit by five armour-piercing bombs. Three of these pierced the hull and caused an inrush of water, following which she was ordered back to Brest for repairs.* (Author's collection)

and became PoWs. Jarvis suffered from acute depression after the war as a result of his experiences in captivity, possibly during the terrible marches from the approaching Russian forces in the winter of 1944/5.

On 22 July the *Scharnhorst* slipped out of Brest and disappeared. Its absence was discovered by an RAF photo-interpreter who examined the print of a photograph of the port brought back by a photo-reconnaissance Spitfire, and the alarm was raised. In a hunt on the following day the battlecruiser was discovered moored to a dock at La Pallice, where the Kriegsmarine seemed to believe that there was less danger from the relentless bombing of Brest by the RAF.

RAF Bomber Command brought forward a major daylight raid on Brest which was already being planned. Three newly-acquired Flying Fortresses, eighteen Hampdens and seventy-nine Wellingtons were dispatched in the afternoon of 24 July, escorted by three squadrons of Spitfires, but the German fighter defence was stronger than expected. Ten Wellingtons and two Hampdens were brought down by fighters or flak. There was no damage to the other German warships but civilian casualties were recorded as seventy-five killed and eighty-one injured. It was estimated that that this raid brought the total of civilians killed by bombing of Brest to over 500.

In addition to this major raid, fifteen Halifaxes were dispatched to La Pallice without fighter escort. Five were lost by German fighters or flak and all the others were damaged, but three armour-piercing bombs penetrated the hull of the *Scharnhorst* without exploding while two others exploded on the deck. The warship shipped over 3,000 tons of water and was ordered back to Brest, where repair facilities were available. She left during the night.

Our squadron also carried out two operations during this episode. The first was on the night of 23/24 July when eight Beauforts were dispatched to La Pallice, carrying Magnum parachute mines. One pilot was forced to turn back with engine trouble but the others dropped their mines and returned safely. It was believed that one mine exploded on the docks and that another might have hit the *Scharnhorst*.

Six other Beauforts of our squadron were sent out in the morning of 25 July to hunt for the *Scharnhorst*, which was known to be heading northwards. Their role was to attack the escorts, leaving the battlecruiser clearer for torpedo-carrying Beauforts of 22 Squadron. Incredibly, they were carrying Magnums, apparently by order of Coastal Command. It was very difficult to achieve a direct hit on a stationary target with these mines and quite impossible on a target in motion.

Three officers of 217 Squadron at RAF St Eval in the early summer of 1941. Left to right: Pilot Officer Jim Hunter (air observer; Flying Officer Jack Gibson (air observer and Squadron Navigation Officer); Pilot Officer Tom Kitching DFC (pilot). Jack Gibson and Tom Kitching survived their operational tours. Jim Hunter was in a Beaufort shot down on 25 July 1941 while attacking an escort to the Scharnhorst on her return journey from La Pallice to Brest; he was picked up and became a PoW for the rest of the war. (The late Jack Gibson)

Only one Beaufort of our squadron located the enemy. It was flown by an Australian in the RAF, Flight Lieutenant A.G. 'Digger' Collings, and it failed to return. His loss caused a young lady who lived near St Eval to burst into tears, but fortunately Collings survived, albeit wounded. He dived on the destroyer *Erich Steinbrinck*, but light flak killed the wireless operator Sergeant Alaric J. Appleby and also caused the Magnum to fall away. Then heavier flak hit the Beaufort, wounding Collings in the legs, but he made a good ditching. He was picked up, together with the air observer Pilot Officer W. Jim Hunter and the air gunner Sergeant Taylor.

In about six weeks, our squadron had lost seven aircraft and six complete crews. This was about a third of our nominal strength. There was another problem, since several of our crew members who had flown from the days of Ansons were declared 'tour-expired' and posted away from the squadron, leaving us even more depleted. One of these was Flying Officer Jack Gibson, our Squadron Navigation Officer. I was appointed to replace him, while continuing in my additional position of Squadron Photography Officer.

Our squadron continued as usual, but once more on a reduced scale while awaiting new crews and aircraft. This was a period when Britain was mainly on the defensive in the war. The danger of invasion had been eliminated but our forces had been defeated in the Balkans and Greece, while they were retreating in the Western Desert. On the Russian front, the German steamroller seemed to be crushing all opposition in its advance to Moscow.

Churchill had said 'Only the Air Force can win us the war . . . the fighters are our salvation but the bombers alone can provide the means of victory'. However, the reaction of our people in the Blitz indicated a strengthening of resolve and it did not seem likely that Germany could be bombed into submission. All we could do in our squadron was to continue operating and hope that somehow world events would turn in our favour.

The Blackburn Skua of the Fleet Air Arm was armed with four Browning .303in machine-guns in the wings and a single Lewis gun in the rear cockpit. Some were based at the Royal Navy's Operational Training School at St Merryn airfield, only a few miles from RAF St Eval. (Author's collection)

On 1 August our crew was one of four dispatched on daylight anti-shipping patrols in the Bay of Biscay, carrying general-purpose bombs. We saw nothing on our lengthy flight, apart from a few tunny fishing boats but, when approaching St Eval at about 19.00 hours, Ken Reeves reported a Blackburn Skua diving down on us. Then the pilot opened fire with his four front guns. Percival took skilful evasive action and the tracer missed us. Reeves offered, rather sorrowfully, to shoot down the attacker, but Percival forbade this and managed to escape into a convenient cumulus cloud.

These Skuas were based at the Fleet Air Arm training airfield of St Merryn, a few miles north of us, but the crews could land at St Eval for operational reasons. The sky was clear when we came out of cloud, and we landed. A Fleet Air Arm lieutenant was ahead of us in the debriefing room and we listened while he gave a vivid description of his attack on a 'Heinkel He 111', which escaped into cloud 'with smoke streaming from an engine'. He sank back deflated when Percival broke in with some caustic comments about his ability and then hastily disappeared, doubtless to return to St Mirren and keep quiet about his exploit.

Our squadron achieved its first sinking of an enemy vessel at midnight on 5/6 August. A Beaufort flown by the audacious Pilot Officer Peter Graham flew inland to Nantes on the Loire and spotted a ship moored in the docks. He made a dive-bombing attack and his stick of 2,000lb of general-purpose bombs straddled the target. It was the German merchant vessel *Leesee* of 2,624 tons, which duly sank. Graham was awarded an immediate DFC.

In daylight on 12 August, our squadron lost another aircraft. This was flown by Flying Officer E.A. 'Tip' Ranee, a tall and elegant pilot with a keen sense of humour, who sometimes wore a monocle. His Beaufort was shot down when it was one of several making an attack on a tanker off Saint-Nazaire. The wireless operator, Flight Sergeant Arthur Chiplin, lost his life, but Ranee and the other two crew members, Sergeants A.G. Wilson and S.J. Austin, were picked up and became prisoners.

Yet another was lost in an anti-shipping 'Rover' patrol in daylight on 21 August. It was flown by Peter Graham, but the circumstances are not known. He probably found a ship to attack near Saint-Nazaire and was shot down. The body of Pilot Officer John A-V. Stockley was recovered but those of Graham, Sergeant Edgar A.C. Williams and Sergeant Ralph Marshall, are commemorated in the Runnymede Memorial.

While these events were taking place in August, those of us in Percival's crew were ordered to carry out several daylight anti-shipping patrols and others

A Beaufort I of 217 Squadron flying over Land's End in Cornwall, the most southwesterly point of England, when returning to RAF St Eval from an operation on 24 August 1941. (Author's collection)

An oblique photograph of a model of Lorient, facing south, used by the author in 1941 as a target map for bombing attacks and minelaying sorties. These models were made in rubber by the RAF's Model Section, so that they could be rolled up for ease of transport to various RAF stations. (Author's collection)

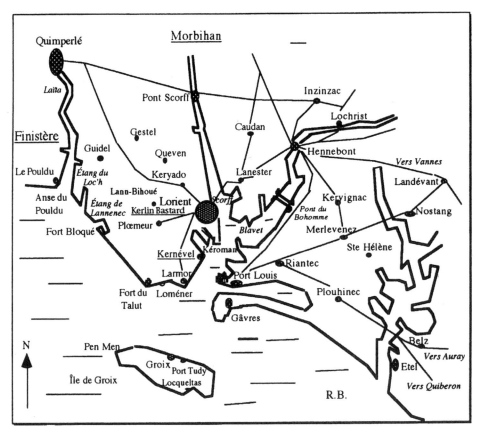

Environs of Lorient. To the south of Lorient is the district of Kernevel where Admiral Karl Donitz, commander of the Kriegsmarine's U-boat Arm, established his operational headquarters on 16 October 1940.

dropping mines at night. The latter were usually off Lorient, which we found trickier than those off Brest or Saint-Nazaire. The flak was more frequent and concentrated, from the nearby islands and enemy vessels. On 21 August (the day when Graham and his crew were lost), I spotted a dummy town near Lorient, on the right of the point where the river Blavet entered the sea. It was obviously a trap, since the lights were switched on invitingly as we approached. We altered course hastily to avoid a reception from flak gunners.

I reported this incident at de-briefing in the operations room back at St Eval. These occasions were always much the same. First, mugs of hot tea were provided and a round tin containing cigarettes was pushed towards us. Notes were then taken from the navigator's log. Our Station Intelligence Officer was Flight Lieutenant Cuthbert W.P. Selby, who had lost an arm in the First World War (he still managed to drive a car, controlling the steering wheel with his knees when changing gear). His assistant was Flying Officer Eddie A.A. Shackleton (later Lord Shackleton), the son of the explorer Sir Ernest Shackleton. Our Squadron Intelligence Officer was Flying Officer E.H. Gould. On this occasion, the de-briefing was carried out by Eddie Shackleton. He was very sceptical about my report, but the fact was later confirmed by an agent in France.

On 28 August, our crew was ordered to carry out a minelaying operation at night off La Pallice, the naval port for La Rochelle. This was a longer flight than any of our previous operations but the weather was clear and there was a bright moon. Moreover, there seemed to be no flak ships as we approached the harbour and I could clearly see two lines of buoys leading to the entrance. Our mine was dropped exactly between these lines and we returned without incident. It seemed to be most satisfactory and I was delighted when, about three days later, I was told that a tanker had been sunk in this position. I entered this fact in my flying log book. However, a post-war examination of German records shows that no sinking occurred in that position over the next few days. It now seems that we were sometimes told of such favourable results in order to boost squadron morale.

Our next sortie, which took place in daylight on 30 August, was a welcome change from the usual minelaying and bombing at night. We were one of three crews ordered to escort what was believed to be the first major convoy to reach port via the south coast of Ireland. We took off at 08.45 hours and met the convoy about an hour later, identifying ourselves and then counting twenty-four merchantmen and two destroyers. We circled these for three hours, hoping to spot a U-boat and bomb it, but there was no sight of one. The next Beaufort relieved us and we flew, as instructed, to Carew Cheriton in South Wales, where a ground party from St Eval had arrived. Our orders were to remain there and await further orders, presumably to escort another convoy, but after another two days all three crews were sent back to St Eval.

On 4 September we were one of several crews ordered to attack shipping in the docks at La Pallice. This turned out to be quite a dramatic occasion which was later reported in the newspapers. We took off at 20.20 hours on a clear night and I navigated the Beaufort so as to attack the docks from a southerly direction, from a height of 500 feet. On the final approach, it was clear that there were no ships and a quick alteration was made to attack some long buildings in the north, which looked like warehouses. There was intense flak and I pressed the switch to release our stick of six general-purpose bombs.

Then something peculiar happened. On the bomb distributor beside me there was a red light which came on when the bombs were armed. A pointer moved across this distributor as the bombs fell away and then the red light should have gone out, but it failed to do so. I yelled over the intercom 'Reeves, did the bombs fall off?' There was no reply, for Reeves was busy with his favourite trick of firing down a searchlight beam to scare the Germans with the tracer. So I shouted a warning to Percival. He nodded and turned back to the target, dived, pulled out and then pressed his bomb release switch, while more flak streamed up at us. There were two metallic thumps beneath the aircraft and I thought we had been hit. But Reeves came on the intercom and confirmed that only four bombs had fallen away during the first attack and the other two during the second. Evidently two bombs had 'hung up' on the first occasion. We later learnt that we had bombed the Compagnie Industrielle des Pétroles.

After this successful flight, our next two operations were disappointments. On 10 September we were ordered, in company with another Beaufort and an escort of three Beaufighters, to find and attack a U-boat believed to be making its way to the docks at Brest. We took off in daylight and set course for Ushant but had to return owing to unfavourable weather conditions.

Next, we were ordered to attack the docks at Saint-Nazaire, taking off at 01.00 hours on 13 September. For some unexplained reason, we had to bomb

Oil Ship and Factory Hit by RAF

TWO Beauforts went to bomb ships on Thursday night. One found a 300ft.-long tanker outside Granville Harbour, North-West France, low in the water and heavily laden.

The pilot attacked in a shallow dive, and after he had dropped a stick of medium and heavy bombs his rear-gunner reported a large cloud of white smoke rising from the tanker.

The other Beaufort flew to La Pallice, recent haven of the German battle cruiser Scharnhorst.

The roads were empty of shipping, but the factory of the Compagnie Industrielle des Petrolles, north of the port, stood out clearly.

The pilot bombed it, and his rear-gunner saw débris flung high by the explosion.

'Mike' Failed

But at that moment the microphone of the inter-communication set failed. So did the light on the bomb distributor, which remained on as if the bombs had not dropped.

So the pilot flew on to the docks, where ships were at anchor, and, in spite of intense anti-aircraft fire, he pressed home a " bombless " attack.

Then the rear-gunner got word to the pilot of the success of the factory bombing, and the plane came home.

The Daily Mail *6 September 1941.*
This report on the second Beaufort is inaccurate. The 'mike' did not fail. The air gunner firing his machine-gun and could not reply immediately.

The Bofors 40mm anti-aircraft gun, designed and produced in Sweden, had an effective ceiling of about 16,000 feet and could fire at the rate of about 100 explosive shells per minute. It was adopted by Germany, Britain, the USA, Russia and Japan. (Author's collection)

from 10,000 feet. We duly made our way over the sea to the target, gradually increasing height, and I was able to pick out our exact position from the lines of surf on the coast. But the dock area was covered with mist and we flew to and fro over it for almost an hour, under intermittent heavy flak, hoping for a clear spell. Eventually, we had to return to the coast, pick out our exact position again, fly carefully back to the target area for a few minutes and drop our bombs on ETA. By then, we had used up so much fuel that we had to return directly over enemy territory and were fired at again when over the area of Lorient.

There was always an additional worry when bombing these French ports, particularly from high level, since we might kill or injure Frenchmen working as forced labourers in the docks. We were told that some construction was taking place but had no idea that it consisted of gigantic concrete bunkers to shelter U-boats, military personnel, torpedoes and other supplies. In fact, this huge

The German equivalent of the Bofors gun was their 37mm flak gun. (Author's collection)

programme had begun during January 1941 in Brest, Lorient, Saint-Nazaire, La Pallice and Bordeaux by the Todt Organisation backed by the great German manufacturing companies such as M.A.N., Holtzmann and Siemens. There were tens of thousands of labourers drawn from all the countries annexed or conquered by Germany. These worked in daily twelve-hour shifts and their conditions were no better than slavery. Our conception of the suffering of the people in Occupied France under a cruel and ruthless dictatorship was not entirely correct, according to post-war analyses of this early period. The main reason was Hitler's belief that France could be allied with Germany in his 'thousand year plan' of domination of the whole of Europe. Coupled with his directive, the occupying German forces found their lives very agreeable. They liked the climate, the scenery, the cafés and the food. Any trangression on their part could result in a far less favourable posting, such as to the Russian Front.

Of course, the French population had been bewildered and dismayed at the unexpected German victory in 1940, and they loathed this occupation. They were subjected to restrictions such as curfews, rationing, the introduction of German currency and the transfer of industries to German war production.

A Luftwaffe unit raising barrage balloons at Brest, as protection against bombing attacks by low-flying RAF aircraft. (Archives Municipales de Brest, ref: 2Fi 10643, via Mme Geneviève Moulard)

Over 1.5 million French servicemen remained PoWs in Germany, held hostage and forced to work, apart from a few who had worked in French agriculture which had become valuable to German war production.

Our next operational flight was intended to be a night bombing attack from medium level against the docks of Lorient, but it came to an unexpected end. We took off at 19.15 hours on 16 September and headed on the usual series of courses over the sea to the target. Twenty minutes after leaving Land's End, when we were at 2,500 feet, I spotted a small orange light below us and moving across our bow from port to starboard. Although I could not see the shape of the aircraft, we knew of the night-fighter version of the Junkers Ju 88, fitted with two upward-firing 20mm cannons which the Germans nicknamed *Schräge Musik* (oblique or jazz music). I called a warning to Percival.

Our Beaufort was fitted with an automatic pilot and there was a clank as Percival disengaged this and dived to starboard in order to confuse the enemy.

AVIS OFFICIEL

Par ordre des autorités d'occupation, il est rappelé à la population qu'en vertu de l'ordonnance relative à la protection contre les actes de sabotage en date du **10 Octobre 1940**, quiconque cache ou héberge chez lui des prisonniers de guerre évadés ou des prisonniers de guerre non possesseurs d'un certificat de libération ou de congé, sera puni de mort.

Il en est de même pour quiconque cachera ou hébergera des membres d'une formation militaire ennemie (par exemple équipage d'un avion ayant fait un atterrissage forcé, parachutistes, etc...).

Quiconque faciliterait la fuite de ces personnes, s'expose en conséquence, aux peines les plus sévères.

VANNES, le 7 Juillet 1941.

Le Préfet,

H. PITON.

Translation: Official Notice

By order of the authorities of occupation, the population is reminded that in pursuance of the ordinance concerning protection against acts of sabotage dated 10 October 1940, whoever hides or shelters in his home any prisoners of war who have escaped or any prisoners of war not in possession of a certificate of liberation or of leave, will be punished by death.

The same applies to whoever hides or shelters members of any enemy military unit (for example the crews of an aircraft which has made a forced landing, parachutists, etc . . .).

Whoever assists the flight of such people is in consequence subject to the most severe penalties.

Vannes, 7 July 1941

Chief Magistrate

H. Piton

(This notice was displayed in Nantes, about thirty-five miles west of the administration centre of Vannes)

'V for Victory'

French Flash "V" Sign to R.A.F.'s Night Bombers

Flying over France on the way to attack the industrial shipbuilding centre of Nantes last night, Beauforts, of Coastal Command, swept so low over towns and villages in the brilliant moonlight that people rushed from their houses to flash the victory sign on pocket torches.

"As we crossed Northern France," said one pilot, quoted by the Air Ministry this afternoon, "we saw cottage doors being thrown open. Light streamed out and silhouetted in the beams were men and women peering up at us."

When the Beauforts arrived over Nantes, the crews saw two large buildings—"as big as half a dozen hangars," said one pilot—outlined by the moon. They were part of an extensive factory.

Sticks of high explosive and incendiary bombs were unloaded on the buildings, which were left wrecked and in flames.

People in French towns and villages flashed the Victory sign on pocket torches to Beauforts on their way to bomb Nantes and St. Nazaire.

Bright Lights

One pilot said light streamed from the open doors of cottages, and in the beams he saw men and women peering up.

The jubilant attitude of these French people, however, was not shared by the Vichy authorities. Vichy radio stated that 17 were killed and 25 injured in the raids.

The commentator added: "The damage caused to railway sheds in Nantes is very important."

The German communique referred to the bombing of "residential quarters on the coast of Heligoland and in the Baltic."

Reports leaking out of Italy say that 300 people were killed in Sunday night's raid on Turin and that the damage was tremendous.

FRANCE FLASHES ••• TO R.A.F.

Royal Air Force pilots flying low over France last night in brilliant moonlight, were greeted by peasants and townspeople, who rushed out of their houses flashing the V sign with torches.

The pilots, flying Beauforts and Blenheims of the Coastal Command, were on their way to attack the industrial and shipbuilding centres of Nantes and St. Nazaire.

"As we crossed Northern France," said one of the pilots today, "we saw cottage doors being thrown open, and, silhouetted in the beams at us. Many of them flashed the letter V on their torches."

The R.A.F. kept up the offensive today with a big daylight raid. About midday a large force roared out across the Channel east of Folkestone.

The planes returned after about half an hour, and within a short time the sky was filled with fighters.

Evening Standard *1 October 1941.*   The Daily Mail *2 October 1941.*   The Star *1 October 1941.*

Although people in the Occupied Zone had little to fear from the average German serviceman, those who committed acts of sabotage or who helped RAF crews shot down in their locality faced torture and execution if they fell into the hands of the Gestapo (Geheime-Staats-Polizei) or the S.D. (Sicherheits-Dienst) security police. The French in the ports over which we operated longed for deliverance, their morale buoyed by clandestine listening to the BBC's daily broadcasts in French, always preceded by the four notes of Beethoven's Fifth Symphony which corresponded to the Morse dit-dit-dit-dah (V for Victory). They sang their own words to the popular song Auprès de ma Blonde, in which their refrain called on us to bring hope on our wings.

As They Flew Over France

V SIGN WAS FLASHED TO R.A.F.

Flying over France on their way to attack the industrial and shipbuilding centres of Nantes and St. Nazaire during the night, Beaufort aircraft swept so low over towns and villages in the brilliant moonlight that people rushed from their homes to flash the Victory sign on pocket torches.

One pilot said: "We saw cottage doors being thrown open. Lights streamed out, and silhouetted in the beams were men and women peering up at us. Many of them flashed the letter V on their torches."

The Evening News *1 October 1941. There were several occasions when 'V for Victory' signals were flashed in Morse to Beauforts flying at about 700 feet over French ports. It was usually the air gunners in the mid-upper turrets who saw these signals, while their pilots and navigator/bomb aimers were concentrating on the target and dropping their sticks of bombs. The gunners often fired down the searchlight beams of the defences and scanned the ground either side of the aircraft's track.*

A Junkers Ju 88 night fighter fitted with nose-mounted radar aerials. (Author's collection)

Then he flew lower and lower, always turning towards the light. Reeves spotted the Ju 88 and wanted to open fire on it, but Percival refused to disclose our position. When we were at about 200 feet above the sea, he decided to abort the operation, still carrying our bombs but switching on the IFF (Identification Friend or Foe). We carried a small coding device called a Syko machine and on this I encrypted a message for Davies to send: 'Returning base chased by night-fighter ETA 21.40'. This caused some excitement in our Operations Rooms. After we landed, they told us that an enemy aircraft had crashed into cliffs near Penzance, but this may have been a ruse to boost our morale.

For some weeks before this abortive operation, Percival had been suffering from sinus trouble, sometimes holding his head in his hands while sitting at the controls. He had to go into hospital for an operation, leaving Reeves, Davies and myself once more without a pilot. At this time, our squadron was partly inactive with the arrival of eight new crews from the Torpedo Training Unit at RAF Abbotsinch, near the Firth of Clyde. Their pilots had been trained in the tricky art of dropping torpedoes but they and their crews needed to settle down in their new environment. A few of our other pilots were also qualified in torpedo work and it seemed clear that this would eventually become the primary role of our squadron.

Instead of waiting for a new pilot, I approached Wing Commander Bower and asked him if a replacement could be found as quickly as possible. This was not an act of bravery on my part. The weather was mostly fine and I wanted more operational time in my Flying Log Book, which registered about 150 hours. After another fifty hours, I would have completed my first operational tour and given less dangerous duties for a while.

Meanwhile, our squadron suffered another loss. On 26 September, a Beaufort flown by Pilot Officer James R. Harrison was returning in daylight from an uneventful anti-shipping search when it crashed into a quarry near Helston, about two miles inland from the coast of south Cornwall. All four crew members were killed instantly. The navigator's log, partly burnt, was passed to me for examination and the final entry read 'Attempting to get out storm', which they did by coming down through cloud. I used it in the squadron as an example of the folly of doing this, unless certain of flying over sea.

The oil tanks at Donges, part of the 'Consummateurs de Petrole', on the north bank of the river Loire, which were attacked by two Beauforts of 217 Squadron on 28 September 1941. (Author's collection)

A salvo of bombs falling from the wings and bomb-bay of a Coastal Command aircraft when attacking an enemy port at low level, through tracer from light flak. Bombs in such attacks were fitted with eleven-second delay fuses so that they did not explode directly under the aircraft, but the blasts always rocked it and their effect on the target could be seen by the mid-upper gunner in a Beaufort. (Author's collection)

This gravestone in the island of Noirmoutier bears the name of Pilot Officer Walter S.P. Griffiths, the pilot of Beaufort I serial W6501 of 217 Squadron which took off from RAF St Eval on the night of 28/29 September 1941. His target was the oil installation at Donges on the north bank of the Loire, about 40 miles north-north-east of Noirmoutier. His body was evidently washed ashore, since the Beaufort came down over the sea. The other three crew members also lost their lives. (Dr Jacques Ilias collection)

On 28 September, our crew was ordered to fly on a sortie with another pilot. He was Sergeant Lloyd H. Morgan, who had joined our squadron in the previous April and was thus experienced operationally in Beauforts. Of course, he was also well known to Davies and Reeves. Our target was new to us. Three Beauforts were to make a low-level attack at night on the oil tanks of the refining centre at Donges, on the north bank of the Loire estuary about nine miles east of Saint-Nazaire.

We took off at 18.00 hours in clear weather and flew on the familiar courses to the mouth of the estuary. The night was starry when we reached the coast, south of the target, but there was some haze inland, possibly industrial. However, I was able to pick out the leaf-shaped island in the estuary just south of Donges

Sergeant aircrew members of 217 Squadron at RAF St Eval, on the beach at Treyarnon Bay in Cornwall. This was close to a hotel which had been taken over as their Mess. They were demonstrating to a press photographer the 'V for Victory' sign which was always relayed in Morse by the BBC to Occupied France at the beginning of their news programmes. It was sometimes flashed by French civilians with torches – 'dit-dit-dit-dah' – to low-flying Beauforts. (Author's collection)

Two sergeant aircrew members of 217 Squadron at RAF St Eval, shrimping with nets borrowed from children on the beach at Treyarnon Bay in Cornwall. In the foreground is Lloyd Morgan, a pilot who was awarded an immediate DFM after two operations on 28 and 30 September 1941. On both occasions he shook off enemy night-fighters before making low-level attacks against targets on the west coast of France. (Author's collection)

and we turned north for our bombing run, flying at 500 feet. The oil tanks were clearly visible when two searchlights suddenly caught us and a night-fighter with a light in its nose appeared on our tail. Reeves acted immediately. He fired a quick burst at the night-fighter, which sheered away, and then a longer burst at a searchlight, which dowsed it.

Some light flak came up from Donges, but I dropped our load of two 500lb and three 250lb general-purpose bombs, together with a canister of incendiaries, directly on the tanks, These blew up with reddish-brown flames, which we could still see when twenty-five miles back on our return flight over land. We returned safely after shaking off another night-fighter.

The Beaufort behind us flew into this burning target and added to the flames but the other was shot down over the sea, probably by a night-fighter. The bodies of Pilot Officer Walter S.P. Griffiths and Sergeant Selwyn C.E Sapwell were washed up, but those of Sergeant Edward D. Suggett and Sergeant Joseph W. Ball were not recovered.

On 30 September three crews were ordered to attack the docks at Nantes, further east along the Loire. With Lloyd Morgan at the controls, we took off at 18.00 hours and headed around the coast of France. The night was clear but we were slightly off course when I identified Belle-Ile on the approaches to the Loire estuary. Then Ken Reeves shouted a warning that a night-fighter was on our tail. Morgan dived and turned towards it. Turning side-to-side while low over the sea, we seemed to have shaken off our pursuer.

Still carrying our bombs, the same load as on our previous sortie, Morgan headed back to our target and I map-read our way to where the port of Nantes straddled a small island in the middle of the river. We circled for a few minutes while I picked out the Port Maritime on the north bank. There was slight haze but we came down even lower and I could see some factory buildings. Light flak came up at us but then I released the load, with the usual result of a buffeting explosion and a red glow behind us. Reeves saw one of two tall chimneys collapse and then a large fire, which was still visible from twenty miles away when we headed for the north coast of France.

Then something remarkable happened when we were flying low over small villages and hamlets. Winking lights were flashed at us in Morse, dit-dit-dit-dah. Oppressed French people had listened to the BBC and were telling us that we were bringing 'hope on our wings'. It was primarily the gunners who saw these lights, keeping watch from their turrets, and all three reported them at our de-briefing. Examining the maps, the intelligence officer was able to tell us that our crew had bombed a chemicals factory. But it was the winking lights that captured most attention. The information was passed to the national press and reporters arrived at Treyarnon Bay to interview and photograph the gunners. On 8 November, Sergeant Lloyd H. Morgan was gazetted with a Distinguished Flying Medal for his part in these two operations.

Chapter 7

New Beauforts and New Stations

Percival returned to RAF St Eval in the first week of October 1941, having undergone a minor but unpleasant operation on his sinuses. He was pronounced fit to fly and joined his old crew of Reeves, Davies and myself. Our next operation took place on 11 October when we were one of three crews ordered to drop magnetic mines in Brest Estuary. The other two were flown by Sergeant 'Hank' Hanson-Lester and by Sergeant Kenneth W. Perry.

We took off at 18.38 hours and flew on the familiar courses to the estuary, dropped our mine at 19.47 hours and returned home safely. Hanson-Lester also returned without major incident. But Perry and his crew 'failed to return' and we did not know what had happened to them. Years later, in November 1985, I received a letter from the sole survivor of the missing crew. He was the wireless operator, Sergeant Frank J. Gornall, who had joined 217 Squadron in August 1941 and with his crew had flown on a number of number of anti-shipping patrols. The operation to Brest Estuary was their first mining operation. At about 20.00 hours, when somewhere near Brest harbour, a shell exploded in the forward section of the Beaufort. This probably killed the pilot and navigator immediately. The latter was Sergeant Carl C. Thomsen, a Dane who had emigrated to Canada, married and then joined the RCAF. Frank did not know exactly what happened to him, but he found himself in the water and inflated his lifejacket. It is probable that he had been protected from the explosion by his wireless set and its bulwark. He thought that the Beaufort must have broken apart on impact with the sea and the rear section must have sunk with the gunner, Sergeant Charles E. Earl. He kept calling for help but there was no response and he gave up the attempt. But after about forty-five minutes he was picked up by a harbour defence vessel from Brest, probably the one which had shot down his Beaufort. He was not seriously injured and was a PoW until liberated by British troops in April 1945.

We participated in another mining operation which took place on the following night, 12 October, when three Beauforts were dispatched to the waters off Saint-Nazaire. The other two aircraft were flown by Sergeant Lloyd Morgan and

A general view of the Beaufort II, which was powered by 1,200hp Pratt & Whitney Twin Wasp engines. This example has two machine-guns in the nose, above aerials for the Air to Surface Vessel (ASV) radar. (Author's collection)

Sergeant Wharton. All went well with Wharton and ourselves but Lloyd had to abandon his operation and return with an oil leak.

There was a decline in operational activity during October, for several reasons. The continuing loss of aircraft and crews and the trickle of 'tour-expired' members leaving the squadron reduced our capacity. We were expecting the arrival of new aircraft, the Beaufort II, and would need to convert on to this new machine. It had more powerful engines, twin 1,200hp Wasps replacing the 1,130hp Bristol Taurus, and could fly reliably on one engine; there were two forward-firing Browning machine-guns in the wings and two others in the turret; it could carry either bombs or a torpedo.

In addition to these factors, our squadron was preparing to move to another station, RAF Thorney Island in Hampshire, near Chichester. Although we were unaware at the time, this was part of 'Channel Stop', a plan to attack the German warships from Brest if Hitler decided to bring them back to home waters via the English Channel.

I was unexpectedly given a short leave after our two minelaying sorties and left to spend three days at home with my parents and two younger brothers. The

The Beaufort II was fitted with increased armament, including two belt-fed Browning machine-guns in the mid-upper turret, a Vickers K gun in the port waist hatch for the wireless operator and another which could be mounted in a starboard position. (Author's collection)

preparations to change our station were afoot on my return, and our crew did not participate when four Beauforts bombed Lorient on 21 October; all of these returned safely. After that, Wing Commander Bower decided to make a farewell attack against one of our usual targets in France and his choice was determined by knowledge of an event in Nantes.

At this time, the Resistance movement had become active in France and many of its members were from the French Communist Party. This had been banned after the outbreak of the war but, after the German invasion of Russia, the members felt they were fighting in a just cause and a team of three had been sent to Nantes. In the early morning of 20 October two of this team, Gilbert Brustlein and Guisco Spartaco, were armed with revolvers and roaming the streets looking for a suitable target. At 08.15 hours they spotted two German officers walking in the square in front of the Cathedral of St Pierre and St Paul, and decided to follow them. Selecting a target apiece when reaching the rue du Roi Albert, they fired at their backs. Spartaco's revolver jammed but Brustlein fired six shots, two of which hit his victim in the neck. This officer shouted 'Die Shuften!' ('The bastards!') and collapsed on his face. His companion,

DECLARATION DU
Président Roosevelt
SUR LES EXECUTIONS D'OTAGES EN FRANCE

Maison Blanche, Washington
25 octobre 1941

" La pratique consistant à exécuter en masse d'innocents otages en représailles d'attaques isolées contre des Allemands dans les pays provisoirement placés sous la botte nazie révolte un monde pourtant déjà endurci aux souffrances et aux brutalités.

" Les peuples civilisés ont depuis longtemps adopté le principe qu'aucun homme ne doit être puni pour les actes d'un autre homme. Incapables d'appréhender les personnes ayant pris part à ces attaques, les nazis, selon leurs méthodes caractéristiques, égorgent cinquante ou cent personnes innocentes.

" Ceux qui voudraient " collaborer " avec Hitler, ou qui voudraient chercher à l'apaiser, ne peuvent point ignorer cet effroyable avertissement.

" Les nazis auraient pu apprendre de la dernière guerre l'impossibilité de briser le courage des hommes par la terreur. Au contraire, ils développent leur " lebensraum " et leur " ordre nouveau " en s'enfonçant plus bas qu'ils n'avaient eux-mêmes jamais été dans un abîme de cruauté.

" Ce sont là les actes d'hommes désespérés qui savent au fond de leur cœur qu'ils ne peuvent pas vaincre. Le terrorisme n'apportera jamais la paix en Europe. Il ne fait que semer les germes d'une haine qui, un jour, amènera un terrible châtiment."

Franklin D Roosevelt

Translation:

THE HOSTAGES
Declaration by President Roosevelt on the execution of hostages in France, at The White House in Washington on 25 October 1941.

THE HOSTAGES

Declaration by President Roosevelt on the execution of hostages in France, at The White House in Washington on 25 October 1941. 'The practice of mass execution of innocent hostages in reprisal for isolated attacks against Germans in countries temporarily under the Nazi boot is repugnant to a world however already hardened to suffering and brutality. 'Civilised people have for many years accepted the principle that no man should be punished for the acts of another man. Unable to arrest those who have taken part in these attacks, the Nazis, adopting their characteristic methods, massacre fifty or a hundred innocent people. 'Those who wish to 'collaborate' with Hitler or wish to appease him, can never ignore this terrible warning. 'The Nazis should have learnt from the last war the impossibility of breaking men's courage by terror. On the contrary, they increase their 'living space'' and 'new order' by sinking to even greater depths in an abyss of cruelty. These are the acts of desperate men who know deep in their hearts that they can never win. They do no mere than sow the seeds of hatred which, one day,' bring a terrible retribution.' Franklin Roosevelt

(Leaflets dropped over Nantes by Beauforts of 217 Squadron before the USA entered the war)

Hauptmann (Captain) Wilhelm Sieger, called for a doctor, but the man was dead. He was the Feldkommandant (Regional Commander) of Nantes, Oberstleutnant (Lieutenant-Colonel) Karl Friedrich Holtz.

The victim was not a rabid Nazi. Holtz was a cultured man with a doctorate who had worked in Nantes between the wars on engineering projects. He spoke French fluently and was a keen musician who had played in a local orchestra. However, Hitler's response to the killing was typical of a vicious tyrant. On the following day, twenty-one detainees in a camp at Chateaubriant and twenty-one hostages in Nantes (mostly Communists) were loaded into trucks and taken to a place of execution where they were shot in three batches at ten-minute intervals. Then the Germans announced that fifty more hostages would be shot if the assassins were not arrested by 23 October. They also offered a reward of fifteen million francs to anyone who denounced them.

These atrocities shocked the Free World and President Roosevelt of the USA expressed his horror. Hitler was sensitive to his views and the execution was postponed until 29 October. In Britain, leaflets were prepared with Roosevelt's declaration on one side and Churchill's comments on the other. These arrived at St Eval and Wing Commander Bower decided on the target for our last raid against the French ports. On the night of 26/27 October, eight Beauforts were dispatched to Nantes on a bombing raid while dropping these leaflets. All aircraft returned safely. It is not known whether the leaflets had any effect on Hitler but on the following day he announced that he would be 'merciful' and cancelled the executions, conditional on the future 'good behaviour' of the people of Nantes.

Percival and his crew did not participate in this operation. In the morning of 28 October we packed our kit and were among the first crews who flew to RAF Thorney Island in our remaining Beaufort Is. This station was situated on a flat promontory and had been opened in 1938. It had an excellent Officers' Mess with comfortable living quarters. We settled in and Percival, who by then held the rank of Flight Lieutenant, was appointed as Officer Commanding Operations. His wife joined him in nearby accommodation. I had increased administration work as Squadron Navigation Officer. There were no operational sorties for several weeks but Beaufort IIs began to arrive in early November and we then spent much of our time in familiarisation, air-testing and dive-bombing practice with these new machines. In some respects it was a restful period, especially for those of us who had been flying operationally or on standby for many months.

Although there were no operational sorties from Thorney Island in these early days, three crews were detailed to fly back to St Eval in Beaufort Is to carry out an important anti-shipping strike, led by Flight Lieutenant Percival. We left at 11.00 hours on 9 November and awaited instructions after arrival. While there, I met Squadron Leader George Halley and his navigator, my old friend Pilot Officer Charles 'Jock' McLean. They had been away for several weeks on detachment at RAF Chivenor. Jock told me that they had been training with a new device which identified enemy shipping at night, with the intention of testing it off the Dutch coast. I had never heard of this instrument but later learnt that it was the Air to Surface Vessel (ASV) radar.

The anti-shipping strike for our three Beauforts did not materialise and we flew back to Thorney Island in the morning of 11 November. On arrival, we

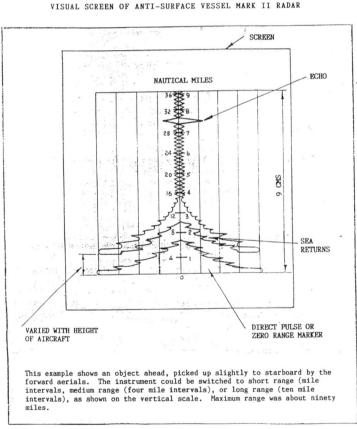

VISUAL SCREEN OF ANTI-SURFACE VESSEL MARK II RADAR

This example shows an object ahead, picked up slightly to starboard by the forward aerials. The instrument could be switched to short range (mile intervals), medium range (four mile intervals), or long range (ten mile intervals), as shown on the vertical scale. Maximum range was about ninety miles.

Visual screen of ASV Mark II radar. This example shows an object ahead, picked up slightly to starboard by the forward aerials. The instrument could be switched to short range (mile intervals), medium range (four-mile intervals), or long range (ten-mile intervals), as shown on the vertical scale. Maximum range was about ninety miles.

A close-up of the nose of the Beaufort II, showing the two Vickers K guns operated by the air observer.
(Author's collection)

learnt that one of our Beaufort Is, flown by Sergeant Peter L. Ankin, had been lost in a training exercise on the previous day. It had descended through cloud and crashed into high ground near RAF Manston in Kent, killing all the crew.

Then, on 15 November, Squadron Leader Halley did not return from an operation, and all four crew members were killed. The bodies of Halley and McLean were never recovered but those of the other two, Sergeant Frank Childs and Sergeant Douglas L. Heald, were eventually washed up on the Dutch coast. The reason for their loss remains unexplained but it seems probable that they located a vessel and attacked but were shot down. The loss of Jock was a blow to me. All our training had been together, we had joined the squadron together and had somehow survived while twenty-three of our Beauforts and crews had been lost. We were almost at the end of our operational tours and had believed that both of us would survive the remainder.

Training exercises with Beaufort IIs continued at Thorney Island but on 25 November the first operational sorties in these machines took place. Two of us took off at about 18.00 hours for a patrol southwards to Cherbourg on the Cotentin peninsula and then down the French coast towards the Channel Islands.

Our crew was in serial AW248 and we were told that this was the first operation in a Beaufort II. The night was very overcast and dark. We saw nothing and the weather clamped down over Thorney Island. We were diverted to St Eval and spent the remainder of the night there, returning during the following morning.

On our return, we learnt that our squadron had suffered a loss on the night of our operation. This was in a Beaufort I flown by Sergeant Mervyn Gill on a minelaying sortie to Brest Estuary. The aircraft had been shot down, probably by a flak ship. Records show that there was only one survivor, the air gunner Sergeant J.A. Cronie, who was picked up and became a PoW.

We were also briefed in advance for an operation to take place on the following morning, 27 November. An enemy vessel of about 6,000 tons from Rotterdam, carrying supplies to the Baltic for the Russian front, was expected to be near the Hook of Holland at about 10.30 hours. We were to lead a formation of three Beaufort IIs, escorted by Spitfires, and make an attack with each Beaufort carrying two 500lb and four 250lb general-purpose bombs.

After an early night and some rather fitful sleep, we took off before the other two Beauforts at 07.15 hours and flew to RAF Coltishall, near Norwich in Norfolk, where we landed at 08.35 hours to meet the pilots of our Spitfire escorts. These were part of 152 Squadron, equipped with Spitfire IIAs, and six had been detailed to escort us on the outward flight.

We then took off from Coltishall at 09.30 hours but, as soon as our wheels left the runway, a flock of seagulls fluttered before us and one of them struck our nose, scattering feathers and blood over the Perspex. Fortunately none of them hit our engines and blocked the air intakes. We then circled, our other two Beauforts and the six Spitfires joined us, and we set course for the Hook of Holland, about forty-two minutes flying time away. Our height was 500 feet and it was comforting to see the other Beauforts and the Spitfires. I felt quite proud to be in the nose of the leading aircraft.

The Hook appeared exactly on time but no enemy vessel was visible. There was a slight mist along the coast but visibility over the sea was clear. We turned to port and flew north-east up the coast, looking for our quarry. After a few minutes a dot appeared and, when we came nearer, turned out to be a vessel which I estimated to be about 1,500 tons. Percival decided to attack, perhaps thinking that this would be better than returning with a nil report. He climbed to starboard, turned to port, and then dived. A stream of tracer came up, some of it seemingly passing just under our nose, and Percival responded with his two .303in Browning guns. This was the only occasion

A distant photograph of the unfortunate minesweeping vessel HS 859 *of the Kriegsmarine, under attack off the Hook of Holland on 27 November 1941. It shows the third Beaufort of 217 Squadron making its dive-bombing run. The photograph was taken from the second Beaufort after it had attacked.* (Author's collection)

This Spitfire VB, serial AD185 of No 19 Squadron based at Matlask in Norfolk, was photographed over the North Sea on 27 November 1941. It was flown by a Czechoslovakian in the RAF, Sgt Sokol, acting as part of the rear cover for three Beauforts of No 217 Squadron from Thorney Island. These were attacking shipping off the Hook of Holland, with the author navigating the formation. (Author's collection)

when I did not drop our bombs. Percival released them before pulling out of the dive and I saw some hit the ship and then explode.

After our bombs exploded the other two Beauforts, flown by Pilot Officer Seddon and Flight Lieutenant Finch, took turns in bombing the stricken vessel. There could have been no survivors from the crew. But all was not well with our Beaufort. I could see a line of bullet holes along the leading edge of our starboard wing, and oil was streaming from the engine. Percival asked sharply if I was all right and I answered in the affirmative. But he was in some trouble. Other bullets had passed low through the fuselage, severing some control wires, and one had gone through the outside of his right flying boot, grazing above his ankle.

However, we were in a Beaufort II, serial AW248, which could fly on one engine. The Spitfires had left us and we turned west for home, flying over six motor torpedo-boats, zigzagging on a south-westerly course. Some gunfire came up from them but it was not accurate. Six other Spitfires appeared, a rear cover from 19 Squadron at Coltishall. One flew alongside us and I flashed 'ENGINE U.S.' in Morse at him with my Aldis lamp. He waved and eventually flew off.

Spitfire pilots of 19 Squadron at Matlask in Norfolk, in September 1941. Left to right: Flight Sergeant Vernon, Flight Sergeant Strihavka (Czech), Sergeant Brown, Sergeant Charnock; Sergeant Sokol (Czech). Seated in front, holding a cat: Sergeant Lysicky (Czech). (Zdeněk Hurt collection)

Many years later, I learnt that he was one of some Czech pilots in the squadron, Sergeant Sokol.

I took the precaution of preparing a message on my Syko coding machine. This gadget consisted of a set of narrow slides engraved with letters of the alphabet and numerals. These were slid with a pointer so that the message read 'in clear' on a datum line. On the tops of the slides the coded letters and numerals appeared on a card which changed daily. I prepared 'SOS DITCHING------N------E', ready to fill in the latitude and longitude for Davies to send in the few moments before we ditched.

However, all went well. One of the other Beauforts appeared and followed us. We flew on with a smoking engine and crossed the coast at Gorleston-on-Sea, south of Yarmouth. With immense skill, Percival made a smooth landing at Coltishall, at 11.25 hours. He taxied to dispersal and got out to examine our Beaufort. The underside of the nose was pitted with bullet holes. These had passed under my seat but fortunately I had been sitting sideways, alternately looking over my right shoulder at the target and writing my log on the chart table. Percival took off his right flying boot and rolled down his sock. There was a blueish weal above his ankle, grazed by the bullet.

Our crew split into two parties and boarded the other two Beauforts for the return journey to Thorney Island, leaving our damaged aircraft behind. We were all in a relieved and happy mood.

In December it was proposed that our squadron should become part of an anti-shipping 'Strike Force', operating in daylight with our Beauforts carrying

A torpedo-carrying Beaufort of 217 Squadron setting off on a daylight raid against enemy shipping in late 1941, escorted by Spitfires. (Author's collection)

torpedoes while escorted by Spitfires and cannon-armed Beaufighters. These would attack enemy vessels sailing along the coasts of northern France and southern Holland. Thus some Beauforts were detached to RAF Manston, near Ramsgate in Kent. An additional plan was to carry out 'blind bombing' of enemy vessels at night, employing the new ASV radar fitted to our aircraft and then dropping flares to identify any vessel shown as a blip.

The former plan might have been successful if other squadrons had been allocated for the purpose and combined training carried out. The latter proved useless on the one occasion when it was attempted, since the flare dropped from 3,000 feet was extinguished by the time the Beaufort dived down to make an attack. Nothing could be seen.

Percival and his crew were not part of these plans since we were not trained in the specialist work of dropping torpedoes, nor at this stage did I have any experience with the ASV. However, three Beauforts carrying 500lb general-purpose bombs were dispatched without escort from Manston in the afternoon

The port wing of the Beaufort of 217 Squadron flown by Pilot Officer Arthur H. Aldridge on 9 December 1941. This shows the end sheared off by a bracing wire of a mast on the German cargo liner Madrid, *when flying over the vessel.* (Arthur H. Aldridge DFC)

Crew members of one of the Beauforts of 217 Squadron which bombed and sank the 9,777-ton German cargo liner Madrid *off the Dutch coast on 9 December 1941. Left to right: Pilot Officer Arthur H. Aldridge; Sergeant Vince Aspinall; Sergeant Alan Still; Sergeant Grimmer.* (Arthur H. Aldridge DFC)

of 9 December to attack a convoy reported off the Dutch coast. They did not carry torpedoes since the waters in the area were too shallow.

They found the convoy off Ijmuiden and the pilots made their attacks in sequence against the largest vessel. The first was the leader, Flight Lieutenant Arthur Finch, who scored several hits while his aircraft was slightly damaged by flak. The next was Pilot Officer Mark Lee but his port engine was hit and caught fire; the Beaufort crashed into the sea and all crew members were killed. The last was Pilot Officer Aldridge, who scored more hits but the tip of his starboard wing was sheared off by the bracing wire of a mast. Both Finch and Aldridge returned safely, leaving the enemy vessel on fire and sinking. It was a U-boat depot ship, the former liner *Madrid* of 8,777 tons. Both pilots were awarded immediate DFCs.

Another strike was attempted on 16 December when three Beauforts carrying torpedoes flew up to RAF Coltishall and linked up with an escort of three Beaufighters and nine Spitfires. They headed to the Dutch coast for an attack

One of 217 Squadron's torpedo-carrying Beauforts, escorted by Beaufighters and Spitfires, flying from RAF Coltishall to attack an enemy convoy off the Dutch coast on 16 December 1941. (Author's collection)

The 5,700-ton enemy vessel Knute Nelson *under attack by a Beaufort of 217 Squadron, off the Dutch coast on 16 December 1941, with a flak ship firing its anti-aircraft armament.* (Author's collection)

against a vessel which was later identified as the *Knute Nelson* of 5,700 tons. This vessel was not damaged but one of the Beauforts was hit by a 20mm shell fired from an escorting flak ship, causing much difficulty with the controls on the return flight.

At this time, all of us in Percival's crew were declared 'tour-expired'. This notification came as a relief to Percival and myself, and probably to Davies and Reeves. There had been some boost to morale on 7 December when the USA

The white roof of the U-boat bunker at La Pallice shows clearly in this reconnaissance photograph, taken on 9 November 1942 from a Spitfire PR IVB of 543 Squadron flown from RAF St Eval by Flying Officer D.K. McQuaig. It was later camouflaged. The two lock gates, at the entrance to the dock basin from the outer harbour, were considered prime targets by the RAF and the USAAF. (Author's collection)

Flight Lieutenant G. Alan Etheridge, DFC, one of the pilots who survived his operational tour with 217 Squadron. (The late G. Alan Etheridge, DFC)

Beaufort II serial AW196. One of three aircraft from RAF St Eval which attacked an enemy tanker in harbour at La Pallice on the night of 30/31 December 1941. The pilot, Pilot Officer G. Alan Etheridge, bombed from 200 feet and the Beaufort's tail was hit by 20mm cannon shells. The rudder trimmer tab became jammed to port and Etheridge had to make the long return flight with both legs braced against the opposite rudder bar. (Author's collection)

declared war on Japan, Germany and Italy, immediately after the Japanese attack on Pearl Harbor, but I was feeling very tired after being on duty every day for almost eleven months apart from two very short periods of leave. During that time, I had flown on fifty operational sorties and been on standby for many more. Most of my friends had been posted as 'missing' from operations or had left the squadron. However, both Percival and I remained on the squadron while RAF Personnel decided on our next postings, making ourselves useful on non-operational flights or in administrative work.

On 30 December, three of our Beauforts from a detachment based at St Eval were dispatched on a bombing raid at night against a tanker reported moored at La Pallice. One of these, flown by Pilot Officer Alan Etheridge, descended to 200 feet so that his navigator, Sergeant Stanley Clayton, could drop the bombs accurately. The Beaufort was hit by 20mm flak which jammed the rudder trimming tab to port. Etheridge flew all the way back to St Eval with both legs strained against the opposite rudder bar, and managed to land safely. He and Clayton were told by an intelligence officer that they had hit a supply vessel of the *Altmark* class, but this cannot be substantiated by post-war examination of German records.

This sortie was the last made by 217 Squadron against any of the ports in western France. Also, all the squadrons of Coastal Command were relieved of the task of minelaying outside enemy ports. Henceforth, our squadron was engaged primarily on anti-shipping sorties, mainly when carrying torpedoes but also with the capacity to carry bombs.

January 1942 brought days of unfavourable weather which restricted operational flying. There were several 'Rover' patrols from St Eval, where a large detachment of our squadron were being held, without any notable result. There was a very unfortunate accident at Manston on 6 January when a new pilot, Sergeant Eric H. Voy, crashed on take-off and was killed. I navigated Wing Commander Bower to St Eval and back on one occasion. His tenure as our CO ceased on 28 January and he was posted to the headquarters of Coastal Command's No 16 Group. Wing Commander Howard R. Larkin took over but was lost on his first sortie, a patrol off Dunkirk on 8 February. All the crew were picked up and became PoWs. Command was taken over temporarily by Squadron Leader George Taylor, who normally commanded A Flight.

On 7 February, Percival and I took off in a Tiger Moth from Thorney Island in order to test my suitability for resuming training as a pilot. He was surprised to find that I could take off and land smoothly as well as perform the various

Halifaxes over the port of Brest on 18 December 1941, part of forty-seven Halifaxes, Stirlings and Wellingtons which were despatched on a daylight raid against the battlecruisers Scharnhorst *and* Gneisenau *which were sheltering there, together with the cruiser* Prinz Eugen. *They met intense flak and a smokescreen and the warships were not hit although six bombers were lost.* (Author's collection)

acrobatics, and strongly recommended my resumption. However, by this time I was reluctant to become a pupil pilot once more. I had been promoted to Flying Officer, was experienced operationally and had become very interested in astro-navigation. I hoped that, perhaps after a break in Group Headquarters, I could transfer on to a squadron of larger aircraft. Five days later, on 12 February, 217 Squadron was heavily involved in the chaotic conditions when the German warships escaped from Brest to home waters. This operation, later known as the 'Channel Dash', had been anticipated and even welcomed by the Admiralty, for it would remove a major threat to Britain's lifeline with the USA. Counter-measures were planned under Operation 'Fuller'.

Hitler's intuition, reputed to be infallible, had been exploited. He was known to be very sensitive about the possibility of a British invasion of Norway. Plans for such an invasion had been deliberately leaked in London. Then, on 27 December 1941, Bomber Command had raided the airfield at Herdla, near Bergen, and provided cover for Commandos storming the nearby islands of Vaasgo and Maaloy, with considerable success. This had been enough for Hitler

An enlargement of part of another photograph of Brest taken on 18 December 1941, showing the dock area partly obscured by the smokescreen and the aircraft in the other photograph. RAF photo-interpreters were able to identify (1)Scharnhorst (2) Gneisenau, in dry docks with their previous white camouflage missing; (3) a dry dock under construction; (4) burnt out oil tanks. (Author's collection)

to order the return of his warships via the English Channel in a suitable period of bad weather, under the command of Vizeadmiral Otto Ciliax and code-named Operation 'Cerebus'. Air cover had been entrusted to the fighter ace Oberst (Colonel) Adolf Galland.

Ciliax decided to leave Brest in the evening of 11 February, with a weather forecast of low loud, rain and mist for the following day. His squadron, consisting of the *Scharnhorst, Gneisenau, Prinz Eugen* and six destroyers, left at 22.45 hours through a channel cleared by minesweepers. Six other destroyers, fifteen torpedo boats and a flotilla of motor torpedo boats (known as E-boats by the British) were scheduled to join them from French and Belgian ports. Once daylight broke, Galland moved his fighters from airfield to airfield along the coasts.

Part of the German escort to the Scharnhorst, Gneisenau *and* Prinz Eugen *on 12 February 1942 – a destroyer, a torpedo boat and Messerschmitt Bf 110s.* (Author's collection)

The battlecruisers Scharnhorst *and* Gneisenau *steaming up mid-Channel during their escape from Brest on 12 February 1942. The photograph was taken from the heavy cruiser* Prinz Eugen. (Author's collection)

Everything went well for the squadron for sixteen hours. The submarine HMS *Sealion* in Brest Estuary withdrew after being bombed by a Dornier Do 17. A Hudson on a 'Stopper' patrol from St Eval had to return with a faulty ASV. Another from Thorney Island was ordered to return owing to fog. Radar stations along the British coast suffered from German interference.

At 10.00 hours, operators in the radar station at Beachy Head insisted that something major was in progress. Four Spitfires of No 11 Group went up to investigate and the pilots reported the ships. Then there was a delay in finding the Air Officer Commanding 11 Group, Air Vice-Marshal Trafford Leigh-Mallory. The alarm was not raised until 11.30 hours.

The squadron reached the Straits of Dover at 12.19 hours and coastal batteries opened fire, using radar sighting but without scoring hits. Six motor

The German fighter ace Egon Mayer, Staffelkapitän of 7./Jagdgeschwader 2, who flew during the Channel Dash. By 5 February 1944, he had been credited with 100 victories on the 'Channel Front'. He was killed in combat with P47 Thunderbolts of the USAAF on 2 February 1944, while leading one of his groups, and was buried in the cemetery at Beaumont-le-Roger, south-west of Rouen. (Jean-Louis Roba collection)

This Messerschmitt Bf 109E-7 of 7./Jagdgeschwader 1 took off from Brest on 12 February 1942 to form part of the escort for the German squadron, but suffered engine trouble when over the Channel. The pilot, Feldwebel Heinz Beyer, headed for Octeville airfield near Cherbourg, but the engine cut out and he made a forced landing. The machine tipped over and Beyer hung upside down for a quarter of an hour before being pulled clear by French civilians, having suffered nothing worse than shock, various bruises and a broken nose. He did not require hospital treatment and the Messerschmitt was rated as 50 per cent damaged. (Jean-Louis Roba collection)

Oberleutnant Johannes Naumann (right) explains with the aid of a painting how he shot down two Fairey Swordfish in his Focke-Wulf Fwl90-1 of 9./Jagdegeschwader 26 on 12 February 1942. (A. Richard Chapman collection)

torpedo boats had been sent out from Dover but could not close with enemy. Six Fairey Swordfish of the Fleet Air Arm's 825 Squadron took off from Manston at 12.25 hours, led by Lieutenant-Commander Eugene Esmonde. They made rendezvous with ten Spitfires of the RAF's 72 Squadron and attacked the *Prinz Eugen*, which dodged their torpedoes. All six Swordfish were shot down by Fw 190s or flak and only five of the eighteen crew members were picked up. Esmonde was awarded a posthumous Victoria Cross.

By this time, the squadron had cleared the Straits of Dover and was steaming past Dunkirk to the Belgian coast. Then, at 14.32 hours, the flagship *Scharnhorst* set off a magnetic mine off Flushing and came to a halt. She got under way again after half an hour, following the other warships at a reduced speed. Meanwhile, six destroyers based at Harwich but dispersed at sea were ordered to close with the enemy off the Hook of Holland. Five managed to do so and fired their torpedoes but scored no hits. One destroyer was badly damaged by gunfire but all returned to Harwich.

The main hope of crippling the ships rested with the four squadrons equipped with Beaufort torpedo bombers. At Thorney Island, 217 Squadron had four aircraft racked up with torpedoes and three with bombs. My role on that day was that of Squadron Duty Officer and I had to gather the crews for the sorties. Four Beauforts with torpedoes and ASV took off at 13.25 hours for a rendezvous with Spitfires over Manston, although the crews were simply told to find an enemy convoy off the Hook of Holland. The Spitfires were fog-bound and two Beauforts landed for further instructions. The other two headed off, hunted fruitlessly, eventfully returned to Manston, refuelled and headed off again, but again without result.

Meanwhile, the armament in the other three Beauforts at Thorney Island was changed from bombs to torpedoes. The crews were briefed more accurately and took off at 14.30 hours for Manston. Together with the two Beauforts which had earlier landed for instructions, they took off and found the German ships. They dropped their torpedoes but all missed. A Beaufort flown by Flight Lieutenant Arthur Finch was shot down and all four men were killed.

The next to attack were nine torpedo-carrying Beauforts of 42 Squadron which had flown down to Coltishall from Leuchars in Fife. These took off and circled over Manston until they were joined by five bomb-carrying Hudsons of 407 (RCAF) Squadron from North Coates in Lincolnshire. The formation set off and found the German squadron at about 16.00 hours. No torpedoes scored hits and two Hudsons were shot down.

A Mark XII torpedo being wheeled to a Beaufort I fitted with a blister under the nose, armed with a rearward-firing .303in Browning machine-gun. (Author's collection)

Meanwhile, twelve Beauforts had arrived at Thorney Island from St Eval, flown by a mixture of crews from 22, 86 and 217 Squadrons. After briefing and being racked up with torpedoes, they flew to Coltishall to meet a Spitfire escort. These did not arrive and they set off at 17.04 hours in an attempt to find the warships in the gathering darkness. One from 217 Squadron, flown by Flight Lieutenant Matthew White, was shot down; all four men were killed but three bodies were recovered and buried in Holland.

Another from 217 Squadron, flown by Pilot Alan Etheridge, found the crippled *Scharnhorst* near the Hook of Holland but his Beaufort was hit by a 20mm shell which wounded the wireless operator, Sergeant Frank Williamson, and damaged some flying controls. Etheridge turned back to England, switched on his navigation lights, and was guided by beckoning searchlights of the Royal Artillery to RAF Horsham St Faith, near Norwich. He made a skilful belly landing, on top of his torpedo.

Apart from these actions by Coastal Command, Bomber Command dispatched 242 aircraft but only thirty-nine found the enemy and fifteen failed

Sergeant Stanley Clayton, Sergeant Frank Williamson, Pilot Officer Alan Etheridge, standing by their damaged Beaufort II at RAF Horsham St Faith on the day after their attack on the Scharnhorst. *The torpedo is still underneath.* (Stanley Clayton collection)

to return. Fighter Command put up 398 aircraft and lost seventeen of them. The Luftwaffe lost only seven aircraft. The German ships suffered two more setbacks, however. At 19.55 hours the *Gneisenau* was damaged by a magnetic mine off Terschelling and at 21.34 hours the *Scharnhorst* was further damaged by another magnetic mine in the same area. All the German vessels reached home ports, although the heavy warships achieved nothing further in the remainder of the war. Grossadmiral Erich Raeder described the Channel Dash in his memoirs: 'It was a tactical victory and a strategic defeat.'

The British set up a Board of Enquiry which produced a highly secret report of thirty-four pages on 2 March 1942. The authors greatly praised 'the countless acts of gallantry' which came to their notice, but stated that the Admiralty and the RAF did not provide sufficient forces or training to deal with the situation. They also stated the main weakness was the failure to detect the enemy earlier. However, French records tell a different story. They state that on 7 February the secret agent 'Hilarion' (Lieutenant de Vaisseau Philipon) in Brest sent the message 'De Hil. Stop. Appareillage de 'Scharnhorst', de 'Gneisenau' et du 'Prinz Eugen' imminent. Stop'. This was quickly followed with another message, 'Mefiez-vous particulièrement de la période de la nouvelle lune'. ('Beware mainly

The 14,800-ton heavy cruiser Prinz Eugen *escaped damage during the Channel Dash but was hit by a torpedo fired by the submarine HMS* Trident *on 23 February 1942, when off Trondheim. She suffered severe damage to her stern but managed to reach the port for temporary repairs. Fitted with a jury stern, as shown here, she headed for Kiel for permanent repairs, escaping damage by a large force of Blenheims and Hudsons on 17 May 1942 while* en route. *(Jean-Louis Roba collection)*

of the time of the new moon'). The squadron left on 11 February, the precise date of the new moon. If these messages were received by British Intelligence, the Admiralty and the RAF were not alerted.

After this day of shambles and sacrifice, RAF Coastal Command decided that our squadron should be sent up to the east coast of Scotland, from where our torpedo-carrying Beauforts might be able to attack the battleship *Tirpitz*. This huge sister-ship to the *Bismarck* was moored in a Norwegian fjord near Trondheim, from where she threatened to wipe out convoys carrying vital war supplies to North Russia.

Our next station was RAF Leuchars, near St Andrews in Fife. This was a comfortable place which had been opened as early as 1918. The whole squadron move took several days but Percival and I arrived there on 16 February, having flown as passengers in one of our Beauforts. Our new commanding officer

RAF Skitten in Caithness, just south of John O'Groats, was a satellite of RAF Wick. It was the base for 217 Squadron from 16 to 31 February 1942, when the crews were on standby to make a torpedo attack against the battleship Tirpitz *returning to Trondheim Fjord in Norway.* (Author's collection)

The Focke-Wulf Fw 200 Condor was adapted from a passenger airliner to serve as a long-range anti-shipping bomber. The Fw 200C-3 version, shown here, entered service in the summer of 1941. The Condor achieved many successes against British shipping, becoming known as the 'scourge of the Atlantic'. (Author's collection)

A low-level photograph of the battleship Tirpitz *in Aasfjord, near Trondheim, taken in February 1942 by a Spitfire of No 1 Photographic Reconnaissance Unit of Coastal Command. Other vessels around her and camouflage netting draped between her port side and the shore were intended to break up her outline from the air.* (Author's collection)

had also arrived. He was Wing Commander Samuel M. 'Mac' Boal, a highly experienced and well-liked pilot who had served in our squadron in the days when it was equipped with Ansons.

However, Percival and I left on the following day, ferried in an old Anson to RAF Skitten in Caithness, a small satellite of nearby RAF Wick. This remote airfield was about five miles south of John O'Groats on the north-east tip of Scotland. We were part of a detachment available to attack the *Tirpitz*, although both of us were 'tour-expired' and unlikely to be sent unless another crew was unavailable. We lived in a snow-bound wooden hut with a roaring fire and a gramophone which had a few records played over and over again. We remained there for a week while a blizzard raged outside, awaiting further orders but nothing came.

On 27 February, we all flew back to Leuchars in our Beauforts. Soon afterwards, Percival left on embarkation leave, for he was posted as a staff pilot in No 31 Air Navigation School in Canada. He sailed to his native country with his wife Peggy. Meanwhile, I waited at Leuchars for my orders.

On 4 March the *Tirpitz* put to sea, escorted by three destroyers and with Vizeadmiral Otto Ciliax in command, in order to intercept Convoy PQ12 outward bound for North Russia. This convoy had been spotted by a Focke-Wulf Condor. A German signal was decrypted by the Government Code and Cypher School at Bletchley Park and Coastal Command's No 18 Group at Pitreavie Castle in Dumferline was alerted. An order was issued on 7 March. Three Beauforts of 86 Squadron, which by then were at Skitten, were to fly to RAF Sumburgh in the Shetlands, as were six Beauforts of 217 Squadron and six of 42 Squadron based at Leuchars. These fifteen Beauforts were to form a strike force ready to make a torpedo attack on the German battleship.

The three squadrons complied with these orders but two of the Beauforts in our squadron did not reach their objective after taking off from Leuchars on the following day. One was forced to land with engine trouble at RAF Arbroath in Angus. Another, flown by Sergeant Roy W.G. Stephens, flew into a cloud-covered hill near Montrose and all four men were killed. Our other Beauforts first landed at Wick and then flew on to Sumburgh on 9 March.

Meanwhile on the early morning of 9 March, the *Tirpitz* (by then without her destroyers, which had had to return for want of fuel) was nearing Convoy PQ18 when twelve Fairey Albacores appeared and made a torpedo attack. Two of these were shot down and all the torpedoes from the others passed astern. The Albacores were from the Fleet Air Arm's 817 Squadron and had flown off the aircraft carrier HMS *Victorious*. This was part of the Home Fleet, which had sailed from Scapa Flow on 3 March under the command of Vice-Admiral A.T.B. Curteis to protect Convoy PQ12 and the homeward-bound convoy QP80. A reconnaissance aircraft had spotted the *Tirpitz* and Curteis was anxious to bring her to battle.

Soon after dawn on 10 March, the Beauforts at Sumburgh were lined up wingtip to wingtip facing the runway, ready to take off in turn when a green Very light was fired. The exact number of aircraft or the names of the crews are not recorded but there were four from 217 Squadron and the formation was to be led by Wing Commander Mervyn F.D. Williams of 42 Squadron. It seemed likely to be a one-way sortie for most or even all of them, for they had no fighter escorts and it was believed that they would face the guns of the *Tirpitz* and her destroyers as well as the Luftwaffe stationed near Trondheim. It was recommended that those in difficulties after the attack should head across to neutral Sweden and either force-land or bale out, while air-sea-rescue craft would be stationed ready to pick up any which ditched on an attempted return journey.

At last, a Very light was fired, but it was red and not green. Another German message had been decrypted. The *Tirpitz* had been ordered to return and had done so during the previous night, not to Trondheim but to Narvik, on the Norwegian coast over 600 miles to the north. She was moored and no longer at sea, and would make for Trondheim only when conditions were favourable. The Beaufort operation was cancelled. All those of 86 Squadron could return to Skitten and those of 217 Squadron to Leuchars, but the detachment from 42 Squadron remained at Sumburgh to await further orders.

For several days after this episode, unfavourable weather restricted operational flying from Leuchars. In this period, I received orders for my next posting. To my surprise, this proved to be a move to RAF Cranage, an 'Advanced Flying Unit' near Middlewich in Cheshire, where I was to be trained as an instructor. I left 217 Squadron on 22 March.

No 2 Instructors Course at the School of Air Navigation, RAF Cranage in Cheshire. The photograph, taken in March 1942, includes instructors as well as trainees. Most of the trainees were air observers who had already completed operational tours in RAF squadrons. The course was very intensive, covering ground subjects as well as practical flying in Avro Ansons. It lasted for three months, after which the trainees became qualified navigation instructors. The author is third from left in the bottom row. (Author's collection)

Chapter 8

The Last Three Years

After the 'Channel Dash' of 12 February 1942, French citizens in the port of Brest experienced some respite from the incessant attacks by the RAF. Sea mining from the air continued but the heavy aircraft of RAF Bomber Command were diverted to a new strategic project. The War Cabinet had decided that the only effective method of supporting the Soviet Union was to begin 'area bombing' of major German industrial centres to reduce their capacity to supply the armed forces and to demoralise the civilian population. This appeared feasible with the advent of new bombers such as the Lancaster with its enormous carrying capacity.

The man chosen to carry out this task was Air Chief Marshal Sir Arthur Harris, who was appointed as Commander-in-Chief of Bomber Command on 22 February. He had a success four nights later when forty-nine aircraft were sent to bomb Kiel and a heavy bomb hit the bows of the unlucky *Gneisenau*. This killed 116 of the crew and put the vessel out of action for rest of the war. But Harris's first heavy raid took place on the night of 3/4 March, not over Germany but against the Renault factory at Boulogne-Billancourt, west of Paris. This was manufacturing an estimated 18,000 lorries a year for the Wehrmacht. Harris dispatched 235 bombers at low level in several waves, the greatest number so far in the war. It was estimated that 40 per cent of the factory was destroyed but 367 French people were killed and 341 badly injured. Many of the latter died later.

This was the period called the 'Second Happy Time' by the U-boat crews. For a while after the entry of the USA into the war, her merchant ships continued to sail unescorted along her eastern seaboard. In January 1942, a group of the new and larger Type IXC U-boats became available to harry merchant vessels, and these picked off such victims with impunity. At the same time, the smaller Type VIIB U-boats operated further north, off the coasts of Newfoundland. Moreover, Dönitz had had the foresight to develop some large U-boats as 'Milk Cow' tankers, supplying the torpedo-carrying U-boats with fuel and other supplies. The latter were thus able to spend longer times on patrol. When the US Navy developed an escort system for the merchant vessels off the eastern seaboard, Dönitz moved his U-boats to the Caribbean, and the rate of sinkings continued.

The victorious U-boats usually returned to the French ports, their conning towers often festooned with life buoys from the merchant vessels they had sunk. They were greeted by military bands playing triumphal music while the crews were welcomed with bunches of flowers and bottles of wine. Any commander who had sunk enough vessels would be awarded a Knight's Cross and hailed as a national hero.

The U-boat men also had the benefit of progress made by the Todt Organisation with the massive bunkers in the French ports since the German occupation in June 1940. The first to come into service were in Lorient during October 1941 and named by the Germans Keroman I and Keroman II. Each contained chambers for seven U-boats. Keroman II also housed a shelter for up to 1,000 men with a canteen, library, hospital, central heating, air-conditioning, a stage for entertainment and special rooms for officers. Work on these huge structures had been little delayed by RAF bombing, but some kitchens and toilets were in separate annexes above ground; these had been destroyed by RAF bombs at the end of 1941.

However, Fritz Todt did not live long enough to receive accolades for his achievements. During a meeting with Hitler in East Prussia in February 1942, he felt safe enough to express the view that Germany could not win the war. On the 8th of that month, the aircraft carrying him back exploded and all the passengers and crew were killed; the accident could not be explained. He was succeeded as Minister for Armaments and War Production by Albert Speer, who also took over control of the Todt Organisation. This continued under the same name, its officials wearing paramilitary uniforms with shoulder badges of rank. They had an inexhaustible supply of slave labour, with 65,000 men in Lorient alone.

By the beginning of 1942 the U-boat men probably felt secure in their shelters, especially since the nightly bombing raids by the RAF had ceased. However, any complacency was shattered on the night of 28/29 March when an assault on Saint-Nazaire planned by Combined Operations (ComOps) took place. The main purpose of this was to deny the use of the dry dock to the *Tirpitz* if the battleship broke out from Norway to create havoc with the Atlantic convoys. This would be done by ramming a warship up against the lock gates, loaded with explosives timed to explode after the crew had vacated the vessel. At the same time, Commandos would storm ashore to attack other targets in the docks, while a diversionary raid would be provided by RAF Bomber Command.

The enterprise was code-named Operation 'Chariot' and a small flotilla of vessels and crews was prepared in great secrecy. An ancient escort destroyer was selected to serve as the blockship. This was HMS *Campbeltown*, formerly the USS *Buchanan*, one of fifty destroyers of First World War vintage mothballed by the Americans but obtained in September 1940 from President Roosevelt by Winston Churchill in exchange for the lease of British bases in the Caribbean. She was modified to provide a silhouette similar to that of the German *Moewe* class of 924-ton torpedo-boats. A 'four-stacker', the aft two funnels were removed while the one next to them was shortened. The heavy armament in her aft section was removed and replaced with eight small turrets armed with 20mm Oerlikon guns. Twenty-four depth charges were packed into her bow, weighing a total of four tons and concealed under the fuel tank. She was commanded by Lieutenant-Commander Stephen H. Beattie.

Over 250 Commandos formed the land assault force in the operation, some of whom were already veterans but others had been more recently trained. Most of them were to be embarked in sixteen Harbour Defence Motor Vessels (HDMLs) of 40 tons, each with a crew of eight but also capable of carrying up to eighteen armed men with full equipment. Their normal range was insufficient to reach Saint-Nazaire but they carried extra fuel in special rubber containers. Two of these HDMLs were also adapted with torpedo tubes.

Another vessel was *MGB 314*, a Motor Gun Boat of 110 tons, with a crew of thirty-nine and armed with one 40mm and two 20mm cannon. She was fitted with rudimentary radar and her roles were to lead the flotilla and also to act as a kind of command ship. She was commanded by Lieutenant Dustin Curtiss. Also on board were Lieutenant-Colonel A. Charles Newman of the Commandos and Commander Robert E.D. Ryder of the naval force. Lastly, there was one Motor Torpedo Boat (MTB), capable of thirty-five knots but of such a short range that it had to be towed.

The flotilla left Falmouth on Thursday 26 March, escorted at first by the destroyers HMS *Atherstone* and HMS *Tynedale*, and set course in the direction of La Pallice to confuse the enemy. At 07.20 hours on the next day, *Tynedale* spotted an object which *MGB 314* identified as a U-boat. It was in fact the Type VIIC *U-593*, commanded by Kapitanleutnant Gerd Kelbling, making its way from Kiel to Saint-Nazaire. Depth-charged by *Tyndale*, it resurfaced and disappeared once more after coming under fire. It was not damaged and sent a message to base. The Germans thought that the British were either minelaying or heading for Gibraltar. They dispatched two torpedo-boats from Nantes to investigate, but these found nothing.

After darkness fell the convoy turned back towards the north-east, to make rendezvous with the submarine HMS *Sturgeon* stationed about fifty miles from the mouth of the Loire Estuary. The submarine flashed lights and contact was made. Then the two escorting destroyers and the submarine headed for home while the assault flotilla headed due east at high speed to the estuary. On the final approach, *MGB 314* moved into the lead, followed by the two launches equipped with torpedoes. Then came *Campbeltown*, with the other launches containing Commandos in columns either side of her.

At 00.30 hours, shortly before the flotilla entered the estuary, the RAF began its diversionary attack against the docks at Saint-Nazaire. Thirty-eight Whitleys and twenty-seven Wellingtons arrived, with the crews under orders not to bomb unless they could see their targets clearly. Unfortunately the sky was cloudy and visibility extremely poor. They circled overhead, under fire and looking for gaps, but only four were able to bomb. Six others bombed secondary targets elsewhere and one Whitley was lost. Their attack ceased at 01.10 hours, when the flotilla entered the estuary, with *Campbeltown* flying the flag of the Kriegsmarine.

Of course, the Germans in Saint-Nazaire on the left bank spotted the flotilla and the alarm was raised. A searchlight played on *Campbeltown* and a challenge was flashed when she passed the flak-ship *Sperrbrecher 137* on her starboard side. A German-speaking sailor flashed back a signal saying that casualties from a sea battle were being brought into port. There was a short delay and then fire was opened on the flotilla and was returned.

The launches with their Commandos on the port side of *Campbeltown* peeled off to land on the Vieux Mole to the west of the docks.[12] Lieutenant-Commander Samuel Beattie on the old destroyer hoisted the White Ensign, increased speed to her maximum of 19 knots and headed straight for the gates of the dry dock. She struck these violently at 01.34 hours and her bows jammed about twelve metres above them. The Commandos aboard her dropped ropes and abseiled down to destroy the pumping room and the machine house that operated the gates.

Meanwhile, the Commandos in the launches which had been on the starboard side of *Campbeltown* headed for the entrance to the main dock, named the Bassin de Saint-Nazaire. They were covered by fire from *MGB 314*. The two launches

---

12. Partly visible on the extreme left of the air reconnaissance photograph taken afterwards.

The destroyer HMS Campbeltown *in the early morning of Saturday 28 March 1942, rammed on the outer gate of the dry dock at Saint-Nazaire. The twenty-four depth-charges on board, weighing four tons, exploded shortly before midday. The gate was destroyed and the sea rushed in. About 360 German soldiers and sailors who had clambered on board as sightseers or souvenir-hunters were blown to pieces.* (Bundesarchiv, Koblenz, ref: 101ll-MW-3719-24, via Tim Carroll)

fitted with tubes fired torpedoes at the dock gate. Return fire sank two launches but the other Commandos stormed ashore and Lieutenant-Colonel Newman set up his headquarters near the entrance. The Commandos set about their work of demolition but came under more fire, partly from the roof of the almost completed U-boat bunker on the north of the dock. They faced heavy losses, for the port was strongly garrisoned. Some casualties were ferried back to the gunboat, which had a small medical team aboard.

Newman decided to lead all the remaining Commandos into the town and make a break for open country, but more of them were killed or wounded. Almost all the others had to surrender; only five men eventually managed to make the long journey into Unoccupied France and then to the escape line through Spain. Commander Ryder ordered Lieutenant Curtiss in *MGB 314* to head west with the wounded, and this was done under cover of a smoke screen.

By mid-morning, all the fighting in Saint-Nazaire had died down and normal life seemed to be resuming. Hundreds of curious German soldiers and sailors clambered on board the stricken destroyer to examine its structure and collect souvenirs. Then, shortly after mid-day, a colossal explosion occurred, shattering

Saturday 28 March 1942 at Saint-Nazaire. The Germans had gathered together these wounded Commandos before transporting them to the military hospital l'Hermitage at La Baule. The man in the centre, with the bandaged head, is Private Tom MaCormack of the Queen's Own Cameron Highlanders, who died in the hospital. The book Saint-Nazaire sous l'occupation *by François Bertin is dedicated to him.* (Bundesarchiv, Koblenz, ref: 1011-065-2302-31, via Tim Carroll)

windows in the town and showering debris from the sky. A huge mushroom-cloud of black smoke rose, the bows of *Campbeltown* disintegrated and the lock gate was blown off its hinges. Sea water poured into the dry dock and the tankers *Passat* and *Schlitstadt*, under repair, were engulfed. Subsequent records showed that 60 German officers and 320 other ranks were killed.

A total of 345 sailors and 266 Commandos set out on Operation 'Chariot'. Of these, eighty-five sailors and fifty-nine Commandos were killed and most of the others became PoWs, many of them wounded. When the results of their achievements became known, almost a quarter of these men received honours. There were five Victoria Crosses, to Lieutenant-Commander Stephen Halden Beattie, Sergeant Thomas Frank Durrant, Lieutenant-Colonel Augustus Charles Newman, Commander Robert Edward Dudley Ryder and Able Seaman William Alfred Savage. Apart from these, there were four Distinguished Service

The results of the combined attack of 28 March 1942 against the port of Saint-Nazaire are shown in this RAF photograph. Photo-interpreters labelled (A) The lock gate, badly buckled and blown off its sill, at the entrance to the Bassin de Penhouet. (B) Damage to the concrete dam by the Bassin de Saint-Nazaire. (C) Damage to the machine house that operated the lock gates. In addition, the U-boat bunker can also be seen; it is the white rectangular building by the Bassin de Saint-Nazaire at the top of the photograph, before being completed and camouflaged. (Author's collection)

Orders, seventeen Distinguished Service Crosses, eleven Military Crosses, four Distinguished Gallantry Medals, five Distinguished Conduct Medals, twenty-four Military Medals and fifty Mentions in Despatches.

After this combined attack, Hitler ordered Dönitz to move his headquarters from Lorient to Paris, fearing he might be the target of a similar operation. He departed on 29 March, being allowed back for only short periods. The German authorities in Saint-Nazaire allowed the evacuation of many women and children into the surrounding countryside.

However, RAF Bomber Command restricted its activities mostly to sea-mining at night, usually with the older machines such as Whitleys, Hampdens and Wellingtons. The danger from the skies came from the US Eighth Air Force, which had begun its European operations in June 1942 with daylight attacks against ports in northern France. The first attack on a U-boat port took

The port area of La Pallice was attacked once more by the US Eighth Air Force, on 16 September 1943, when forty-four B-17 Flying Fortresses were despatched. One Fortress was shot down and six others damaged, but the bombing was effective. Bombs fell in the U-boat locks at 'A' and the pens at 'Is', both in the rectangle. Another salvo fell on the dispersal area of an airfield, as circled. (Author's collection)

place on 21 October 1942 when sixty-six B-17 Fortresses, escorted by twelve P-38 Lightnings of US Fighter Groups and about 100 RAF Spitfires arrived at mid-day over Lorient. The bombs fell mostly in the dock area, killing forty-eight forced labourers and ten Germans. Thereafter, the U-boat ports in France became frequent targets for the US Eighth Air Force.

A very audacious plan for another raid on a French port was proposed by Major Herbert G. 'Blondie' Hasler and considered by Vice-Admiral Lord Louis Mountbatten, the head of Combined Operations (ComOps). This involved paddling two-man canoes up the Gironde during the hours of darkness and blowing up some of the blockade runners which were bringing special metals to the German war industry. It was considered feasible and codenamed Operation 'Frankton'.

*Two 2,000lb general-purpose bombs
falling from a B-17 Flying Fortress
on the port of Lorient during a
daylight raid on 21 October 1942
by sixty-six Fortresses and twenty
B-24 Liberators of the US Eighth
Air Force. The U-boat shelter is on
the left near the top of the bombs
while part of the Ile de Saint-
Michel is to the left of their noses.
Considerable damage was caused to
the dock area and many Germans
and forced labourers were killed.
Three Fortresses failed to return.*
(Author's collection)

On the night of 7 December 1942 the submarine HMS *Tuna* launched five collapsible canoes (nicknamed 'Cockleshells') near the mouth of the Gironde Estuary. Each carried two Royal Marine Commandos, who had to paddle about 75 miles. They encountered a very strong rip tide and one capsized, resulting in the deaths of two men. The crew of another was captured while sheltering in daylight. Another canoe became holed and the men were also captured. Only two canoes reached the docks at Bordeaux, on the third night. The four men planted limpet mines on four vessels totalling about 17,000 tons. These sank but the Germans were able to repair and raise them.

The remaining four men had to make their way to the escape line at Marseilles, a problem made more difficult since the Germans had begun to occupy Vichy France on 11 November. Two men were captured and, together with the other four prisoners, executed by firing squad. Only two men, Hasler and Marine Bill Sparks, reached Gibraltar via the 'Marie-Claire' escape line. Hasler was awarded the Distinguished Service Order and Sparks received the Distinguished Service Medal.

The first three months of 1943 brought increased tragedy for the people of Lorient and Saint-Nazaire. This stemmed from the intensity of U-boat activity in the Atlantic. In the last quarter of 1942, over 1,500.000 tons of Allied shipping had been sunk as a result of the increased production of U-boats and their perfection of 'Wolfpack' attacks in which they formed picket lines across the routes of convoys and then gathered for coordinated attacks when one was spotted. On 14 January 1944 the War Cabinet approved the 'area bombing' of the U-boat ports in France, giving the order of priority as (1) Lorient (2) Saint-Nazaire (3) Brest (4) La Pallice.

The response of RAF Bomber Command was immediate. On the night of 14/15 January, 122 heavy bombers were dispatched to Lorient, using the method of sending picked crews of the Pathfinder Force in advance to mark the target. The main force followed, dropping a deadly mixture of high-explosive and incendiary bombs. The result was devastation in the residential area of Lorient, overwhelming the rescue services. Seven such attacks followed, the last being on the night of 16/17 February. By this time, Lorient was a shattered and uninhabited wreck, with over 450 civilians believed to have been killed. The survivors had fled into the countryside. The RAF then turned to Saint-Nazaire on the night of 28 February/1 March with 417 bombers, destroying 60 per cent of the town. Most of the population had already left but twenty-nine of those remaining were killed. Two more heavy attacks were made in March, with the bombs falling mainly in the dock area.

By the end of March, it was apparent from air photographs and intelligence reports that the U-boat bunkers were immune from these bombs and that the Germans had moved their essential services out of the towns. A total of 2,946 bombers had been dispatched and fifty-one had been lost, without any military gain. Further heavy attacks were called off, Brest and La Pallice being spared this type of destruction. Bombing of the dock areas was left mainly to the US Eighth Air Force operating in daylight. However, RAF Bomber Command continued to despatch small numbers of aircraft to drop sea mines at night. These had a more detrimental effect on the operations of U-boats than all the area bombing, destroying some of them and also creating difficulty for the Kriegsmarine which had to operate a continuous programme to locate the magnetic mines and explode them.

This procedure for bombing the U-boat ports continued until D-Day, 6 June 1944, when all branches of the RAF and USAAF concentrated on supporting the landings in Normandy. RAF Bomber Command was able to operate in daylight, with the protection of RAF Fighter Command, in attacks on German

Eighty-three B-17 Flying Fortresses of the US Eighth Air Force were despatched on 4 July 1943 to bomb the lock gates at La Pallice, as part of the Battle of the Atlantic. Most of the 275 1,000lb general-purpose bombs fell accurately in the target area. In addition to other damage, a Sperrbrecher *(heavily armed flak ship and mine-exploding vessel) received a direct hit. One aircraft failed to return.* (Author's collection)

German troops discussing the destruction of an oil tank in the Caverne-Saint-Loubes storage area of Bordeaux. The photograph was probably taken after RAF Bomber Command despatched 109 Lancasters, 101 Halifaxes and five Mosquitos to bomb oil depots at Bordeaux and La Pallice on the night of 10/11 August 1944. The attacks were effective and no aircraft were lost. (Archives de Bordeaux, via Geneviève Moulard)

The US Eighth Air Force despatched thirty-eight B-17 Flying Fortresses on 29 May 1943 to attack the lock gates at Saint-Nazaire. They dropped almost 200 tons of bombs and caused considerable damage to the dock area, without losing any aircraft. (Author's collection)

gun positions and communications, as well as the launch sites for V-1 flying bombs. The Allies broke through the German lines and the German garrisons in Lorient, Saint-Nazaire, La Pallice and Bordeaux became blockaded from sea and land. The exception was Brest, for the Allies intended to seize this port to receive supplies being sent by sea from America.

The original garrison at Brest consisted of about 9,000 Germans, mostly older men engaged on anti-aircraft duties, but in early August the defences were hugely strengthened by a division of battle-hardened paratroopers under the command of the tough General Bernard Ramcke. In addition, scattered groups from other units arrived from the fighting in Brittany. Ramcke then commanded a total of about 50,000 men. The civilian population numbered about 80,000 and Ramcke decided to evacuate all save those required for essential services. This began on 4 August and about 60,000 left the potential area of combat, in which Ramcke formed five defensive lines facing east.

The task of capturing Brest was given to the Third US Army commanded by the charismatic General George S. Patton, who ordered his VII Corps under

The U-boat bunker at La Pallice was almost unchanged in 1963. This photograph was taken from low level by an F95 camera with a 12in lens in an English Electric Canberra PR.7 of 31 Squadron, flying on a training exercise from Laarbruch in Germany. (Air Commodore Graham R. Pitchfork collection)

General Troy H. Middleton to begin moving against the port. This consisted of an armoured division, three infantry divisions and 'Task Force A' of chosen men to act like Commandos on special missions.

Meanwhile, the U-boat pen at Brest received daylight visits from Lancasters of the famous dam-busting 617 Squadron on 5, 12 and 13 August. These did not carry bouncing bombs on their attacks, but a total of twenty-six 12,000lb 'Tallboy' bombs were dropped from heights of 16,000 to 18,000 feet, for the loss of one Lancaster. Nine of these huge bombs hit the bunker but five did not penetrate both roofs, one of which was constructed above the other. Four penetrated both roofs but the bombs appeared to have been deflected. No U-boats were damaged, but four men were killed.

However, the activities of U-boats from French ports came to a sudden end after this episode. On 15 August, Allied forces invaded the south of France in

Feldmarschall Erwin Rommel (centre, wearing white scarf) at La Pallice on 11 February 1944 during a tour of inspection of the 'Atlantic Wall'. (Archives departmentales de la Charente-Maritime, ref: 62 Fi 755, via Geneviève Moulard)

Operation 'Dragoon' and moved rapidly inland. Three days later, Hitler ordered all U-boats to abandon the French ports. Twenty-four of them did so but nine others under repair had to be broken up or scuttled.

The VII Corps had to complete operations elsewhere, and it then had to advance over 150 miles before reaching the outskirts of Brest on 24 August. The battle began after Bomber Command dispatched 324 aircraft on that night against enemy artillery positions. The Americans advanced into the town, in close combat against stubborn defence, and there were heavy casualties on both sides. The attackers had the advantage of support from Republic P-47 Thunderbolts of the US Ninth Air Force, each carrying rockets and up to 750lbs of bombs. The Germans retreated until mid-September, when they became concentrated in the rocky Crozon Peninsula south of Brest, and could not hold out for much longer. Ramcke surrendered on 19 September, having suffered over 10,000 men killed. About 38,000 of his men were taken prisoner, including the wounded. The town of Brest lay in complete ruins and the Americans suffered 9,831 casualties, including the wounded.

In contrast to such carnage Bordeaux was liberated in the same period, but without combat. There had been numerous acts of sabotage in the town and

Ecstatic French people in the town of Laballe in Brittany, greeting two American liberators in a jeep. A lieutenant is being presented with a bouquet while his driver is almost obscured by the cheering crowd. They were driving towards Brest, about 100 miles to the west, where the German garrison under General Ramcke surrendered to the American forces on 19 September 1944. (Author's collection)

surrounding area by the Maquis, but by August these scattered groups of patriots had been gathered into the new Forces Français de l'Interior (FFI), formed as a regular fighting division and armed by the Allies. A battle for Bordeaux seemed imminent but on 24 August the French municipal authorities approached the German garrison for a peaceful solution. On 28 August the Germans quit the town. The FFI entered the following day, to an ecstatic welcome from the population, without a shot being fired.

The German garrison of about 4,500 men moved north-west into the Medoc district, shaped like a rough triangle bounded on the west by the Atlantic and on the east by the Gironde. They remained almost undisturbed until 14 April, when the FFI was strongly reinforced by troops released from the German front and able to mount an attack with aid from the air. The defenders were pushed

Some of the Germans from the garrison of Cherbourg, which surrounded to American forces on 26 June 1944, marching through the liberated port to a prisoner-of-war stockade. A statue of Napoleon is in the background. (Author's collection)

northwards until 20 April 1945, when they reached the Pointe de Grave on the southern entrance of the estuary and were forced to surrender.

The other three U-boat ports, Lorient, Saint-Nazaire and La Pallice, remained in German hands until their country surrendered on 5 May. The garrisons marched out under armed guard to an uncertain future. Many of the colossal bunkers they left behind are still there today, symbols of four years of humiliation and oppression but also of hope and ultimate victory.

During the period I served in 217 Squadron, from late January 1941 to late March 1942, we lost thirty-six aircraft and crews. This was twice our nominal strength of eighteen aircraft and crews, although we never seemed to be built up to that number. Not all the 144 men lost their lives, for a post-war examination shows that twenty-one became PoWs. Several of these were wounded, some severely.

By any standards, this was an appalling rate of attrition. Unknown to the few survivors, this was confirmed on 16 November 1942 when the Air Member for Training, Air Marshal Sir A. Guy R. Garrod, sent a table of RAF operational casualties to the Air Member for Personnel, Air Marshal Sir Bertine E. Sutton. This contained the following figures:

Percentage Chance of Survival

	One Tour	*Two Tours*
1. Torpedo bomber	17.5	3
2. Light bomber	25.5	6.5
3. Fighter reconnaissance	31	9.5
4. Night fighter	39	15
5. Bomber reconnaissance	42	17.5
6. Day Fighter	43	18.5
7. Heavy and medium bombers	44	19.5
8. Light general reconnaissance landplane	45	20
9. Medium general reconnaissance landplane	56	31.6
10. Long-range fighter	59.5	35.5
11. Sunderland flying boat	66	43.5
12. Heavy general reconnaissance landplane	71	50.5
13. Catalina flying boat	77	60

The Bristol Beaufort occupied the unenviable place at the top of this list. Although it often carried bombs instead of torpedoes, it was still classed as a torpedo bomber by the RAF and its losses formed the main base for these statistics up to November 1942. The fault for the heavy losses did not lie in any major defect in the aircraft itself. Although not perfect, it was a sturdy and reliable machine by the standards of the time.

The reason for those losses can be attributed to two main causes. One was that its operations usually involved flying at low level, sometimes in daylight, when it was vulnerable to direct fire from enemy flak gunners or sometimes from fighters. The other reason was that it was necessary to carry out 200 hours of operational flying before completing a tour in the RAF. A sortie in a Beaufort was on average about four hours, so that the aircrews had to complete

Wing Commander Samuel McC. 'Mac' Boal, who rejoined 217 Squadron in February 1942 as Commanding Officer. He lost his life on 1 April 1942 when leading a torpedo strike of three Beauforts from RAF Leuchars in Fife against a German convoy off Stavanger Fjord in Norway. Two of his crew were picked up by German sailors to become PoWs. (Author's collection)

Sergeant John Sinclair photographed as a cadet at Initial Training Wing. (John Sinclair)

Sergeant Maurice Mayne. (Maurice Mayne)

Sergeant Stan Clarke. (Maurice Mayne)

fifty sorties before reaching that total. This can be compared with the average of thirty sorties by aircrews of Bomber Command, who flew longer distances before reaching their targets.

In mid-April 1942, before these statistics were compiled, 217 Squadron received orders to prepare flying to Ceylon, equipped in the torpedo-bomber role. The purpose was to help protect the island against a possible invasion by the Japanese forces which had conquered Malaya and occupied Singapore. But the squadron was unable to comply immediately, for it was not completely equipped with torpedo-carrying Beaufort IIs or with trained crews.

Moreover, on the first day of that month, Wing Commander 'Mac' Boal had failed to return from a torpedo attack against a German convoy near Stavanger Fjord in Norway. This convoy had consisted of ten vessels carrying supplies to the German forces occupying Kristiansand, escorted by three trawlers converted

A Beaufort I in a dispersal pen at Luqa airfield in Malta, photographed in 1942. It has two Vickers K guns in the nose, operated by the navigator, an ASV radar aerial beneath the fuselage, and a large air filter above the engine cowling. (Author's collection)

into flak ships. Boal had led two other Beauforts into the attack but had been shot down. He and the wireless operator Sergeant Stan Clarke had been killed. The navigator Sergeant John Sinclair and the air gunner Sergeant Maurice Mayne had been wounded but both had been picked up to become PoWs for the rest of the war. The other two Beauforts had dropped their torpedoes; these had missed but the aircraft had returned safely.

The preparation for the flight to Ceylon proved very protracted. Wing Commander W.A.L. Davies arrived to command the squadron. New crews joined from the Torpedo Training Unit, some after a rather skimpy course. New Beaufort IIs fitted with torpedo racks were slow to arrive. After several weeks, the crews began to fly down to Portreath in south-west Cornwall, where long-range tanks were fitted for the long flight ahead. The first leg of this was to be over neutral Portugal to Gibraltar. The next would be to the besieged island of Malta, and then a longer flight to Cairo in Egypt. It was not until 10 June that a first section of nine Beauforts arrived at RAF Luqa in Malta, with six more on the next day. Seven others eventually trickled in but another made a forced landing in Portugal, and the crew were interned. The arrival of these Beauforts was a bonanza for the Air Officer Commanding, Air Vice-Marshal Sir Hugh Pughe Lloyd, for he was able to employ them temporarily on operations which were far more urgent than a possible Japanese invasion of Ceylon. While heavily bombarded from the air, Malta was vital for the protection of Allied convoys carrying supplies to the British Eighth Army in North Africa. Some Beauforts of 22 Squadron had already arrived but the newcomers were also required to torpedo warships of the Italian Navy as well as to sink Axis vessels taking supplies to the Afrika Korps.

When the first Beauforts of 217 Squadron arrived in Malta, the island was so short of supplies that it could barely hold out any longer. Fuel and food were the most critical. However, two Allied convoys were approaching. One, code-named 'Harpoon', had left the Clyde and passed Gibraltar. The other, code-named 'Vigorous', had left Alexandria in Egypt and was also nearing the island. Both were under constant attack, mainly from the Luftwaffe, and had already suffered severe losses.

On 14 June the crew of a Baltimore reported spotting an Italian naval force converging on 'Vigorous'. Nine Beauforts of 217 Squadron were ordered to attack at dawn the following day, led by Wing Commander Davies. Eight took off at about 04.00 hours but the other, flown by Flying Officer Arthur Aldridge, was delayed by another aircraft blocking the exit from his sheltering blast pen.

Soldiers constructing blast pens in dispersal points around RAF airfields in Malta, to protect aircraft during raids. They are using limestone blocks from bombed buildings. (Author's collection)

Aldridge decided it was too late to link up with the other Beauforts and set course directly for the enemy fleet which, unknown to him, consisted of four cruisers and four destroyers. It arrived a few minutes before sunrise and the Italian gunners did not open fire, believing that a solitary aircraft flying out of the twilight must be friendly.

Aldridge circled and picked out a large vessel leading the formation. He flew at an angle of 45° ahead of it and released his torpedo from about 800 yards. The torpedo ran true while he turned away. It struck the 10,500-ton heavy cruiser *Trento* in the bows and exploded. At this point five of the other Beauforts arrived and attacked, while the remaining three headed north to hunt for two Italian battleships which had also been reported. Both formations flew into intense fire. All dropped their torpedoes but the Italians were able to 'comb their tracks'. The action against the cruisers had been witnessed by the commander of the submarine HMS *Umbra*, which closed with the stricken vessel and put another torpedo into her. The *Trento* heeled over and sank, with heavy loss of life. The

The Italian heavy cruiser Trento *was of 10,500 tons displacement and armed with eight 8in guns, as well as twelve 3.9in and eight 37mm anti-aircraft guns. She was torpedoed and badly damaged east of Malta in the early morning of 8 June 1942 by a Beaufort of 217 Squadron flown by Flying Officer Arthur H. Aldridge. About four hours later she was sunk by the submarine HMS* Umbra. *(The late Chris Davies collection)*

submarine then moved north to the Italian battleships and fired four more torpedoes, but all of these missed.

All the Beauforts returned to Malta but the crews were told to take off again, after replacing two damaged aircraft and one wounded gunner. They did so but found no targets, for the Italian warships had headed back to Taranto. Nevertheless, the 'Vigorous' convoy turned back to Alexandria, since its gunners had expended almost all their ammunition. Only two merchant ships from the 'Harpoon' convoy arrived at Malta, on the following day. The two convoys lost one cruiser, five destroyers, two minesweepers and six merchant ships, but they had brought some relief to Malta.

The next operation took place on 20 June when twelve Beauforts set off for an Axis convoy near the toe of Italy. Two aircraft which were last to take off were attacked by two Junkers Ju 88s. One flown by Sergeant Hutcheson managed to evade but the other, flown by Flying Officer Frank Minster, was shot down and there were no survivors. The other Beauforts did not find the convoy and returned without loss.

On the following day, nine Beauforts in three vics led by Squadron Leader Robert Lynn set off to attack a heavily-defended convoy bound for Tripoli in Libya. They were escorted by six Beaufighters of 235 Squadron. All three Beauforts in the first vic were shot down during the attack. Lynn and his crew lost their lives. The pilots of the other two managed to ditch; the crews were picked up by the convoy, some of them wounded. Two more Beauforts were hit, but they and the other five managed to return to Malta, albeit with some wounded. The formation had torpedoed and sunk the German merchant vessel *Reichenfels* of 7,744 tons.

On 23 June, Wing Commander Davies led seven Beauforts of his squadron, together with five of 39 Squadron, to another convoy off the toe of Italy. They hit and damaged the 6,835-ton Italian merchant vessel *Mario Roselli* but two Beauforts of 39 Squadron were shot down. One of the pilots in a Beaufort of 217 Squadron was wounded in the leg and crash-landed in Malta. A respite followed until 3 July, when Squadron Leader Patrick Gibbs led a mixed force from 39 and 217 Squadrons to attack a convoy off the south-west coast of Greece. Torpedo hits were claimed but two Beauforts of 217 Squadron were shot down; these were flown by Sergeant Russell Mercer and Sergeant James Hutcheson, and there were no survivors.

This poem was written by Sergeant George L. Hodson, a WOp/AG in 217 Squadron, He did not live to experience post-war conditions. At the age of nineteen years, he was one of eight sergeants of his squadron who 'failed to return' to Luqa in Malta from a strike on 3 July 1942 against an enemy convoy off the coast of Greece. All eight crew members have 'no known grave'. The poem was found in his effects by his friend Sergeant Harry Mallaby of 217 Squadron.

Sometimes I wonder
Will I live
To see the fight for freedom won,
And then begin the fight again
Against the men of greed and gain.
Who would our land in post war years
Fill it once more with grief and tears
With promises heard once before
A land for heroes fit to live in.

Is this the land from whence we heard
Those words that now are scorned
By men who from the last Great War remain
Some blind, some gassed, some maimed
The rest returned for peace and rest
For which they fought their level best.
Only for some was meant this peace
For others it meant begging in the streets
Long waits in queues for jobs that never came.

Sometime I wonder
Will I live
To see it all again.

After this attack, 217 Squadron was released for over a fortnight. Its losses had been severe and there was a problem with sickness among the surviving aircrews in all three Beaufort squadrons, some of whom were suffering from tick fever, dysentery or scabies. Rations were down to near-starvation level, which exacerbated these problems.

The first attack after this recovery period took place on 21 July when Squadron Leader Gibbs led three Beauforts of 217 Squadron with four of 86 Squadron and two of 39 Squadron to a convoy near the Greek island of Cephalonia. They claimed some success and all returned safely.

On 22 July, Wing Commander Davies returned to the UK. Patrick Gibbs was promoted to Wing Commander and took over the remainder of 39, 86 and 217 Squadrons in Malta. These began to function as a single unit, sometimes with men from different squadrons flying in the same aircraft.

An attack with this composite unit took place on 24 July, with three Beauforts of 217 Squadron and three of 86 Squadron, escorted by nine Beaufighters of 235 Squadron. Their target was a large merchant ship which had been spotted near Cephalonia, escorted by two destroyers and two flak-ships. The Beaufighters and the three Beauforts from 86 Squadron attacked first, but all the Beauforts were shot down by an intense barrage. However, the three from 217 Squadron attacked from the opposite direction, taking the enemy gunners by surprise, and scored two torpedo hits on the Italian *Vettor Pisani* of 6,339 tons, which caught fire and burnt out. Four of the men from 86 Squadron were killed but eight were picked up to become PoWs.

An attack which took place on 28 July resulted in one of the most extraordinary events of the Second World War. Nine Beauforts were racked up with torpedoes and took off under the leadership of Gibbs to attack a merchant ship escorted by two destroyers south-west of Greece. Two Beauforts of 217 Squadron were shot down. Three crew members of the aircraft flown by Pilot Officer R.I.C. Head were picked up by one of the destroyers. The four men in the other Beaufort, flown by Lieutenant Ted Strever of the SAAF were picked up by an Italian Cant floatplane and taken north to the Greek port of Prevesa. On the following day, they were taken in another Cant towards Taranto in Italy, but managed to overpower the armed guard and the Italian crew. They flew the Cant to Malta and landed in a bay, despite being attacked by Spitfires.[13]

---

13. For a detailed account of this episode, see *Reported Missing* by the author, published by Pen & Sword Books Ltd in 2009.

Tracks of the Beaufort and the Cants.

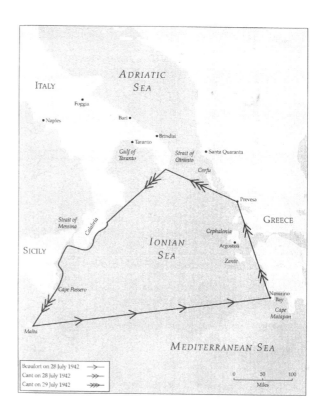

Captors and prisoners on the wings of the skyjacked Cant in St Paul's Bay in Malta, photographed from the approaching air-sea-rescue craft. (The late William H. Dunsmore DFC, via Roy C. Nesbit)

Prisoners and captors in friendly mood in Malta. Left to right: Pilot Officer Bill Dunsmore, Corsican guard, Italian flight engineer, Lieutenant Ted Strever, Tenente *Mastrodicasa, Sergeant John Wilkinson,* Tenente *Chafari, Sergeant Ray Brown, Italian wireless operator.* (The late A. Raymond Brown DFM, via Roy C. Nesbit)

Another convoy for Malta, code-named Operation 'Pedestal', entered the Mediterranean via Gibraltar on 10 August. Five merchant ships reached Grand Harbour, the last being a crippled tanker on 15 August. The convoy had suffered the loss of an aircraft carrier, two cruisers, a destroyer and nine merchant ships, but it had brought enough fuel and supplies to keep Malta viable for two months. At last, 217 Squadron was released to continue its flight to Ceylon, but it could muster only eight crews and Beauforts from the original twenty-one which had landed at Luqa. The aircraft were fitted with long-range tanks for the flight ahead.

The last crew left Malta on 28 August. The flights to Ceylon took place in a series of hops to RAF landing grounds or stations. From Cairo the usual route was south to the northern tip of the Red Sea and then east across Iraq to Habbaniya, near Baghdad. The next stage was south-east down the Persian Gulf to Bahrein. Then they turned east once more, to Karachi in India. The

Soldiers, sailors and airmen joined crowds of civilians at Grand Harbour in Valletta on 15 August 1942 to cheer the arrival of survivors of the 'Pedestal' convoy. Only five of the fourteen merchant ships in the convoy reached Malta but one of these was the vitally important tanker Ohio. *(Author's collection)*

final stages were south-east via Bombay and Bangalore to RAF Mimmeriya in central Ceylon. The squadron's ground party had already arrived by sea and then overland.

After a few weeks, the crews converted from Beauforts to Lockheed Hudsons. New crews arrived and Wing Commander A.D.W. Miller assumed command in November. The squadron became employed in anti-submarine patrols over the Indian Ocean. Detachments were sent to Ratmalana, close to Colombo in the south-west of the island.

These patrols in Hudsons proved uneventful and in February 1943 the squadron moved about fifty miles north to RAF Vavuniya, where living conditions were slightly more comfortable. Wing Commander R.J. Walker took over the squadron in March and the crews converted to Beauforts again during April. Together with 22 Squadron on the same station, they formed a torpedo-carrying strike force against Japanese warships, but the latter were engaged on more urgent matters in the Pacific and failed to appear. One crew from 217

Squadron was lost during torpedo practice on 26 August 1943, having probably hit the sea while flying at very low level.

This inactivity with Beauforts lasted for over a year and became so irksome to the aircrews that they called themselves 'The Ceylon Home Guard'. However, torpedo-carrying Beaufighter TFXs ('Torbeaus') arrived in June 1944 and the aircrews began to convert on to them. Wing Commander John G. Lingard DFC took over 217 Squadron in the following August. The aircrews began to train with deadly rocket projectiles (RPs) and by the end of the year their squadron became a very effective fighting force. At this time, 22 Squadron was similarly equipped and began moving to the Burma theatre.

In early 1945 a new operation was devised for 217 Squadron by the RAF's No 222 Group in Colombo. This consisted of an attack against the Japanese fleet in Singapore and was code-named Operation 'Jinx'. However, the Beaufighters could not reach Singapore from Ceylon, a distance of about 2,300 miles, and it was decided that they would operate from the tiny group of the Cocos Islands,

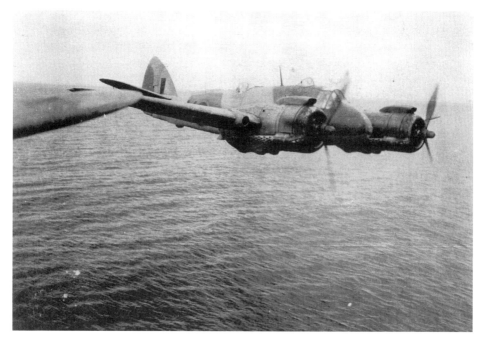

Beaufighter TFXs of 217 Squadron from RAF Vavuniya in Ceylon, practising formation flying in 1945 in preparation for Operation 'Jinx', the torpedo attack against the Japanese fleet in the Lingga Roads near Singapore. (John H. Simons collection)

about 1,040 miles from Singapore provided they crossed the mountainous range of Sumatra. The operation was sanctioned by Vice-Admiral Lord Louis Mountbatten, Supreme Commander of South-East Asia Command.

Huge efforts were made to prepare a staging post on the Cocos Islands for the operation. There was already a small party of Royal Engineers in a cable station on one of them, named Direction Island, and an advance party of airmen from 217 Squadron was landed there by cruiser in early March. These were followed by three large transports bringing over 200 airmen with building materials and supplies which included eighty-one torpedoes. 'Station Brown', with buildings and a runway of pressed steel planking on crushed coral, had been cut from the jungle at the end of April, under the command of Air Commodore A.W. Hunt.

Meanwhile the aircrews of 217 Squadron were practising long-distance flights of about eight hours in twelve Beaufighters fitted with extra fuel tanks. They knew they had to fly to the Cocos Islands and were told that their targets in Singapore included three battleships, an aircraft carrier and several destroyers,

Stores arriving by landing craft on one of the Cocos Islands in 1945, during the construction of an airfield for use in the proposed Allied invasion of Malaya, as well as a staging post for transport aircraft flying between Australia and Ceylon. Coconut palms grew down to the narrow beach. (Author's collection)

Coconut palms being cleared by a bulldozer in April 1945 during the construction of an airstrip on one of the Cocos Islands. The airstrip was codenamed 'Station Brown'. (Author's collection)

protected by fighters from three airfields. It was obviously an extremely dangerous operation, and possibly suicidal.

On 3 May, the men of 217 Squadron learnt that the operation had been cancelled. They were not told of the reason and were furious at their wasted effort. In retrospect it seems that the directive came from Mountbatten, for he had become intent on Operation 'Zipper', an invasion of the Malayan mainland near Phuket Island planned to begin in late August. All secondary operations were cancelled to conserve resources.

No 217 Squadron was ordered to move to RAF Gannavarum, south of Madras on the east coast of India, and to practice rocket and cannon firing in preparation for this new operation. The ground and air parties completed this move on 22 June, but Operation 'Zipper' never took place. As the world knows, the atom bombs were dropped on Japan and the country surrendered unconditionally on 14 August. On 30 September of that year, 217 Squadron was disbanded.

Many years after the war I was able to establish from RAF documents released by the Public Record Office (now The National Archives) that a former member of 217 Squadron was flying from Ceylon at the same time as his old squadron.

A detachment of Liberator Vs from 321 (Dutch) Squadron were the first aircraft to operate from the Cocos Islands. They arrived from RAF China Bay in Ceylon on 2 July 1945, in preparation for the invasion of Malaya. This Liberator letter Y, flown by Lieutenant-Commander J. de Bruyn, was photographed taking off from West Island on 7 July for the first operational flight, a reconnaissance of the Sunda Straits. (Author's collection)

This was Flight Lieutenant John F. Percival, the Canadian pilot with whom Davies, Reeves and myself had flown the majority of our operational sorties. On 3 January 1944 he joined 160 Squadron based at RAF Sigiriya in the heart of the jungle and equipped with four-engined Consolidated Liberator Vs. It was mainly engaged on long-range anti-submarine patrols of fifteen hours in length. After several of these sorties, he was appointed a flight commander and promoted to Squadron Leader.

On the dark night of 13 April 1944, Percival and his crew of eight took off from Sirigiya in Liberator serial BZ864 letter B for another long sortie. A few seconds after the wheels left the runway, the Liberator swung to port and lost height. The port wheel struck a gun site near the end of the runway and the aircraft crashed into low trees about a hundred yards away.

Within two minutes the crash tender and the ambulance had broken through the perimeter fence, followed by five men including the Commanding Officer, Wing Commander G.R. Brady. Two of the men staggered from the rear of the wreckage, dazed but unhurt. The CO and his men scrambled into the wreckage and pulled out four of the crew, alive but unconscious; of these, two died on the way to hospital and another shortly afterwards. The Liberator began to burn fiercely and a fire tender was unable to extinguish the flames immediately. The bodies of Percival and the other two men were not recovered until later.

A Court of Inquiry was unable to ascertain the cause of the crash but it appears to have been sudden engine failure; servicing was difficult in the tropical conditions of the jungle. The six men who died in the crash were buried with military honours on the following day, at Levermentu Cemetery, Flower Road, Colombo.

Junkers Ju 88 at RAF Chivenor

A very strange event took place on 26 November 1941, resulting in amazement and even hilarity among the RAF men who witnessed it. The cause was Junkers Ju 88A-5, radio code M2 + MK, works number 6073, of Küstenfliegergruppe 106, which took off at 16.00 hours GMT from Morlaix in northern France for an anti-shipping sortie over the Irish Sea. This was part of Luftflotte 3, the main air force that operated over south-west England bombing airfields, ports and shipping.

The Ju 88A-5 was a formidable aircraft, equipped with high quality anti-shipping radar and capable of carrying 5,500lbs of bombs. Most were armed with one 13mm and five 7.9mm machine-guns. However, the crew members

Junkers Ju 88A-5, radio code M2 + MK, of Küstenfliegergruppe 106, which took off from Morlaix in Northern France on 26 November 1941 on an anti-shipping sortie and landed in error at RAF Chivenor in North Devon. It has been given RAF roundels and the serial HM509. (Author's collection)

of M2 + MK were not highly experienced on operational work. The pilot was Unteroffizier (Sergeant) Erwin Herms, the navigator Obergefreiter (Senior Aircraftmen) Ernst Kurz, the wireless operator Gefreiter (Leading Aircraftman) Heinrich Klein, and the air gunner Obergefreiter Friedrich Krantier.

This crew headed north to the Irish Sea at about 7,000 feet and spent several hours at night hunting for shipping between Eire and Wales. Their radar did not pick up any targets and they turned southwards for home at about 19.45 hours. Unfortunately for them, the navigator had underestimated the wind velocity, which had strengthened and pushed them to the north-east. When they arrived at a coastline, they thought it was north Devon, whereas it was the north coast of the Pembroke peninsula of Wales. Then they saw searchlights at Pembroke, which they thought must be Plymouth.

At this point, they jettisoned their bombs and continued south. Then they flew over coastline near Plymouth but thought they must have crossed clean over the Brittany peninsula and arrived at the coastline of the Bay of Biscay. So they turned north again, very worried about their lack of fuel.

At 21.25 hours they saw a flarepath, which they hoped was Morlaix. In fact it was RAF Chivenor in north Devon, where trainee aircrews of No 3 Operational Training Unit (OTU) were practising night flying in Beauforts. Meanwhile, British radar operators had plotted the aircraft as RAF coming back to its base. Herms fired a red-white cartridge, the German signal for the night, followed by a red-green, which in the Luftwaffe meant 'I am in danger and am going to land.' As it happened, red-green had been the RAF identification signal for part of the night, but it was challenged with a '0' flashed in Morse by an Aldis lamp on the ground. Herms did not understand this request but put on his navigation lights. Flying Control had switched off the landing lights, but switched them on again. Of course, Chivenor was primarily a training station, and trainees in the air could sometimes make mistakes. Herms made a good wheels-down landing.

When Herms taxied into the beam of the 'chance light' at the end of the runway, RAF men were startled to see black crosses and swastikas outlined in white on a dark green fuselage and fin. Squadron Leader W. 'Len' Harvey, the officer-in-charge of nightflying at Chivenor, jumped into his jeep and sped to the operations block, accompanied by Pilot Officer P.J. Twomey of the RAAF. He grabbed a Thompson submachine-gun, which was available for emergencies, and rushed out again. He tried to instruct the pilot to switch off his engines, by signalling with a torch. When Herms failed to respond, he fired two short bursts, consisting of seven bullets in all, into the cockpit. At this, a German shouted 'Don't shoot!' in English, and they all came out to surrender. Kutz had a small nick above the elbow from a bullet, but otherwise they were unhurt.

The Station Medical Officer attended to this slight wound, while the Germans were separated and each placed under armed guard. They were stripped of their uniforms and required to wear pyjamas. An interrogation officer from the Air Ministry arrived during the night and the whole story of their misfortune came out. The Germans must have felt very sheepish, but at least they were safe in a PoW camp for the remainder of the war.

The Junkers was repaired at Chivenor. While there, flying instructors trooped into the hangar to examine such an unusual arrival. They thought it was a fine machine and were deeply impressed by the elaborate radar array protruding from the nose. About a fortnight later, it was flown under escort to the Royal Aircraft Establishment at Farnborough and from there to 1426 (Enemy Aircraft) Flight at RAF Duxford in Cambridgeshire. It received specialist examination and was given RAF roundels and the serial number HM509. German markings were repainted for 'fly-on' parts in British war films, including Noel Coward's *In Which We Serve*. It was 'struck off charge' on 26 July 1944.

Appendix B

Kenneth Campbell's Victoria Cross

A t 14.50 hours on 7 April 2000 a memorial plaque to Flying Officer Kenneth Campbell was unveiled at his home town of Saltcoats in North Ayrshire. The impetus for this public recognition came from Bill Brady, a management consultant in South Africa who had been born in Saltcoats. He became fascinated by the story of the attack on the *Gneisenau*, visited Scotland and met Kenneth Campbell's elder brother James, who at the age of ninety was still active in his firm of solicitors.

What began as a small family affair grew into an occasion on 7 April 2000 organised by North Ayrshire Council. A gathering of those involved took place

The occasion at Saltcoats in Ayrshire on 7 April 2000. Left to right: Ron Bramley, the only living crew member of the four Beauforts of No 22 Squadron which took off to attack the Gneisenau *on 6 April 1941; James Campbell, age 91, elder brother of Kenneth Campbell VC; Wing Commander David A. Simpson, Officer Commanding No 22 Squadron; Bill Brady, holding the Victoria Cross), who was largely responsible for the occasion.* (Author's collection)

The Standard Party of No 22 Squadron at Saltcoats in Ayrshire on 7 April 2000 during the dedication of the plague to Kenneth Campbell VC. (Author's collection)

at the Lauriston Hotel. Among these was a party from No 22 Squadron at RAF Chivenor in North Devon, headed by their Commanding Officer, Wing Commander David Simpson. This had flown up to Saltcoats in Sea King helicopter serial XZ595 and landed in a nearby field.

At the end of the luncheon, Mr James Campbell donated the Victoria Cross to No 22 Squadron, stressing that it must be regarded as an award of all four members of the Beaufort and that it should be held indefinitely by the squadron. In his reply, Wing Commander Simpson stated that it was the only Victoria Cross awarded to any torpedo-bomber squadron in the RAF and that this was the proudest moment in his entire career.

Immediately afterwards, everyone moved to the plaque in the Ness Garden, Saltcoats, where youngsters from the local Air Training Corps were smartly lined up as a guard of honour. Wing Commander Simpson was followed by No 22 Squadron's Standard Party, with the standard bearing the squadron's battle Honours. Then the Deputy Lieutenant, Colonel John Henderson, arrived and inspected the guard of honour. An opening address was given by the Convenor of the North Ayrshire Council, Councillor Sam Taylor. This was followed by the citation in the *London Gazette*, read by Wing Commander Simpson.

The plaque was then unveiled and a prayer of dedication and blessing was given by the Reverend Sandy McCallum. The Sea King helicopter then arrived, flying very slowly with a huge Royal Air Force Ensign fluttering from it, to gasps of admiration from the crowd of onlookers. The ceremony ended with a traditional lament, played on the pipes by Mr Jim Butler.

Ron Bramley and I attended the occasion, on behalf of the Beaufort Aircrews Association. Ron flew as an air gunner in one of the other three Beauforts of No 22 Squadron which took on the operation in which Kenneth Campbell made his attack. We were allowed to handle the Victoria Cross. It seemed surprising modest for the highest British military award for valour, with its plain red ribbon and small cross made from the dull metal of a cannon captured at Balaklava in the Crimean War.

The Victoria Cross was flown in the Sea King helicopter back to No 22 Squadron's headquarters at RAF Chivenor. This squadron has since moved its headquarters to RAF Valley in Anglesey, which is also a training station. One of its pilots in 2011 was Prince William, with the rank of Flight Lieutenant.

The memorial plaque on a wall at Saltcoats in Ayrshire, which was dedicated on 7 April 2000 by the Reverend Sandy McCallum. (Author's collection)

Appendix C

Beaufort Aircrews Association

T hose who flew in RAF Beaufort squadrons and survived the war found that there was little recognition of their activities in official histories, despite their successes in anti-shipping attacks which had helped gain victory in the Battle of the Atlantic as well as immobilise the Axis forces in North Africa. These efforts had been at the expense of a casualty rate which was notoriously the highest of all RAF activities.

Some accounts had appeared in commercial books. The first was *Not Peace but a Sword* written by Wing Commander Pat Gibbs DSO, DFC and Bar, published in 1943; this described his operations in 22 Squadron, which took place before

The Bristol Beaufort II at the Royal Air Force Museum at Hendon, built from parts of aircraft manufactured in Australia. The Secretary of the Beaufort Aircrews Reunion, Eddie Whiston, is standing in front of the machine. (Michael Whiston collection)

he was posted to Malta and eventually led the combined remnants of Beaufort squadrons on numerous attacks. Another was the more general book *The Ship Busters* published in 1947; this was written by Ralph Barker, an air gunner in Beauforts who had become a journalist after the war. Then there was *Beaufort Special* by Bruce Robertson, published in 1976; this was a large-format book based partly on his collection of wartime photographs. Lastly, there were several books concerning anti-shipping operations which included Beauforts, written by myself from research at the Public Record Office coupled with first-hand accounts from survivors.

My books resulted in numerous letters from former aircrew members who served in Beaufort squadrons. Among these correspondents was Eddie Whiston, who had trained as a torpedo pilot in Canada and then joined 217 Squadron in Ceylon when it was equipped with Beauforts, later receiving torpedo-carrying Beaufighters (Torbeaus). He proposed setting up a Beaufort Aircrews Association, together with the assistance of his friend John Porter. The latter had volunteered as RAF aircrew but been turned down since he was somewhat colour-blind; he had also joined 217 Squadron in Ceylon, serving as an electrician.

I passed names and addresses of several Beaufort aircrews to Eddie and he began collecting more names by personal contacts and a notice in *Air Mail*, the periodical circulated by the Royal Air Forces Association. Membership grew rapidly to about a hundred by 1984, although this number included several honorary members who had contributed to the history of Beaufort squadrons. There was no charge for membership, which depended solely on small private donations. Eddie became the secretary while a former torpedo-pilot in 22 and 39 Squadrons, Squadron Leader Norman Hearn-Phillips AFC, DFM, accepted the position of treasurer. I was given the role of chairman.

The first reunion took place in the evening of 1 November 1986 at the Royal Air Force Club in Piccadilly, London. Fifty-four members attended, each paying for his dinner in the club's ballroom, which had been converted for the function. The procedure was similar to that of a 'dining-in night' at an RAF officers' mess, with a Loyal Toast, another to absent friends, and a talk from a distinguished guest speaker. The latter was Wg Cdr Jerry A. Stewart from 42 Squadron, which by then was equipped with Hawker Siddeley Nimrods. The occasion proved a great success. It is unlikely that any of the veterans had discussed their wartime experiences in detail with their families, but there was no such reluctance among former crew members. The whole evening was animated and cheerful.

Roy C. Nesbit in the chair at the
RAF Club in Piccadilly on Saturday
11 November 1989, as Chairman of
the Beaufort Aircrews Association
(Squadron numbers 22, 39, 42, 47,
86, 217).

My functions in these arrangements were to locate and invite the guest speakers, to chair the reunions and then to write newsletters which were printed and circulated by Eddie Whiston. Much of the information in these newsletters was gained from our members. They sometimes included short accounts from members who had been shot down, taken prisoner and later attempted to escape. Perhaps the most dramatic of these was the story of a crew of 217 Squadron from Malta which had been shot off the coast of Greece and picked by Italians in a Cant floatplane. On the following day, when being flown to the Italian mainland, they managed to overpower the Italian crew and fly the Cant to Malta, despite an attack by Spitfires.

The numbers of our association continued to increase, topping 150 by the next year. Our annual reunions were always held at the same venue and continued to be well attended. The guest speaker on the third occasion, held on 5 November 1988, was one of our honorary members, Roger Hayward from the MoD. He had spent much of his spare time compiling a summary of all the Beauforts built as

Part of the first Reunion of the Beaufort Aircrews Association, held on 1 November 1986 at the Royal Air Force Club in Piccadilly, London. (Author's collection)

well as the ultimate fate of each. We were surprised to learn that a large number had been built in Australia and that as many as seventeen RAAF squadrons had operated with them in the South Pacific, where they proved very effective in low-level bombing and torpedo attacks. Moreover, there was a present-day RAAF Beauforts Squadron Association, much larger than our Association, which was engaged on rebuilding a Beaufort to flying condition. Roger's book, entitled *The Beaufort File*, was published in 1990, providing an excellent reference for those interested in the subject.

Our annual reunions and periodic newsletters continued, but Norman Hearn-Phillips died on 19 June 1994. The loss of this immensely experienced and knowledgeable committee member was a sad blow to us, but his function was taken over by Lloyd Morgan, DFM, a pilot in 217 Squadron with whom I had flown on a couple of sorties in 1941. We decided to transfer our reunions to luncheon functions, making travelling simpler for our ageing veterans.

Our reunions and newsletters continued but inevitably our membership dwindled and the health of some of our remaining aircrew members became impaired. The last reunion took place on 22 May 1999 but the newsletters continued, often in increased length and sometimes containing copies of photographs. We were able to report witnessing events such as the presentation of Kenneth Campbell's Victoria Cross to 22 Squadron on 7 April 2000 and the tribute to Coastal Command and its successor formations at Westminster Abbey on 16 March 2004.

With much sadness, we had to announce the death of our committee member John Porter on 8 February 2004, followed by the death of our Secretary Eddie Whiston on 19 August 2004. The function of distributing the newsletters was taken over by Lloyd Morgan. We decided to continue for as long as possible and reported the luncheon at Buckingham Palace on 10 July 2005 to commemorate the 60th anniversary of the end of the Second World War. Then there was the opening of a memorial hangar in Malta 29 September 2005, with a plaque dedicated to crews of the four Beaufort squadrons who lost their lives flying

Three members of a Beaufort crew in 217 Squadron who flew together on two successful low-level bombing operations, photographed at the Royal Air Force Club. Left to right: Lloyd Morgan, DFM (pilot), Roy Nesbit (observer), Ken Reeves (air gunner). (Author's collection)

from the island. This was followed by the adoption of St Eval Church on 16 October 2005 as the spiritual home of the Coastal Command and Maritime Air Association.

Information from our ex-aircrew members began to dwindle over the next few years, as their number declined. By 2009 it became clear that our association could not carry on much longer, with some of these members in their 90s and the others in their late 80s. Similar conditions were happening with the RAAF Beaufort Squadrons Association, which announced in that it would discontinue in May 2010.

With great regret, we wound up our Beaufort Aircrews Association in April 2011 and donated our remaining funds to the Royal Air Forces sssociation. We had been in existence for about twenty-five years. Eddie Whiston's inspiration and drive had rekindled the comradeship of a group of men who had flown in some of the most dangerous RAF activities of the Second World War. It had been well worth while.

Appendix D

Air-Laid Mines and U-boats: Coastal Waters
of Western France

The Type VIID *U-102* left Kiel on 22 June 1940 for its first war cruise, under the command of Kapitänleutnant Harro von Kiet Heydenheldt, and headed for the North Atlantic. It sank two merchant vessels on 20 June and sent its last message thirteen days later when about 100 miles west of Ushant. It was lost some time later with all forty-three crew members. There are no relevant records of attacks by Allied warships or aircraft. It seems possible that it detonated an RAF mine when nearing the French coast.

The Type IXC *U-165* left Kiel on 7 August 1942 on its first war cruise and headed for the Canadian coast, under the command of Korvettenkapitän Eberhard Hoffmann. It sank two merchant vessels and a Canadian patrol yacht, and also damaged four other vessels. It then headed for Lorient but by 28 August had disappeared with all fifty-one crew members. It was believed to have detonated an RAF mine when nearing the port.

The Type IXC *U-171* left Kiel on 17 June 1942 for its first war cruise, under the command of Kapitänleutnant Günther Pfeffer, and headed for the Gulf of Mexico. It sank three large merchant vessels before turning east towards France, but detonated an RAF mine on 8 October when off Lorient. German vessels rescued thirty of the crew, including Pfeffer, but twenty-two were lost.

The Type IXD1 *U-180* left Bordeaux on 22 August 1944 for its second war cruise, after conversion to a transport, bound for Penang under the command of Oberleutnant zur See Rolf Reisen. Its first cruise had taken place from Kiel under, the command of Kapitän zur See Werner Musenberg, during which it had sunk two large merchant vessels off South Africa, handed over the Indian Nationalist leader Chandra Bose to the Japanese submarine *I-29*, and collected valuable war materials. Soon after leaving Bordeaux, it exploded an RAF mine in the Gironde estuary and was lost with all fifty-six crew members.

The Type VIIC *U-263* left La Pallice on 19 January 1944 under the command of Kapitänleutnant Karl Nölke for its second war cruise. It had sunk two merchant vessels on its first cruise but on 22 November 1942 had been badly damaged by Hudsons of 407 (RCAF) Squadron based at St Eval. Extremely lengthy repairs and conversions had then taken place. This second cruise lasted only a few hours, for its sank the following day with the loss of all fifty-one crew members. It was believed to have detonated an RAF mine.

The Type VIIC *U-206* left St-Nazaire on 29 November 1941 for its third war cruise, commanded by Kapitänleutnant Herbert Opitz and bound for the Mediterranean. It had sunk a merchant vessel and an RN corvette on its second cruise, and also rescued six RAF airmen. It disappeared on 30 November and was believed to have detonated an RAF mine. This was confirmed after the war with the discovery of its sunken wreck.

The Type VIIC *U-415* left Brest on 14 July 1944 for its eighth war cruise, commanded by Oberleutnant Herbert Werner. It had sunk two merchant vessels and an RN destroyer on its previous cruises but had been forced to return early on three occasions, once with defects and twice with damage from air and sea attacks. It detonated an RAF mine when outside Brest harbour and sank with the loss of three men, all the others being rescued.

The Type IXC *U-519* left Lorient on 30 January 1943 for its second war cruise, bound for the North Atlantic under the command of Kapitänleutnant Günther Eppen. It disappeared without trace shortly afterwards with the loss of all fifty crew members. Although believed to have been sunk by US air attack, this has now been disproved by post-war research. It seems likely that an RAF mine was the cause of its loss.

The Type IXC/40 *U-526* left Bergen on 11 February 1943 for its first war cruise, under the command of Kapitänleutnant Hans Moglich, to operate in the North Atlantic. It sank no vessels but on 16 April detonated an RAF mine when approaching Lorient, with the loss of forty-two crew members, including Moglich. Twelve other men were rescued by German vessels which included the nearby Type IXC *U-513*.

The Type 1X1/40 *U-547*, commanded by Oberleutnant Heinrich Niemeyer, detonated an RAF mine in the Gironde estuary on 13 August 1944. It had previously completed two war cruises under Fregattenkapitän Kurt Sturm and sunk two merchant vessels as well as an anti-submarine trawler. Damage from the mine did not cause it to sink but resulted in de-commissioning. After repairs, it left Bordeaux on 23 August for home waters and arrived in Marviken six days later. It was finally scrapped at Stettin on 31 December 1944.

The Type VIIC *U-981* completed a war cruise in the North Atlantic under the command of Oberleutnant de Reserve Walter Sitek, and then another in the Bay of Biscay under Oberleutnant Günther Keller, without achieving any sinkings. On 7 August 1944 it left Lorient for Lorient under Keller, heading for La Pallice, but five days later detonated an RAF mine in the Gironde estuary. While still on the surface, it was bombed by a Halifax from 502 Squadron based at St David's in Pembrokeshire. It then sank with the loss of twelve men, but forty survivors including Keller were rescued by the Type VIIC *U-309*, which happed to be nearby on passage from Brest.

Appendix E

Air-Laid Mines and Enemy Surface Vessels: Coastal Waters of Western France

Date	Name	Description	Tonnage	Result	Position
30 Aug 1940	*Vivagel*	Aux. Patrol	1,096	Sunk	E of Cheaveau
5 Sep 1940	Not known	Tug	30	Sunk	Off Lorient
7 Sep 1940	Not known	Fishing vessel	60	Sunk	Off Lorient
23 Sep 1940	*M.1604*	Aux. Minesweeper	474	Sunk	Off Lorient
30 Sep 1940	*Abeille 24*	Tug	361	Sunk	Off Brest
14 Oct 1940	*Euler*	Cargo vessel	1,879	Sunk	4711N 0218W
14 Oct 1940	*Cincour*	Cargo vessel	250	Sunk	Off He de Yeu
19 Nov 1940	*Mourillon*	Tug	50	Sunk	Off Rochfort
7 Jul 1941	*H.S. 209*	Aux. Defence vessel	162	Sunk	Off Lorient
7 Sep 1941	*M.4030*	Aux. Minesweeper	120	Sunk	Off Brest
23 Oct 1941	*M.6*	Minesweeper	750	Sunk	Off Lorient
16 Nov 1941	*Echo*	Navigation vessel	133	Sunk	Off La Pallice
3 Dec 1941	*Flotarde*	Fishing vessel	150	Sunk	Off Lorient
9 May 1942	*Albatros*	Tug	119	Sunk	Off lie d'Oleron
26 May 1942	*Charmeuse*	Fishing vessel	25	Sunk	Off Brest
12 Jun 1942	*M.4212*	Aux. Minesweeper	125	Sunk	4337N 0134W
10 Jul 1942	*M.4401*	Aux. Minesweeper	339	Sunk	4458N 0134W
11 Jul 1942	*Faroud*	Cargo vessel	150	Sunk	Off Belle Ile
3 Aug 1942	*Crepuscule*	Not known	60	Sunk	Off Ile d'Oleron
27 Aug 1942	*Perserverence*	Fishing vessel	57	Sunk	Loire Estuary
30 Sep 1942	*M.4408*	Aux. Minesweeper	264	Damaged	Not known
13 Oct 1942	*Les Balaineaux*	Tug	186	Sunk	Off La Pallice
26 Nov 1942	*NL23 Argus*	Aux. Netlayer	196	Sunk	Loire Estuary
4 Dec 1942	*Bique*	Salvage crane	264	Sunk	4527N 0049W
14 Jan 1943	*Pen Hir*	Tug	120	Sunk	Gironde estuary
6 Mar 1943	*Jeune Marthe*	Not known	75	Sunk	Off lie d'Oleron
14 Jun 1943	*Sperrbrecher 23*	Aux. Mine Destructor Ship	160	Sunk	Off Lorient
17 Jun 1943	*FL.07*	Minesweeper	750	Sunk	Gironde estuary
?? Jul 1943	*Albatros*	Not known	203	Sunk	Not known
?? Jul 1943	*Charles*	Not known	50	Sunk	Not known
?? Jul 1943	*Bordue*	Not known	149	Sunk	Not known
?? Oct 1943	Not known	Fishing vessel	90 or 100	Sunk	Not known
11 Nov 1943	*Dresden*	Cargo vessel	5,567	Damaged	Not known
11 Dec 1943	*V.602*	Aux. Patrol craft	290	Sunk	Not known
?? Dec 1943	*Eifel*	Cargo vessel	1,429	Sunk	Off Lorient

Notes

1. Some details cannot be ascertained from the available enemy records, mainly towards the end of the period.
2. It is probable that the above were sunk or damaged by magnetic mines dropped close to the shorelines by RAF Coastal Command, RAF Bomber Command and the Fleet Air Arm. However, horned mines were laid by the Royal Navy and magnetic mines by Allied submarines, all further out to sea. It is possible that some of the enemy vessels were struck by these.

Researched by aviation and naval historian Roger Hayward.

Appendix F

St Eval Church

S unday 1 October 1989 was a remarkable day for some of us who had served at RAF St Eval, as well as for many parishioners and guests who gathered at their church for a service of dedication.

St Eval Church was perhaps unique in that, when work began on the new Coastal Command airfield in 1938, it stood on a mound which was incorporated within the station boundaries. This church then continued to play a part in the life of the station until the latter was closed down on 6 March 1959 and its activities were transferred to nearby RAF St Mawgan.

The Parish Church of St Eval, near Padstow in Cornwall, was originally built in Norman times. It stood within the boundary of RAF St Eval from the opening of the station on 2 October 1939 to its closure on 6 March 1959. This photograph was taken on 21 July 1973. It was refurbished as an RAF Church by local parishioners and dedicated at a service on 1 October 1989. (St Eval Church)

The church dated back to Norman times but was rebuilt in the thirteenth century, although some of the original stonework remains today. The tower fell down in 1700 but was restored a few years later by Bristol merchants, being whitewashed to act as a landmark for mariners sailing along the rocky coast of north Cornwall. The church then gradually deteriorated once more until another restoration around 1889. In this form, it eventually became a landmark for RAF aircrews returning from their sorties.

The new RAF station opened on 2 October 1939 and became one of the largest and best-known of Coastal Command's bases, housing numerous RAF squadrons and even USAF groups. Many types of aircraft flew from it, including Ansons, Beauforts, Blenheims, Halifaxes, Hudsons, Hurricanes, Lancasters, Liberators, Mosquitos, Sea Otters, Shackletons, Spitfires, Warwicks, Whirlwinds and Whitleys. During the Second World War, strikes were often flown against enemy ports, warships, blockade runners and coastal convoys. Photo reconnaissance sorties also took place from the airfield, meteorological aircraft flew far out into the Atlantic, long-range fighters sought German aircraft, anti-submarine aircraft hunted U-boats, and search-and-rescue operations were carried out.

With all this activity, casualties were heavy at times, from sorties, accidents and enemy bombing attacks. In 1988, Squadron Leader Jim Greenaway MBE, who had served on the station during the war, made a donation to start an appeal for an RAF memorial to commemorate these losses. The appeal fund was then coordinated by the Rector of St Eval Church, the Reverend Bryan Gadd, together with the C of E Chaplain of RAF St Mawgan, Padre Edward Core.

It had been met with an astonishing response, from the small but generous local parish, from RAF stations and associations, and even from abroad. Unhappily, Jim had died at the end of 1988, but not before he knew his appeal had been successful.

The fund was able to provide more than a single memorial. A stained glass window for the Lady Chapel had been commissioned from Mr Crear McCartney, a Scottish artist who had served in RAF Transport Command. A memorial plaque was erected and Squadron Badges were purchased. In addition, a Book of Remembrance was in course of research and preparation, to contain the names of all those who had lost their lives at St Eval or flying from the station.

Applications from those who wished to attend the service of dedication on 1 October 1989 had been so numerous that they had to be chosen by ballot. The church could seat only 200, but a large marquee had been erected outside to seat another 300, with the service relayed to this additional congregation. When

The stained glass Memorial Window at St Eval Church was commissioned from Crear McCartney. It includes the badge of Coastal Command with its motto 'Constant Endeavour' as well as the badge and representation of the Church and the motto 'Faith in our Task'. The stained glass includes the RAF's colour blue and the RAF motto 'Per Ardua ad Astra'. The RAF Search and Rescue theme is represented by 'De Profundis Clamavi' (Out of the Depths have I cried to thee, O Lord). (St Eval Church)

the RAF decides to mount a ceremony, the results are always impressive. The winding pathway to the church entrance was lined by airmen and airwomen, spaced out in pairs facing each other. As groups of guests passed between them, each pair snapped to attention. These guests included representatives of the governments of Canada, Australia, New Zealand and the United States, as well as members of various RAF associations. The date had been chosen as the 100th anniversary of the restoration of the church. It also commemorated exactly 50 years of the existence of RAF St Eval.

The interior of the small church had been refurbished, partly from the appeal fund, and looked beautiful. The first lesson was read by the Church Warden, Mr Warwick Cowling, and the second by the Officer Commanding RAF St Mawgan, Group Captain C.T. Moore. A sermon was then delivered by the Chaplain-in-Chief of the RAF, The Venerable B.N. Halfpenny, and a description of the stained glass window was read by Mr David Pugh. The patron of the fund, Lord Shackleton, who had served as an intelligence officer at RAF St Eval, unveiled the memorial plaque, and the Dedication was delivered by the Lord Bishop of

The official badge of RAF St Eval, containing a representation of St Eval Church and the motto 'Faith in our Task'. The Church was always a landmark for crews of the squadrons who flew from the station. (St Eval Church)

Truro, The Right Reverend Peter Mumford. A bugler then sounded the Last Post, followed by Reveille. The Intercession was led by Chaplains of the RAF. After the National Anthem, The Blessing was given by the Bishop. An hour later, there was a flypast by a Nimrod Mark II from RAF St Mawgan.

There remained the matter of the Book of Remembrance, which had not been compiled at the time this service took place. In our Beaufort Aircrews Association, we had been aware of this need well in advance, partly from the local resident Roy Dunstan who, in his youth, had witnessed many landings and take-offs from St Eval and was one of our Honorary Members. In September 1988 our Secretary, Eddie Whiston, had urged me to undertake the work of researching the material, in the knowledge that I had spent several years examining RAF records in the Public Record Office (PRO).

I was willing to undertake this voluntary work but was under contract with publishers at the time and first had to fulfil these obligations. All I could do in the interim was to write to the Chaplain at RAF St Mawgan, The Reverend Edward Core, who was supervising the preparation. My letter enclosed a sizeable cheque from our association as a contribution to the cost of artwork in the Book of Remembrance. It also set out a method of carrying out the research. The outcome was a reply authorising our Treasurer, Norman Hearn-Phillips, AFC, DFM and myself as our Chairman, to act on behalf of the St Eval Memorial.

The problem of research was unusual in that it depended initially on the Operations Record Book (ORB) of RAF St Eval, rather the records of a single squadron. I knew from practical experience that this book, although of major importance to RAF researchers, was not perfect. Like many other war diaries, it was compiled from information gathered in extremely difficult and stressful conditions. Names of those who 'failed to return' could be misspelt while others were not recorded at all. Although likely to be accurate with those squadrons based on the station, there were many other squadrons on temporary attachment and their losses might not be included, although the names would have been passed to

IN THIS BOOK

ARE RECORDED

THE NAMES OF THOSE

WHO LOST THEIR LIVES

WHILE SERVING

AT R·A·F St EVAL

DURING THE SECOND

WORLD WAR

The RAF Book of Remembrance at St Eval Church was worked on by Mrs Wendy Selby of Newquay, a Fellow of the Society of Scribes and Illuminators, and dedicated at the Battle of Britain Service on 20 September 1992. (St Eval Church)

their parent stations. Thus the records of many other squadrons would also have to be examined, and in turn these might not be perfect. It was also possible that some ground staff at St Eval had been killed accidentally or by enemy bombs, and their names had been missed.

One other major problem was that units of the US Eighth Air Force and US Navy Air Force flew from St Eval in 1943, and their records were not in the PRO. Fortunately this matter was resolved by Bernard J. Stevens, who had specialist knowledge of this subject and volunteered to research the losses from American records.

Norman and I thus concentrated solely on RAF losses, from documents in the Public Record Office plus numerous checks with the Air Historical Branch (RAF) at the Ministry of Defence and the Commonwealth War Graves Commission. In September 1990 we were able to present a preliminary list of dates, names, service numbers and units to St Eval Church. By then we had examined over 2,000 names and the list contained over 700 of these, including the US personnel. However, we could not be absolutely sure that we had identified every name, and we suggested that provision for an addendum be provided in the Book of Remembrance, in case more names came to light. Indeed, more were discovered over the next two years, by which time the names totalled 823.

In the meantime, The Reverend John G. Slee at RAF St Mawgan and his committee had appointed Mrs Wendy Selby, a Fellow of the Society of Scribes and Illuminators, to work on the calligraphy of the Book, which also included colour copies of squadron badges etc. A service on Battle of Britain Day, Sunday 20 September 1992, was chosen as the day of acceptance of the book into St Eval Church. Both Norman and I were present on the occasion.

Pages in the book could not be photocopied but eventually all were photographed by the Photographic Unit at RAF St Mawgan. Negatives were then held so that prints could be provided for relatives of the fallen, many of whom visited St Eval Church.

In January 1999 I made an unexpected discovery while researching another matter. In August 1942 a detachment of Lancasters from 81 Squadron, Bomber Command, was detached to RAF St Eval from their base at RAF Wyton in Huntingtonshire, in order to join in the war against U–Boats operating from ports in western France. Four of these Lancasters failed to return and all twenty-eight crew members lost their lives. There was no reference to this detachment in the St Eval records. I passed this information on to the Revd John Slee at RAF St Mawgan and suggested that these names should be included in an Addendum.

I then received a letter from Frank Harper, a former flight engineer with 83 Pathfinder Squadron, who had written a book about this squadron which included a Roll of Honour listing 886 airmen killed. He and his wife had moved to Cornwall in 1977 and he had embarked on a mammoth programme of researching all RAF aircraft lost from Cornwall and Devon, eventually finding 2,986 airmen killed. Of these, 152 names were not in the lists provided to Norman and myself. Another fund had been set up to list all these additional names. When the calligraphy was complete, the Book of Remembrance and its Addendum seemed to contain all the names that it was possible to research.

On Sunday 2005 a special service was held at St Eval Church. This was packed and every seat was taken. The occasion was to mark the adoption by the Coastal Command and Maritime Air Association of this parish church as its spiritual home, the Chairman of the Association, Air Commodore Andrew Neal AFC, was escorted to the chancel steps by the churchwardens, who were asked by the Rector if they were willing to accept this proposal. They replied 'We are willing and we welcome them into the parish church in the hope they will regard it as their own.'

Later, the Venerable Brian Lucas, Archdeacon Emeritus of the RAF, gave an address and dedicated the Book of Remembrance.

Appendix G

Memorial at Westminster Abbey

For several years, the Maritime Air Trust under the patronage of the Duke of Edinburgh had worked on a project to prepare a memorial to those who served in Royal Air Force Coastal Command and its successor formations. This was named 'Project Constant Endeavour' in recognition of Coastal Command's motto. It culminated on 16 March 2004 with a service of thanksgiving and the dedication of a Tribute at Westminster Abbey. Among those present were Prince Michael of Kent, High Commissioners, Ambassadors, visiting dignitaries and veterans of the Second World War with their relatives and friends.

I was one of those invited to attend and arrived with my guest, Mrs Jane Cowderoy. The Abbey became packed, with every seat taken, but we were fortunate in being allotted seats Al and A2 in the front row, and thus had an

The relief carving dedicated to RAF Coastal Command in the South Cloister of Westminster Abbey.

REMEMBER THE SACRIFICE & CONSTANT ENDEAVOUR IN DEFENCE OF FREEDOM
OF THE MEN AND WOMEN OF THE ROYAL AIR FORCE COASTAL COMMAND, THEIR SUCCESSORS &
THEIR COMRADES IN THE COMMONWEALTH, ALLIED AND OVERSEAS SQUADRONS

excellent view of the ceremony. The Tribute in the south cloister had already been unveiled by The Queen, accompanied by the Duke of Edinburgh. This is a relief carving in light grey Carrara marble depicting the sky and sea, overlaying an outline of the world above a breaking sea. An eagle depicts mastery of the sky, with the badge of Coastal Command as a watermark. The legend of undulating letters represents the rhythm of the sea. The span is about eight feet.

The Dean of Westminster began the service of dedication. There were addresses from Air Chief Marshal Sir John Barraclough and then from Her Majesty. The Queen's Colour for the Royal Air Force and the Sovereign's Colour for the Royal Auxiliary Air Force were borne through the Abbey and received at the altar. The Book of Remembrance, which had been carefully prepared and contained 10,875 names, was borne to the alter by veterans; it had already been dedicated by the Dean of Liverpool at the Battle of the Atlantic Service in May 2003. There were sermons, hymns, an Act of Remembrance, the Last Post, Reveille and the National Anthem. The Choir of the Abbey and the Central Band of the Royal Air Force were magnificent throughout the Service of Thanksgiving

After the Royal Party had left, the members of the congregation filed out through the South Cloister, where we were able to review the Tribute carving. There was then a flypast at 12.55 hours by a Hawker Siddeley Nimrod of No 206 Squadron from RAF Kinloss in Morayshire and two Panavia Tornados of No 9 Squadron from RAF Lossiemouth in the same county. They arrived precisely on time, in bright clear weather but silhouetted under thin cloud.

Appendix H

Roll of Honour No 217 Squadron

15 November 1939

Sgt Berwick, Ernest A., 515587, RAF, Snettisham (St Mary) Churchyard, Norfolk

31 January 1940

Cpl Ferris, Ernest A., 561539, RAF, Age 29, Plymouth Old Cemetery

6 February 1940

LAC Marsden, Herbert J.N., 528828, RAF, Runnymede Memorial, Panel 23

Flg Off White, John A.C., 39406, RAF, Age 24, Runnymede Memorial, Panel 6

Plt Off Wright, Arthur H.M., 41643, RAF, Age 23, Runnymede Memorial, Panel 10

11 August 1940

Plt Off Coulman, Richard M., 41557, RAF, Runnymede Memorial, Panel 7

Plt Off Gordon-Peiniger, Anthony, 40904, RAF, Age 26, Runnymede Memorial, Panel 8

Sgt Hopperton, Edgar, 625352, RAF, Age 20, Runnymede Memorial, Panel 15

Sgt Mellody, Eric K., 969831, RAFVR, Runnymede Memorial, Panel 17

7 December 1940

Plt Off Brooks, George H., 78459, RAFVR, Age 20, Hospital-Camfrout Cemetery, Finistère

Sgt Eede, Thomas J.G., 527729, RAF, Age 33, Hospital-Camfrout Cemetery,

Flg Off Mussenden, Hugh E., 41198, RAF, Age 23, Hospital-Camfrout Cemetery

Sgt Pratt, John W, 627713, RAF, Age 20, Hospital-Camfrout Cemetery

17 December 1940

Sgt Matthews. Douglas A.G., 566240, RAF, Age 24, La Trinité-Sur-Wa: Cemetery, Morbihan

18 December 1940
Sgt Postill, Henry E., 546900, RAF, Runnymede Memorial, Panel 18

20 December 1940
Sgt Milligan, Peter, 629402, RAF, Age 23, Lanester Communal Cemetery, Morbihan
Sgt Plant, WilliamS., 620004, RAF, Age 25
Sgt Tiplady, Charles M., 745261, RAFVR
Plt Off Webb, Nelson, H., DFM, 44594, Age 23

24 December 1940
Flg Off Robertson, Robert A., 76463, RAFVR, Age 23, Glasgow (Lambhill) Cemetery

26 December 1940
Sgt Bradshaw, Robert A. 905929, RAFVR
Sgt Miflin, William B., 550750, RAF, Age 21
Flg Off Tllson. John H.D., 42030, RAF, Age 23
Sgt Wild, Joseph C., 751369, RAFVR, Age 29

27 December 1940
LAC Hoffen, John G., 537498, RAF, Age 22

25 January 1941
AC2 Penberthy, Frederick G.E., 622890, RAF
AQ Colman, Richard P., 617159, RAF
AC2 Martin, Bigar F, 1188084, RAFVR
AC2 Brough, Herbert, 1012040, RAF
AC1 Yost, Marvin A.G., 654271, RAF, Age 19

1 February 1941
Pornic War Cemetery, Loire-Atlantique
Runnyroede Memorial, Panel 23
Plymouth Old Cemetery
St Eval Churchyard, Cornwall m ii ii
Stoke-on-Trent (Hartshill) Cemetery Stroud New Cemetery, Gloucestershire
Sgt Browning, William S.R., 755933, RAFVR, Runnymede Memorial, Panel 40

Sgt Croker, Arthur J., 527G30, RAF, Age 23, Runnymede Memorial, Panel 41

Sgt Hayman, Arthur G., 580515, RAF, Runnymede Memorial, Panel 44

Flt Lt Oakley, Richard R. A.215, RAAF, Age 23, Phen-Les-Guines Cemetery, Pas de Calais

Sgt O'Byrne, Thomas P., 743014, RAFVR, Age 30, Runnymede Memorial, Panel 49

Sgt Rowley, Kenneth G., 755531, RAFVR, Age 26, Runnymede Memorial, Panel 51

Sgt Rutherford, John B., 519262, RAF, Age 24, Runnymede Memorial, Panel 51

Sgt Wood, John A.D., 623845, RAF, Runnymede Memorial, Panel 55

15 February 1941

Sgt Abbott, William N., 903156, RAF, Age 22, Lannilis Cemetery, Finistère

Sgt Beeden, Arthur W.R., 552724, RAF, Age 18, Lannilis Cemetery, Finistère

Sgt Cowling, Henry, 526616, RAF, Runnymede Memorial, Panel 41

Flg Off Gair, Ronald W., 36171, RAF, Age 22, Lannilis Cemetery, Finistère

Sgt Pusey, Norman V., 58055, RAF, Runnymede Memorial, Panel 50

Sgt Sheridan, James F.J., 905697, RAFVR, Age 25, La Forest Churchyard, Finistère

Sgt Thompson, Joseph, 526413, RAF, Age 23, Runnymede Memorial, Panel 53

Plt Off Williams, Cilmyn G.L., DHl, 45542, Age 30, Runnymede Memorial, Panel 35

18 February 1941

Sgt Webster, Joseph R.H., 958761, RAF, Lannilis Cemetery, Finistère.

13 May 1941

Sgt Ellwood, Dermot E.R. 745448, RAFVR, Age 20, Bayeux Cemetery, Calvados

Flt Sgt Hardwick, Gerald T., 581334, RAF, Age 19

10 June 1941

Flt Sgt Hollely, Peter P., 742265, RAFVR, Age 22, Flint (St Mary) Churchyard, Flintshire

Sgt McIvor, Cyril G.J, 615917, RAF, Runnymede Memorial, Panel 47

Sgt Perrins, Philip T., 974123, RAFVR, Age 19, Runnymede Memorial, Panel 50

Sgt Whadcoat, Kenneth J., 957278, Age 22, Runnymede Memorial, Panel 54

17 June 1941

Flg Off Eyre, John AD, 43359, RAF, Age 33, Urchfont Cemetery, Wiltshire

18 June 1941

Sgt Garbutt, Fred, 992261, RAFVR, Age 26, Runnymede Memorial, Panel 43

Sgt Gosden, Anthony, 916773, RAFVR, Age 20, Pornic Cemetery, Loire-Atlantique

Sgt Hollinghurst, Edmund, 922334, RAFVR, Age 25, Lacanau-Medoc Cemetery, Gironde

Sgt Norris, John D., 957339, RAFVR, Runnymede Manorial, Panel 49

21 June 1941

Sgt Chesterman, Eric, 901481, RAFVR, St Charles de Percy Cemetery, Calvados

Flg Off Welsh, John, 43122, RAF, St Martin de-Re Cemetery, Charente-Maritime

Wheat, Walter J.P., 982331, RAFVR, Runnymede Memorial, Panel 54

17 July 1941

Flt Lt Kerr, Thomas F., 41588, RAF, Pornic Cemetery, Loire-Atlantique

Sgt Allan D. Scott, 401234, RNZAF, Escoubac-La-Boule Cemetery, Loire-Atlantique

Flg Off Whitehead, Eric G., 79200, RAFVR, Age 35

Sgt Windle, Alec, 942630, RAFVR, Age 23

25 July 1941

Sgt Appleby, Alaric J., 949210, RAFVR, Age 25, Runnymede Memorial, Panel 38

11 August 1941

Flt Sgt Qhiplin, Arthur, 746770, RAFVR, Age 28, Runnymede Memorial, Panel 35

21 August 1941

Flt Off Graham, Peter F.R., ISC, 89363, RAFVR

Sgt Marshall, Ralph, 1304739, RAFVR, Age 25

Sgt Williams, Edgar A.C., 39406, RAF, RAFVR, Age 26, Runnymede Memorial, Panel 54

Plt Off Stockley, John A.V., 62677, RAFVR, Age 21, Escoublac-La-Baule Cemetery, Loire-Atlantique

17 September 1941

Flt Lt Carleton, Ridley C, 70846, RAF, Age 28, Lytham St Anne's Cemetery, Lancashire

26 September 1941

Sgt Carter, Harold L., 1162321, RAFVR, Age 25, Lewisham Cemetery, London

Plt Off Harrison, James R., 89822, RAF, Farnborough Churchyard, Kent

Plt Off Opperman, Paul F., 100561, RAFVR, Age 19, Rowde (St Matthew) Churchyard, Wilts

Sgt Ryder, Dennis A., 1255613, RAFVR, Age 21, Enfield Crematorium, Middlesex

28 September 1941

Sgt Ball, Joseph W., 940028, RAFVR, Age 22, Runnymede Memorial, Panel 39

Sgt Sapwell, Selwyn C.E., 401216, RNZAF, Runnymede Memorial, Panel 64

Plt Off Griffiths, Walter S.P., 61267, RAFVR, Age 21, La Gueriniere Cemetery, Vendée

Sgt Suggett, Edward D., 759265, RAFVR, Age 25, Pornic Cemetery, Loire-Atlantique

11 October 1941

Sgt Earl, Charles E., 923291, RAFVR, Age 35, Runnymede Memorial, Panel 42

Sgt Perry, Kenneth W., 918534, RAFVR, Runnymede Memorial, Panel 50

Sgt Thomsen, Carl C., R/60289, RCAF, Age 31, Runnymede Memorial, Panel 62

10 November 1941

Sgt Ankin, Peter L., 748362, RAFVR, Age 21, Cambridge Crematorium

Flt Sgt Wicks, Dudley R., 581367, RAF, Age 20, Reading Cemetery, Berkshire

Sgt Smith. Albert A.. 1152244. RAFVR. Age 25, Stone Cemetery, Staffordshire

Sgt Shield, Cuthbert E., 959713, RAFVR, Age 26, Belford (St Mary) Churchyard, Northumberland

15 November 1941

Sgt Childs, Frank, 955494, RAFVR, Age 21, Bergen General Cemetery, Netherlands

Sgt Heald, Douglas L., 942529, RAFVR, Age 23,

Sqn Ldr Halley, George C, 75362, RAFVR, Age 32, Runnymede Memorial, Panel 28, Runnymede Memorial, Panel 33

Plt Off Mrlean, Charles, 60787, RAFVR

25 November 1941

Sgt Gill, Mervyn, 1181624, RAFVR, Age 20, Brest (Kerfaustras) Cemetery, Finistère

Sgt Griffiths, John R., 1013752, RAFVR

Sgt Boyd Orr, Noel, 1053586, RAFVR, Age 19, Runnymede Memorial, Panel 40

9 December 1941

Plt Off Lee, Mark, 89826, RAFVR, Age 21, Ameland (Nes) Cemetery, Netherlands

Sgt Carter, Henry, 1311031, RAFVR, Runnymede Memorial, Panel 41

Sgt Chadaway, John A. 755149, RAFVR, Age 22, Runnymede Memorial, Panel 41

Flt Sgt Foster, John A., R/58108, RCAF, Age 29, Runnymede Memorial, Panel 60

6 January 1942

Sgt Voy, Eric A. 1258671, RAFVR, Age 30, Charing (Kent County) Crematorium

12 February 1942

Flt Lt Finch, Arthur J.H., EEC, RAF, 39937, Runnymede Memorial, Panel 65

Flt Sgt Fyfe, David Y., 749346, RAFVR, Age 27, Runnymede Memorial, Panel 83

Sgt Hammersley, Basil W., 751236, RAFVR, Age 22, Runnymede Memorial, Panel 84

Flt Sgt Jackson, Albert H.L., 403778, RNZAF, Age 31, Runnymede Memorial, Panel 117

Sgt McNeill, Thorns, 1355426, RAFVR, Runnymede Memorial, Panel 89

Flt Lt White, Matthew, 42928, RAF, Age 21, Hook of Holland Cemetery

Flt Sgt Goldsmith, Hedley A., 957745, RAFVR, Age 25, The Hague (Westduin) Cemetery

Flt Sgt Wilson, John A., 749369, RAFVR, Age 21

8 March 1942

Sgt Hayhurst, Jack, 1122493, RAFVR, Age 21, Rawtenstall Cemetery, Lancs

Sgt Humphrys, Leslie F., 1189555, RAFVR, Fettercairn Cemetery, Kincardineshire

Sgt Stephens, Roy W.G., 1376366, RAFVR, Age 20, Golders Green Crematorium, Middx

Sgt Tofield, Cyril, 1012769, RAFVR, Age 21, Failsworth Jewish Cemetery, Lancs

15 March 1942

Sgt Foulkes. Leslie R., 1100664, RAFVR, Age 22, Manchester Southern Cemetery, Lans

Sgt Harvey, Alexander G., 1325317, RAFVR, Age 32, Runnymede Memorial, Panel 85

Sgt Leaver, Alfred J., 1169627, RAFVR, Age 20, Wigston Lynn Cemetery, Norfolk

Sgt Rout, Sydney J., 116353, RAFVR,

1 April 1942

Wg Cdr Boal, Samuel M., DFC, 37713, RAF, Runnymede Memorial, Panel 64

Sgt Clarke, John S., 953786, RAFVR, Runnymede Memorial, Panel 80

10 June 1942

Sgt Norman, Denis W., 1169618, RAFVR, Malta (Capuccini) Naval Cemetery

20 June 1942

Sgt Bowyer, Joseph A., 923861, RAFVR, Age 21, Alamein Memorial, Egypt, Column 250

Sgt King, Walter A.R., 1226209, RAFVR, Alamein Memorial, Column 261

Flg Off Minster, Frank J.R.T., 63431, RAFVR, Age 22, Alamein Memorial, Column 248

Sgt Moschonas, John, 1377375, RAFVR, Age 19, Alamein Memorial, Column 262

21 June 1942

Sqn Ldr Lynn, Robert G., DFC, 41041, RAF, Malta Memorial, Panel 2, Column 1

Sgt Connell, Jack, 1075371, RAFVR, Age 21, Alamein Memorial, Egypt, Column 250

Sgt Smyth, William D., 1167711, RAFVR, Age 20, Alamein Memorial, Column 262

Sgt Walls, Fred H., 1063090, RAFVR, Age 22, Tripoli War Cemetery, Lybia

22 June 1942

Sgt Frith, Tom, 978528, RAFVR, Age 24, Tripoli War Cemetery, Libya

3 July 1942

Sgt Davis, Denis M., 923060, RAFVR, Malta Memorial, Panel 3, Column 2

Sgt Eennis, Frederick K., 959648, Age 25, Panel 2, Malta Memorial, Column 2

Sgt Hodson, George L., 1259043, RAFVR, Age 19, Alamein Memorial, Panel 4, Column 1

Sgt Hole, Harold, 1186282, RAFVR, Age 29, Alamein Memorial, Panel 4, Column 1

Sgt Hutcheson, James, 1115654, RAFVR, Age 30, Alamein Memorial, Panel 4, Column 1

Sgt Mercer, Russell G., 1179715, RAFVR, Age 21, Alamein Memorial, Panel 4, Column 1

Sgt Weaver, Frank S., 4G4713, RNZAF, Age 26, Alamein Memorial, Panel 5, Column 2

Sgt York, Leonard A., 952913, RAFVR, Age 22, Alamein Memorial, Panel 4, Column 2

22 July 1942

Sgt Wallworth, Jack N., 1288982, RAFVR, Age 36, Malta (Capuccini) Cemetery

9 October 1942

Flt Sgt McGrath, William W., 900875, RAFVR. Age 20, (Lost in SS *Laconia*, sunk by *U-156*) Alamein Memorial, Column 250

29 January 1943

Plt Off Lambert, Stanley E., 123443, RAF, Age 28, Columbo (Kanatte) Cemetery, Sri Lanka

Flg Off O'Brien, William P.G., 60852, RAFVR, Age 30,
Flt Sgt Thompson, Ronald P., 905134, RAFVR, Age 22,
Flg Off Ward, John G., 117660, RAFVR, Age 30,

25 February 1943
Sgt Davies, William R., 536210, RAF, Age 27, Kirkee War Cemetery, India

28 March 1943
LAC Drake, Felix A., 984612, RAFVR, Age 23, Kandy War Cemetery, Sri Lanka

30 April 1943
Flt Sgt Lansdale, Bomb RJ3., 951026, RAFVR, Age 22, Columbia (Kanatee)
    Cemetery, Sri Lanka

26 August 1943
Flg Off Lund, Richard, 125152, RAFVR, Age 21, Singapore Memorial, Column
    432
Sgt Plows, Frank, 1307375, RAFVR, Age 23, Singapore Memorial, Column 426
Flg Off Wallis, Stanley G., 120342, RAFVR, Singapore Memorial, Column 424
Sgt Walmsley, Philip, 1188194, RAFVR, Age 26, Singapore Memorial, Column
    426

19 September 1944
Flg Off Ballantyne, Alexander F., 169868, RAF, Age 25, Arnhem Oosterbeek
    Cemetery, Netherlands

7 December 1944
AC1 Irvin, Charles, 1083159, RAFVR, Age 22, Trincomalee War Cemetery, Sri
    Lanka

11 October 1945
Flg Off Jackson, James C, 196031, RAFVR, Age 22, Kirkee War Cemetery, India
Flt Lt Pratt, Robert E., 151673, RAFVR, Age 23

Notes

1. This has been compiled from a list provided by the Commonwealth War Graves Commission, but rearranged in chronological order.
2. Names and addresses of next-of-kin have not been included.
3. Ages are not available in many instances.
4. Those listed in Alamein Memorial, Malta Memorial, Singapore Memorial and Runnymede Memorial have 'No Known Graves'.
5. Ranks have been abbreviated as follows:

Wg Cdr	Wing Commander
Sqn Ldr	Squadron Leader
Flt Lt	Flight Lieutenant
Flg Off	Flying Officer
Plt Off	Pilot Officer
Flt Sgt	Flight Sergeant
Sgt	Sergeant
Cpl	Corporal
LAC	Leading Aircraftman
AC1	Aircraftman First Class
AC2	Aircraftman Second Class

Bibliography

Ashworth, Chris, *RAF Coastal Command*, Sparkford, Patrick Stephens Ltd, 1992.

Barker, Ralph, *The Ship Busters*, London, Pan Books Ltd, 1957.

Barnett, Correlli, *Engage The Enemy More Closely*, London, Penguin Books Ltd, 2000.

Décamps, Pierre, *Bordeaux sous l'Occupation*, Rennes, Ouest-France, 1983.

Bertin, François, *Saint-Nazaire sous l'Occupation*, Rennes: Ouest-France, 1989.

Bohn, Roland, *Raids Aériens sur La Bretagne durant La Seconde Guerre Mondiale, Tome 1*, Bannalec, 1997.

——, *Raids Aériens sur La Bretagne durant La Seconde Guerre Mondiale, Tome 2*, Bannalec, 1998.

Dunstan, Roy, *My Life with RAF St Eval*, Privately printed.

Extrade, Serge and Lachaise, Francis, *La Rochelle au quotidien sous la botte (juin 1940–juin 1941)*
——, ABC DIF Editions, 2004.

Gilbert, Martin, *Churchill – A Life*, London, Minerva, 1994.

Gildea, Robert, *Marianne in Chains*, New York, Picador, 2004.

Hayward, Roger, *The Beaufort File*, Tonbridge, Air Britain Ltd, 1990.

Kersaudy, François, *Churchill and De Gaulle*, London, Collins, 1981.

Le Berd, Jean, *Lorient sous l'Occupation*, Rennes, Ouest-France, 1987.

McNeill, Ross, *Royal Air Force Coastal Command Losses of the Second World War, Volume 1*, Hinckley: Midland Publishing, 2003.

Middlebrook, Martin and Everitt, Chris, *The Bomber Command War Diaries*, London, Penguin Books, 1990.

Nesbit, Roy Conyers, *Woe to the Unwary*, London, William Kimber, 1981.

——, *Torpedo Airmen*, London, William Kimber, 1983.

——, *Reported Missing: Lost Airmen of the Second World War*, Barnsley, Pen & Sword Books Ltd, 2009.

Péron, François, *Brest sous l'Occupation*, Rennes, Ouest-France, 1981.

Rawlings, John D.R., *Coastal, Support and Special Squadrons of the RAF and their Aircraft*, London, Jane's Publishing Co. Ltd, 1982.

Richards, Denis, *Royal Air Force 1939–1945, Volume 1*, London, HMSO, 1953.

——, and Saunders, Hilary St G., *Royal Air Force 1939–1945, Volume 2*, London, HMSO, 1975.

Tams, F.A.B., *A Trenchard 'Brat'*, Bishop Auckland, The Pentland Press Ltd, 2000.

Index

Page numbers in *italics* refer to illustrations.

Admiral Hipper, 60, 60–1, 64, 70–1
Admiralty, the, 39, 61, 104, 109, 165, 172, 173
Afrika Korps, the 24, 197
Air Mail (publication), 217
Air Ministry, the 21, 74, 212
Air Publication 1234, 67
Air Publication 1528, 67
Albacore, Fairey, 176
Aldis lamp, 5, 72, 157, 211
Aldridge, Plt Off Arthur H., vi, *159*, 160, *160*, 197–8, *199*
Alexandria, 197, 199
Altmark class, 164
Anderson, Wg Cdr L.H., 37–8, 41
Ankin, Sgt Peter L., 154, 239
Anson, Avro, *11*, 12, 21, 23, *24*, 24–8, 36–9, *40*, 42, 47, 54, 131, 175, 228
Appleby, Sgt Alaric J., 130, 238
Arado Ar 196A, 115, *116*, 127
Ardennes, the 7, 29
Ark Royal, HMS, 112–13, *113*, *114*, 118
'Armed Rovers', 81, 85
Associated Institute of Bankers, 2
ASV radar, *149*, 153, *153*, 159, 168, 170, *196*
Athenia, 25
Atherstone, HMS, 180
Austin, Sgt S.J., 132
Ayr, 7
Ayres, Sgt Charles, 47

Baghdad, 203
Bahrein, 203
Balaklava, 215
Ball, Sgt Joseph W., 147, 239
Bangalore, 204
Bank of England, the, 1, 2
Banning, Sgt, 122
'Barbarossa', Operation, 94
Barcelona, 47
Barker, Ralph, 217

Barraclough, ACM Sir John, 234
Battle, Fairey, 14–15, *15*, *16*
Battle of Britain, the, 8, 32, 37, 39
BBC, the, 32, 82, *111*, 141, 147
Beachy Head, 168
Beattie, Lt-Com Stephen H., 180, 181, 183
Beaufort Aircrews Association, 122, 215, 216–21
Belle-Ile, 147
Bennet, Sgt William, 95–6, 98n
Bergen, 103, 165, 223
Betasom, 42
Bismarck, 103–20, *103*, *105*, *106*, *120*, 127, 173
Blavet, river, 134
Bletchley Park, 119, 176
Blitzkrieg, 7, 31, 32, 94
Boal, Wg Cdr Samuel M., 175, *195*, 196–7, 241
Bohn, Roland, 64n
Bolland, Wg Cdr Guy A., 39, 61, *62*, 71, 119–20
Bombay, 204
Bombsight, Course-Setting, 12, 15–17, *17*, 58, *58*
Bordeaux, 31, 32, 35, 42, 47, *48*, 49, 51, 138, 186, *188*, 189, 191–2, 222, 223
Boulogne-Billancourt, 178
Bower, Wg Cdr Leslie W.C., 71, 84, 143, 150, 152, 164
Bowhill, ACM Sir Frederick W., 19, *19*, 122
Brady, Wg Cdr G.R., 209
Brady, William, 213, *213*
Bramley, Ron, *213*, 215
Brest, 32, 33, *34*, 38, 39, *45*, 47, 49, *60*, 61–4, 70, 71, 72–3, 74–81, *74*, *75*, *77*, *79*, 82, 85, *89*, 91–2, 93–6, 98, 103, 110, 116, 119, 121–2, 123, 129, 136, 138, 148, 149, 155, 165, *165*, *166*, 168, 172, 178, 187, 189–91, 223, 224

Briare, 31
Briggs, Fg Off Dennis A., *111*, 112
Bristol, 21
British Expeditionary Force, 29
Bromet, Air Cdre G.R., 61
Brustlein, Gilbert, 150
Butler, Jim, 215
Buckingham Palace, 220

Caen, 96
Cairo, 197, 203
Cambridge, 4, 6–7, 12
Campbell, James, *213*, 214
Campbell, Fg Off Kenneth, 76–80, *77*, *79*, 213–15, 220
Campbeltown, HMS, 180–3, *182*
Canada, 6, 23, 148, 175, 217, 229
Cannon, Sgt C.W.D., 63
Cant floatplane, 201, *202*, 218
Carpiquet, 96
Catalina, Consolidated, 47, *111*, 112, 194
Cephalonia, 201
'Cerebus', Operation, *see* the 'Channel Dash'
Chamberlain, Neville, 1, 25, 31
Chandra Bose, 222
'Channel Dash', the 165–73, *167*
'Chariot', Operation, *see* Sainte-Nazaire, raid on
Cherbourg, 154, *193*
Chichester, 96, 149
Childs, Sgt Frank, 154, 240
Chiplin, Flt Sgt Arthur, 132
Churchill, Winston, 24, *30*, 31, 32, 46, 46, 62, 70, 88, 131, 152, 180
Ciliax, Vizeadmiral Otto, 166. 176
Clarke, Sgt Stan, *195*, 197, 241
Clayton, Sgt Stanley, 164, *174*
Coastal Command and Maritime Air Association, 221, 232
Cocos Islands, 205–8, *207*, *208*
Collings, Flt Lt A.G., 130
Colombo, 204, 205, 209

Compagnie Industrielle des Petroles, 136
Continental Hotel, Brest, 75
Core, Padre Edward, 228, 230
Coward, Noel, 212
Cowderoy, Mrs Jane, vi, 233
Cowling, Henry, 237
Cronie, Sgt J.A., 155
Crozon Peninsula, 106, 191
Curteis, Vice-Admiral A.T.B., 176
Czechoslovakia, 2, 33

Davies, Sgt 'Davey', 84, 85, 90, 91, 92, 94, 98, 110, 112, 121, 123, *124*, 142, 145, 148, 158, 163
Davies, Wg Cdr W.A.L., 197, 200, 201, 209
de Gaulle, Charles, 29, *30*, 32, 82
de la Ferté, Air Marshal Sir Philip, 122, *123*
Denmark Strait, the 103
D.H.4, de Havilland, 23
Direction Island, 206
Dodman Point, 84, 86, 125
Donges, 143, 145–6
Dönitz, Admiral Karl, 35, 35, 42–3, 178–9, 184
Dorchester, 23
Dornier Do 17, 168
Dorsetshire, HMS, 112, 119, *120*
Downing College, Cambridge, 4, 7
Drem lighting system, 125
Dunkirk, 23, 29, 31, 47, 94, 164, 170
Dunn, Plt Off, 72, 81–2
Dunstan, Roy, *20*, 21, 25, 230
Durrant, Sgt Thomas F., 182
Dutch Air Lines, 10

Earl, Sgt Charles E., 148, 239
Edinburgh, HRH The Duke of, 233, 234
Eighth Army, 197
Elizabeth II, HM The Queen, 234
Ellwood, Sgt Dermot E.R., 95–6, 237
Empire Air Training Scheme, 6
Eppen, KL Günther, 223
Epping Forest, 1
Erich Steinbrinck, 130
Esmonde, Lt Comm Eugene, 170
Etheridge, Plt Off G. Alan, vi, *163*, 164, 171, *172*
Eyre, Fg Off John A., 122, 238

Fenton, Fg Off, 28
Finch, Flt Lt Arthur, 157, 166, 170, 240

Flamingo, de Havilland, 31, *31*
Fleet Air Arm
  802 Sqn, 107
  817 Sqn, 176
  825 Sqn, 107, 170
Flushing, 170
Flying Fortress, Boeing, 129, 185
Fokker Airliner, 10, *10*, 12
Forces Français de l'Interieur, 192
Forward, Fg Off, 61
'Frankton', Operation, 185–6
'Fuller', Operation, 165
Fulmar, Fairey, 107

Gadd, Rev Bryan, 228
Gair, Fg Off Ronald W., 61, 237
Galland, Oberst Adolf, 166
Garrod, Air Marshal Sir Guy R., 194
Garrow, Capt Ian, 47
George VI, King, 23, 106
Gestapo, the, 141
Gibbs, Sqn Ldr Patrick, 200, 201, 216
Gibraltar, 47, 112, 181, 186, 197, 203
Gibson, Plt Off Jack E., vi, 60, *130*, 131
Gill, Sgt Mervyn, 155, 240
Gironde, river, 185–6, 192, 222, 223, 224
Glasgow, 12
Gneisenau, 72–3, *73*, 75–81, *80*, 119, 121, 166, *166*, 167, 172, 178, 213
Gordon-Peiniger, Anthony, 38, 235
Gorleston-on-Sea, 158
Gornall, Sgt Frank A., 148
Gosden, Sgt Anthony, 122, 238
Gould, Plt Off Peter 135
Government Code and Cipher School *see* Bletchley Park
Graham, Plt Off Peter, 125, 127, 132, 134, 238
Granville, 84
Great War, the 1, 3, 7, 23
Greenaway, Sqn Ldr Jim, 228
Griffiths, Plt Off Walter S.P., *144*, 147, 239
Guernsey, 37, 84, 98

Halfpenny, Ven B.N., 229
Halifax, Handley Page, 129, *165*, 224, 228
Halley, Sdn Ldr George, 153, 154, 240

Hanson-Lester, Sgt, 148
Hardwick, Sgt Gerald T., 95, 237
Harper, Sgt C.W., 102
Harper, Frank, 232
Harris, ACM Sir Arthur, 178
Harrison, Plt Off James R., 143, 239
Harvey, Sqn Ldr W., 211
Harwich, 170
'Harpoon', Operation, 197, 199
Hasler, Major H.G., 185–6
Hastie, Sgt Archibald, 47
Hayward, Roger, vi, 218
Hayworth, Sqn Ldr Gilbert, 62
Head, Plt Off R.I.G., 201
Heald, Sgt Douglas L., 154, 240
Hearn-Phillips, Sgt Ldr Norman, vi, 217, 219, 230
Heinkel He 59, 37, *38*
Heinkel He 111, *41*, 71, 72, 82, 94, 100, 132
Helston, 143
Henderson, Col John, 214
Henschel He 125, 94
Herdla, 165
Herms, Unteroffizier Erwin, 211
Heydenheldt, KL von Harro, 222
'H', Force, 112, *113*
Highland Division, the, 47
'Hilarion', *see* Jean Phillipon
Hillman, Sgt Ralph W., 78
Hitler, Adolf, 1, 12, 35, 39, 43, 80, 138, 152, 165, 179, 184, 190
Hoffmann, KK Eberhard, 22
Hollely, Sgt Peter F., 122, 237
Holmes, Plt Off Kenneth J., 60, 85
Holtz, OL Karl F., 150–2
Hood, HMS, 104–5, *106*
Hornet Moth, de Havilland, 27
Hudson, Lockheed, *5*, 21, 27, 168, 170, 204, 223, 228
Hunt, Air Cdre A.W., 206
Hunter, Flt Lt, A.V., 61
Hunter, Jim, *130*, *130*
Hurricane, Hawker, 8, 31, 228
Hutcheson, Sgt James, 199, 200, 242
Hyde, Fg Off James R., 78

I-29 submarine, 222
Ijmuiden, 160
Ile de Sein, 82, 127
Irvin jacket, 54, 55, *63*, 90

Jagdgeschwader 77, 64
James, Sgt, 82
Jarvis, Sgt Sidney W., 127–9, *127*

'Jinx', Operation, 205–6
John O'Groats, 175
Junkers Ju 87 Stuka, 29, 33
Junkers Ju 88, 139, 142, *142*, 210–12

Kampfgeschwader 40, 100
Kampfgeschwader 100, 94
Kampfgruppe 100, 82
Karachi, 203
Kelbling, KL Gerd, 180
Keller, OL Günther, 224
Keroman I & II, *43*, *44*, 179
Kerr, Fg Off Thomas E., 127, 238
Kiel, 25, 173, 178, 180, 222
King, Sqn Ldr L.B., 38
King George V, HMS, *108*, 112, *117*, 118, 120
Kitching, Plt Off Tom, 68, 92, *130*
Klein, Gefreiter Heinrich, 211
Knute Nelson, *161*, 162
Krantier, Obergefreiter Friedrich, 211
Kristiansand, 196
Kurz, Obergefreiter Ernst, 211
Kustenfliegergruppe 106, 210

Lancastria, 33
Land's End, 78, 82, 92, *133*, 139
Lannion, 87
Lanvéoc, 47, 100
Larkin, Wg Cdr Howard C., 164
La Pallice, 35, *45*, *46*, *49*, 96, 102, *128*, 129, 135, 138, *162*, 164, 180, *185*, 187, *188*, 189, *190*, 191, 193, 222, 224
Lauriston Hotel, 214
Lee, Plt Off Mark, 160, 240
Leesee, 132
Leigh-Mallory, AV-M Trafford, 168
Lemp, LtsZ Fritz-Julius, 25, 42
Levermentu Cemetery, 209
Levin-Raw, Fg Off D.E.H., 70, 71, 85, 88, 89–91
Lewis gun, 7, *15*
Lindemann, KaptzS Ernst, 105, *107*, *110*, 113, 115, 118, 119
Lingard, Wg Cdr John G., 205
Lisbon, 47
Liverpool, 61, 70, 71, 234
Liverpool Street Station, 12
Lloyd, AV-M Sir Hugh Pughe, 197
Lloyds Bank, 1, 2, 3

London, 1, 12–13, *13*, 32, 57, 59, 165, 217
London Gazette, 80, 215
London, Saro, 21, 71
Lorient, 34, 35, *35*, 42, *42*, 43, *43*, *44*, 49, 61, 70, 71, 84, 85, 96, *133*, 134, *134*, 137, 138, 139, 150, 179, 184, 185, *186*, 187, 189, 193, 222, 223, 224
Lucas, Ven Brian, 232
Lundy Island, 72
Lütjens, Admiral Günther, 105, *107*, 112, 118
Lynn, Sqn Ldr Robert, 199–200, 242
Lysander, Westland, 125, *126*

Maalöy, 165
Madras, 208
Madrid, 47
Madrid, 160
Maginot Line, the, 29
Magister, Miles, 21
'Magnum' Mine, 85–6, 91–2, 129–30
Malaya, 196, 208
Malta, 197–203, *198*, *202*, *204*, 217, 218, 220
Manchester, Avro, 75, 80
Mario Roselli, 200
Maritime Air Trust, the, 233
Marseille, 47, 186
Marshall, Sgt Ralph, 132, 238
Marshalls Training School, 7
Martin, Capt Benjamin C.S., 119
Marviken, 223
Massey, Sgt John Roy, 47, *51*
Matthews, Sgt Douglas, 47, 235
Mayne, Sgt Maurice, 195, 197
McCallum, Rev Sandy, 215
McCartney, Crear, 228
McLean, Charles, 10, 18, 59, 153
Mehl, Sister Cecilia, 96, 98n
Menary, Flt Sgt, 76
Mercer, Sgt Russell, 200, 242
Messerschmitt Bf 109, 38, 46, 63, 64, *169*
Messerschmitt Bf 110, 85, *167*
Middlewich, 177
Milan, 32
Miller, Wg Cdr A.D.W., 204
Minster, Fg Off Frank, 199, 241
Moglich, KL Hans, 223
Montrose, 176
Moore, Gp Capt C.T., 299

Morgan, Sgt Lloyd, 145, *146*, 147, 219, 220, *220*
Morlaix, 210, 211
Morse Code, 5, 17
Moscow, 131
Mosquito, de Havilland, 228
Mountbatten, Vice-Admiral Lord Louis, 185, 206, 208
Müllenheim-Rechberg, Baron Berkhard von, 119
Mulliss, Sgt William C., 78, *79*
Mumford, Rev Peter, 230
Munich, 2
Musenberg, KaptzS Werner, 222
Mussenden, Fg Off Hugh, 47, 235
Mussolini, Benito, 31

Nantes, 47, 132, 140, 147, 150–2, 181
Narvik, 177
National Archives, the, 84n, 119, 208
Neal, Air Cdre Andrew, 232
Needles, The, 49
Ness Garden, 234
Newman, Lt-Col A. Charles, 180, 182–3
Newquay, 18, 19, *26*, 59, 122
New Zealand, 6, 229
Niemeyer, OL Heinrich, 223
Nimrod, Hawker Siddeley, 217, 230, 234
Norfolk, HMS, 105, 112
North Ayrshire Council, 213, 215
Norwich, 155, 171

Oakley, Fg Lt E.A., 61, 237
Opitz, KL Herbert, 223
Oxford, 123

Padstow, 53, 118, 122
Paimpol, 98
Panzerkampfwagen III tank, 29, *29*
'Parachute and Cable Armament', 90
Paris, 29, 31, 32, 178, 184
Passat, 184
Patton, General George S., 189
Pearl Harbor, 164
'Pedestal', Operation, 203, *204*
Pembroke, 72, 211
Penang, 222
Penfeld river, 91
Penzance, 82, 88, 90, 102, 142

Percival, Fg Off John F., 94, 98, 100–1, 103, 110, 121, *121*, 123, *124*, 125, 132, 136, 139–42, 148, 152–3, 155–9, 162, 164, 173, 179, 209
Perry, Sgt Kenneth W., 148, 239
Pétain, Phillipe, 31, 32
Petch, Flt Sgt N.S., 49
Pfieffer, KL Günther, 222
Phillipon, Jean, 79, 80, 172
'Phoney War', the 3, 5, 25, 28
Phuket Island, 208
Pitchfork, Air Cdre Graham R., vi, *52*, 120n
Plumb, Plt Off D.K., 70
Pointe de Grave, 193
Polglase, Wg Cdr F.J., 75
Plymouth, 40, 61, 82, 211
Porter, John, vi, 217, 220
Postill, Sgt Harry E., 49, 236
Prevesa, 201
Prince of Wales, HMS, 104
Prinz Eugen, 103, 105, *105*, 119, 121, *165*, 166, 167, 170, 172, *173*
'Project Constant Endeavour', 233
Public Record Office, the, 7, 94, 119 + n, 208, 217, 230, 231
Pugh, David, 229

Ramcke, General Bernard, 189, 191
Ramsey, 7
Ranee, Fg Off E.A., 132
Red Sea, the, 203
Reeves, Sgt Kenneth, 70, 84, 85, 88, 90–1, 92, 94, 110, 112, 121, 123, *124*, 132, 136, 142, 145–7, 148, 162, 209, *220*
Reichenfels, 200
Reisen, OL Rolf, 222
Renault factory, 178
Renown, HMS, 112, *113*
Repulse, HMS, 105, 112
Revington, Wg Cdr A.P., 23, 37, 90
Reynaud, Paul, 31, 32
Rickard, Sgt Joe, 125
Ritchie, Sgt George A.D., 95, 96, 98n
Robertson, Bruce, 217
Robertson, Fg Off Robert, 51, 236
Rodney, HMS, 112, *117*, 118
Romford, 2
Roosevelt, President F.D., 151, 152, 180

Royal Aircraft Establishment, 212
Routledge, Sgt, 72
Royal Air Force
COMMANDS
Bomber, 5, 7, 14, 20, 39, 61, 62, 70, 74, 76, 80, 82, 91, 93, 94, 109, 116, 121, 129, 165, 171, 178, 179, 184, 187, 191, 196, 232
Coastal, 5, 18, 19–23, 27, 36, 39, 41, 61, 64, 70, 82, 91, 122, 129, 164, 171, 173, 176, 220, 221, 227, 228, 232, 233–4
Fighter, 5, 12, 20, 32, 172, 187
Training, 5–7
GROUPS
No 2, 94
No 5, 110
No 8, 7
No 11, 168
No 15, 61, 70, 73
No 16, 164
No 19, 61, 70, 120
No 222, 205
STATIONS
Abbotsinch, 142
Andover, 125
Arbroath, 176
Boscombe Down, 23, 82, 123, 125
Carew Cheriton, 27, 135
Chivenor, 73, 122, 153, 210–12, 214, 215
Coltishall, 155, 157–8, 160, 170, 171
Cranage, 177
Cranwell, 71
Duxford, 212
Felixstowe, 71
Habbaniya, 203
Halton, 23
Hendon, 23, 31, *216*
Horsham St Faith, 171
Kinloss, 234
Lee-on-Sea, 19
Leuchars, 170, 173, 175–6, 177
Lindholme, 62
Limavady, 70, 71, 73
Lossiemouth, 234
Lough Erne, *111*, 112
Luqa, 196, 197, 203
Manston, 154, 159, 164, 170
Mount Batten, 47
North Coates, 36, 76, 170
North Weald, 1

Northwood, 19, 41
Portreath, 197
Prestwick, 7, 9, 13
Ratmalana, 204
Silloth, 36
UNITS
Air Observer Navigation Schools, 9
Bombing & Gunnery Schools, 13, 59
Elementary Flying Training Schools, 5
Flights, 4, 27
Initial Training Wings, 4
Maintenance Units, 6
Navigation Schools, 6, 175
Operational Training Units, 17, 60, 73, 82, 211
Photographic Reconnaissance Units, 66
Service Flying Training Schools, 6
Torpedo Training Units, 142, 197
Royal Air Force Club, 217, *219*, *220*
Royal Air Forces Association, 217, 221
Royal Air Force Volunteer Reserve, 1–2, 6
Royal Auxiliary Air Force, 234
Rutherford, Sgt J.B., 61, 237
Ryder, Cdre Robert E.D., 180, 182, 183

Saint-Nazaire, 33, *44*, *87*, 93, 94, 95–6, 102–3, 105, 107, 110, 113, 116, 125, 127, 132, 134, 136–8, 145, 148, 187, 189, *189*, 193
  raid on 179–84, *182*, *183*, *184*
Salisbury, 82
Saltcoats, 213–15
Sapwell, Sgt Selwyn C.E., 147, 239
Savage, Able Seaman William H., 183
Scapa Flow, 105, 120, 176
Scilly Islands, 91
Scott, Sgt James, 79, 238
Scharnhorst, 72, 75, 81, *81*, 93, 119, 121, 129, *165*, 166, *166*, *167*, 170–2
Schlitstadt, 183
S.D., 141
Sea King, Westland, 214–15

Sealion, HMS, 168
Seddon, Plt Off, 157
Selby, Flt Lt Cuthbert W.D, 135
Selby, Mrs Wendy, 232
Shackleton, Avro, 228
Shackleton, Fg Off Eddie A.A., 131, 229
Shackleton, Sir Ernest, 135
Sheffield, HMS, 112–13, 115
Sheridan, Sgt James E.J., 63, 237
Sieger, Hauptmann Wilhelm, 152
Siemens, 138
Simpson, Wg Cdr David, *213*, 214–15
Sinclair, Sgt John, 195, 197
Singapore, 196, 205–6
Sitek, OL Walter, 223
Skua, Blackburn, *131*, 132
Slee, Rev John, 232
Smalls Lighthouse, 72
Sokol, Sgt, 157–8, *157*
Somerville, Admiral Sir James, 112
Southern Rhodesia, 6, *9*
Sparks, Marine Bill, 186
Spencer-Schrader, Plt Off, 69, 70
Sperrbrecher 4, 127
Sperrbrecher 16, 122
Sperrbrecher 137, 181
Spartaco, Guisco, 150
Speer, Albert, 179
Spitfire, Supermarine, 8, 66, 75, 98, 129, 155–7, *156*, *158*, 159, 160, *161*, 168, 170–1, 185, 201, 218, 228
St Andrews, 173
St Eval Church, *20*, 21, 24, *25*, 41, 54, 71, 221, 227–32, *227*, 229
St Malo, 84
St Pancras station, 12–13
Stephens, Sgt Roy W.G., 176, 241
Stettin, 223
Stevens, Bernard J., 231
Stewart, Wg Cdr Jerry A., 217
Stockley, Plt Off John, 125, 127, 132
'Stopper' patrol, 81, 168
Stranraer, Supermarine, 21
Stratford, Fg Off A.H., 63
Strever, Lt Edward, 201, *203*
Sturgeon, HMS, 181
Sturm, FK Kurt, 223
Suffolk, HMS, 105, 107, *109*, 118
Suggett, Sgt Edward D., 147, 239
Sumatra, 206
Sunderland, Short, 21

Sutton, Air Marshal Sir Bentine, 194
Syko machine, 142, 158

'Tallboy' bombs, 190
Tams, Plt Off Frank A.B., vi, 61, 62, *63*
Taranto, 199, 201
Taylor, Sgt., 130
Taylor, Sqn Ldr George, 164
Taylor, Sam, 215
The Daily Telegraph, 119–20
Thomsen, Sgt Carl C., 148, 239
Thunderbolt, Republic, 191
Tiger Moth, de Havilland, 7, *8*, *9*, 27, 184
Tilson, Fg Off John H.D., 51
Time Impact Mine, 47, 49, 76
Tirpitz, 173, 175–7, *175*, 179
Todt, Dr Fritz, 43, 179
Tornado, Panavia, 234
Torquay, 9
Tours, 31
Tovey, Admiral John E., 105, 107, *108*, 109, 112, 115, 118, 120
Trento, 198, *199*
Trevisker Farmhouse, *20*, 21, 25
Trevose Head, 69
Treyarnon Bay, 59, 145, 146, 147
Tripoli, 199
Trondheim, 173, 176, 177
Trumble, Peggy, *121*, 123
Tuna, HMS, 127, 186
Twomey, Plt Off P.J., 211
Tynedale, HMS, 180

U-boats
    U-30, 25, 42
    U-102, 222
    U-165, 222
    U-171, 222
    U-180, 222
    U-263, 222
    U-309, 224
    U-415, 223
    U-513, 223
    U-519, 223
    U-526, 223
    U-547, 223
    U-593, 180
    U-981, 223
Umbra, HMS, 198
US Eighth Air Force, 24, 185–7, *186*, *188*, *189*, 197, 231
Ushant Island, 78, 81, 82, 86, 92, 98, 136, 222

Vaasgö, 165
Vancouver, 94
Vannes, 82
Very pistol, 112, 176–7
Vettor Pisani, 201
Vickers K gun, 36, 39, 55, 69, *69*, 150, *154*, *196*
Victorious, HMS, 105–6, 112, 176
V-1 Flying Bomb, 187
'Vigorous', Operation, 197, 199
Vildebeest, Vickers, 21
Voy, Sgt Eric H., 164, 240

Walker, Wg Cdr R.J., 204
Waterbeach Hotel, 123
Watergate Hotel, 59, 123
Webb, Sgt Nelson W., 37, 49, 236
Webster, Sgt Joseph P.H., 64, 237
Wellington, Vickers, 61, 74, 80, 116, 121, 129, 181, 189
Welsh, Fg Off John, 64, 85, 122, 238
Werner, OL Herbert, 223
Western Desert, the 23, 131
Westminster Abbey, 220, 233–4
Wharton, Sgt, 149
Whirlwind, Westland, 228
Whiston, Eddie, vi, *216*, 217, 218, 220, 221, 230
White, Fg Off John, 27
White, Flt Lt Matthew, 171, 240
Whitehouse, Sgt, 84n
Whitley, Armstrong Whitworth, 14, 15, *16*, 61, 181, 184, 228
Wilhelmshaven, 25
William, HRH Prince, 215
Williams, Plt Off Cilmyn G.L., 61, 237
Williams, Sgt Edgar A.G., 132, 239
Williams, Wg Cdr Mervyn F.B., 178
Williamson, Sgt Frank, 171, *172*
Wilson, Sgt A.G., 132
Woodford Green, 1, 12, 53
Wright, Plt Off Arthur, 27, 235
Wybrant, Fg Off, 61

Young, Sgt H.E.C., 122
Ypres, 3

'Zipper', Operation, 208